KT-369-986

New Feminist Library
Dedicated to the memory of Sarah Eisenstein, 1946–1978,
activist, scholar, friend

DOUBLE EXPOSURE

Women's Health Hazards
on the Job and at Home

Edited by Wendy Chavkin, M.D.

Preface by Eula Bingham

Monthly Review Press
New York

Library of Congress Cataloging in Publication Data
Main entry under title:

Double Exposure.

1. Women—Health and hygiene—Addresses, essays, lectures.
2. Industrial hygiene—Addresses, essays, lectures.
3. Housing and health—Addresses, essays, lectures.
I. Chavkin, Wendy.
RA564.85.D68 1983   613.6'2   83–42525
ISBN 0-85345-632-1
ISBN: 0-85345-633-X (pbk.)

Monthly Review Press
122 West 27th Street
New York, NY 10001

Manufactured in the United States of America

10   9   8   7   6   5   4   3   2

10001419977

We bring more than a paycheck
To our loved ones and family

I wanted more pay
But what I've got today
Is more than I bargained for
When I walked through your door

I bring home asbestosis, silicosis,
Brown lung, black lung disease
And radiation hits the children
Before they've really been conceived

Workers, lend an ear
'Cause it's important that you know
With every job there is the fear
That disease will take its toll

If not disease, then injury
May befall your lot
And if not injury, then stress
Is gonna tie you up in knots

So we bring home more than a paycheck
To our loved ones and family

More, more, more, more . . .

> —from "More Than a Paycheck"
> by Ysaye M. Barnwell

Acknowledgments

Many people helped me put this book together. My thanks to the editorial board of the New Feminist Library—I would especially like to acknowledge the hard work of Trude Bennett and Rayna Rapp. Ruth Milkman was ever helpful with facts and figures about women workers. Vilma Hunt, Clara Shiffer, and Zena Stein encouraged and helped me when I first became active in the field of women's occupational health. My thanks to Helen Marieskind and Bobbye Ortiz for their roles in inspiring this project and getting it off the ground. Linda Coleman spent much time and artistic effort gathering together the photographs. Sam Chavkin, Sylvia Chavkin, Nick Freudenberg, Alice Kessler-Harris, Susan Schechter, and Judy Scott all read parts of the manuscript and gave useful critical reactions. Susan Lowes worked very hard whipping the book into shape; I thank her for her excellent work. And of course my thanks to the women's movement, the occupational health movement, the labor movement, and to Bonnie Hill, Deanna Stropes, and Gloria Jordan for serving as such inspiring examples of women who fought back.

Contents

Part 2
Damned If You Do, Damned If You Don't:
Work and Reproduction

Part 3
On the Homefront:
Women at Home and in the Community

Preface

Eula Bingham

The Occupational Health and Safety Act of 1970 guaranteed each American the right to a safe and healthy workplace. Since then we have discovered increasing numbers of hazardous substances that American workers must face every day, and we have learned more of their potentially damaging effects on our health. Yet in many instances, through inverted logic, the blame for getting sick is placed on the victim—the worker—rather than on the conditions of the workplace. This manipulation is particularly clear when it comes to discussing the safety of women who work around substances that may be harmful to reproduction. Here is an example, one that could be duplicated countless times across the country.

A company doctor faces a woman across a desk and tells her, "Honey, I am just trying to protect your unborn child," and then denies her employment in a chemical plant, or in certain areas of the plant. This doctor has not only assumed the role of protector of future generations—and future profits—but has also tacitly ignored the role of the male in the reproductive process and the scientific evidence on the effect of chemicals on the *male* reproductive system. He has also denied the existence of the Occupational Safety and Health Act, and of Title VII of the Civil Rights Act, both of which guarantee equal protection to men *and* to women.

In 1977, I was appointed assistant secretary of labor for occupational safety and health, with the specific task of enforcing these acts. I soon found, to my dismay, that they were being systematically subverted—often with the assistance of occupational safety and health professionals themselves. In the winter and spring of 1978, for instance, there was an upsurge of company policies that prohibited women from certain jobs in the chemical industry. Further, it seemed that the more hazardous a company's operations were (i.e., the more toxic the chemicals it produced, or the higher the number of exposures suffered by its employees), the more "protective" its management was. These policies were not so different from the unwritten policies of the lead industry—whose dangers to reproductive health were noted as early as 1910—where it was simply understood that women were never to be hired. From my point of view, such an approach was archaic. We had entered a new era with the passage of the Occupational Safety and Health Act, and now had a *law* to protect both women *and* men. So in 1978 we issued a new lead standard, one that took into account the need to protect the "functional capacities" of both women and men. This was the same year that four women in West Virginia reported that they had agreed to be sterilized in order to keep their jobs in a lead pigment plant. On investigation, we found that the plant was not even in compliance with the *old* lead standard. And as we examined the policies of company after company, we found the same story. The message was clear: it was easier to exclude women than to clean up the workplace. The irony was that 1978 was also the year in which the Oil, Chemical, and Atomic Workers petitioned for an emergency standard for dibromochloropropane (DBCP), a pesticide found to inhibit spermatogenesis among male workers, and the response from the chemical companies was electrifying! They suspended DBCP operations within days of the announcement of the petition, and both an emergency temporary standard and a permanent standard were issued by the Department of Labor without any threat of litigation from the companies. But while the world thus learned in a dramatic way what many of us in the scientific community had been arguing for years—that chemicals can produce toxic effects on the male reproductive system—the difference in society's response to the reproductive hazards faced by men, as opposed to women, came as a shock even to me. In the case of men, the response was to shut down the plant until the hazard was abated; when women faced similar risks, they were simply *excluded*. But by working with clear-headed, analytical attorneys, experienced in the area of equal opportunity, we were able to begin to develop strategies for overturning this type of injustice.

Nevertheless, no matter what strides such agencies as OSHA make in this direction—and it is not even certain that, under Reagan, these will continue—the health problems faced by women on the job will not be solved by regulation alone. We need more information, and we need other kinds of action. This book puts together information on the health hazards women face not only in industry, but in the office and hospital, in agriculture and in the home. It details not only hazards to reproduction, but the less dramatic but no less damaging hazards to health in general.

The action, however, must come from us. My naiveté about the ability of government to solve these problems has vanished. Covert and less overt discrimination must be attacked in other ways. After working in this area for many years, I feel strongly that many of our problems will not disappear until women take their place in the mainstream of our economic system. And while certain remedial actions can indeed advance women's economic status—such as equal pay for jobs of equal worth—the cultural roadblocks to placing a higher value on women's work must also be removed. And in addition to economic power, I feel that it is imperative that women work through the political system and take their places in legislatures, where votes can mean the difference between having equal treatment or not, and a strong legislative mandate for health and safety can be established. Having women in the executive branches of government is also essential if we are to move toward meaningful health and safety initiatives; no less imperative is the need to increase the number of women in the judiciary. In other words, in order to win the power to make the changes we need, women must move into the political arena. And in order to do that, we need information on the issues we are fighting for. This book takes an important step in that direction.

Introduction

- Women working with lead based pigments at a plant in West Virginia were told that because exposure to lead might endanger a fetus, they could continue to work there only if they could prove that they were unable to bear children. They were urged to undergo a sterilization operation, which the company referred to as "a band-aid operation." Five of the women were sterilized. Two who refused were demoted to lower paying janitorial jobs.
- Two hundred Mississippi women, most of them black, went on strike against the chicken-processing plant that employed them. The women were protesting working conditions, such as speed-ups and sexual harassment, as well as low wages. A *New York Times* article described the health and safety hazards they experienced:

  Employees who unload the chickens often must work covered with feathers, the ones who cut the chickens are covered with gore . . . [which] produces a painful rash on arms and necks. Workers say the line moves too fast. One said that knives often were rusty and that this meant workers could not keep up with the line and often cut themselves. If they cut themselves, they must stay on the line. . . . They also say that they were allowed to leave the line to use the lavatory only three times a week.

- In Love Canal, New York, residents concerned that they were experiencing too many miscarriages from toxic wastes organized a Mother's Day Die-In outside the gates of the Hooker Chemical Company. Subsequently, when they felt the state health department was responding inadequately to their fears, one woman sent the commissioner a Father's Day card with the names of those women who had miscarried.[1]

All across the country women face working conditions that threaten their health. *Double Exposure* describes these problems, their roots, and their place in current conflicts around women's changing role in society. It also documents women's resistance to health hazards on the job and at home. Its goal is to provide women with information so that they can better understand how to change their situations.

The struggle to improve health and safety conditions on the job has gone on for many years—peaks of activity usually occur when working people feel strong enough to put forth demands and protect themselves against retaliatory firings. Through the years organized labor has scored some noteworthy successes, particularly in such heavy industries as mining, auto, and steel. However, in such worksites as cotton mills, garment factories or sweatshops, and electronics plants, where women make up most of the workforce, little progress has been made in safeguarding health. This has transpired not only because of corporate resistance but also because the male-dominated union leadership, especially in the more conservative unions, has placed the issue of women's health and safety on the back burner. In fact, few of these leaders have shown any interest in organizing women into unions in the first place.

The current economic crisis in the United States may force labor leaders to develop a new perspective regarding women workers. Unions are losing members and strength as their traditional stronghold, the industrial sector of steel, auto, and rubber, declines while unemployment and recession persist. In self-defense, unions may try to expand by enrolling women workers. In order to succeed, organized labor will have to demonstrate concern for the situations these women experience—including the hazards on their jobs as well as the needs related to childbearing and childrearing.

It is against the backdrop of these developments that the articles in *Double Exposure* examine the health-threatening conditions faced by women workers, including those whose workplace is the home. It brings together the work of a diverse group of women—academics, organizers, practitioners, workers, activists from the ranks of organized labor and activists from the women's movement. They write both as experts in their areas and as women who understand the experience of being women and workers.

In the last fifteen years in the United States, concern over health has sparked a variety of political movements: the ecology movement; Ralph Nader's consumer-protection drives; anti-nuclear-energy activities; and the current efforts toward disarmament and a nuclear freeze. Among these struggles are movements for occupational safety and health, and for women's health.

This recent round in the fight for improved health and safety conditions on the job was spearheaded by the coal miners. Safety hazards in the mines have all too often been dramatically illustrated by cave-ins and other fatal disasters. In the mid-1960s rank-and-file miners became actively concerned about black lung disease, a progressively debilitating lung condition brought about by chronic exposure to coal dust. The battle for recognition of, and compensation for, black lung disease was led by rank-and-filers and by miners' widows, and was integrally linked with a struggle for internal democracy within the union. In response to pressure from the Black Lung Association, the Association of Disabled Miners and Widows, and a wildcat strike, Congress passed the Coal Mine Health and Safety Act in 1969. The Black Lung Benefits Act followed in 1972.[2]

This coincided with the war in Vietnam and the mass movement organized in opposition to it. The labor shortage characteristic of wartime and the profound social unrest generated by this particular war made the late 1960s a fruitful moment for launching activities for worker safety and health. In fact, the Nixon administration seized upon the issue, hoping both to divert attention from U.S. activities in Southeast Asia and, simultaneously, to appear as the champion of the blue collar worker, the "silent majority." It did not intend the Occupational Safety and Health Act of 1970 to have teeth, and for the first years of its existence the Occupational Safety and Health Administration (OSHA) conducted few inspections and levied few, and minimal, penalties. Only under the directorship of Eula Bingham, appointed by President Carter in 1977, did OSHA begin to take seriously its mandate to ensure healthful conditions in the workplace.

Many 1960s activists perceived that this new movement might provide them with the opportunity to work with labor. The Medical Committee for Human Rights, Committees for Occupational Safety and Health (statewide organizations composed of labor unionists and health professionals, better known as COSH groups), and Nader's Public Interest Research groups all fed into this new meeting ground for leftists, progressive professionals, and unionists.

At the same time, in another manifestation of the general unrest, women were forming groups to tackle reproductive health issues. These early groups varied from those that emphasized "consciousness raising" and learning about the female body, to those that provided "alternative" health services, to those that concentrated on confrontation with established medical institutions. Diverse though they were, they all shared certain assumptions. The central belief was that a woman had the right to control her own body. A further tenet was the importance of demystifying science and sharing knowledge and skills. Toward this end, many alternative services run by these women used lay counselors, paramedics, and patient participation or "self-help." The intention was to empower a woman "patient" and enable her to retain control over decisions affecting her health. As one woman described it, "We see our clinic as a dual model: first, to women [as an example of] self-reliance, taking power through knowledge and sharing it with other women; second, as a model of . . . a nonhierarchical, consumer-run, low-cost, quality-care community clinic."[3]

The women's health movement concentrated on those aspects of female experience that its members felt had been most frequently abused and disrespected: reproduction and sexuality; fertility issues such as birth control, sterilization and abortion; pregnancy and childbirth; gynecological care and surgery; and menopause.

The women's health movement played an influential role in some of the changes of the day. When abortion was legalized by the Supreme Court in 1973, pressure from the movement helped assure that many abortion clinics provided counseling services. The Department of Health, Education, and Welfare passed regulations designed to prohibit coercive sterilization operations and ensure that "informed consent" lived up to its name, partly in response to pressure from groups like the Committee to End Sterilization Abuse. Others, like the National Women's Health Network, scrutinized medical technology and drugs. Side-effects of the pill and the IUD received serious attention and publicity. The drug DES (diethylstilbestrol) was acknowledged to be a carcinogen and a teratogen, and support and advocacy groups for "DES daughters" emerged. Birthing rooms and childbirth preparation classes became widespread within established medical institutions.

Despite the growing activity, the occupational health and safety movement and the women's health movement have scarcely overlapped. The first has focused largely on the problems affecting workers in heavy industry, who are predominantly male. When the hazardous exposures experienced by women workers have received attention, the workers' "femaleness" per se has not been considered particularly germane. Conversely, the women's health movement has not specifically addressed itself to health problems related to work. Assuming that its focus on reproduction and sexuality guaranteed its relevance to every woman, it has reached out to women principally on these grounds. It has not devoted the same attention to other aspects of women's health and experience—for example, the health problems of women as *workers*.

This book starts from the assumption that these two movements have common areas of concern and much to gain from closer cooperation. There are three basic reasons why it is useful to frame occupational safety and health questions in terms of sex, and women's health issues in terms of work: (1) Women work in ghettoized jobs and therefore face the hazards particular to those jobs; (2) women's physical role in reproduction means women have specific health needs at work; and (3) the work women do in the home is not acknowledged to be work, so that hazardous conditions there and on the community level are not taken seriously. These issues are inseparably related. The excuse for restricting women to "female" occupations is that they are considered to be less productive workers—precisely because of their reproductive capacity and role. The definition of women as *essentially* wives and mothers is used to pay them less in every job category.

This book intends to begin an exploration of these issues and their impact on women's health. The first section, "Women at Work," examines the health-damaging conditions present at some jobs performed primarily by women. These are diverse jobs, but they have certain important features in common. First, the workers in them are rarely unionized. The women's movement and labor movement share a troubled history. Alice Kessler-Harris describes in chapter 7 how the very issue of health at work became a battleground between the two as many unions seized upon laws ostensibly protecting women's health as a means of excluding them from jobs. Protective labor legislation that prohibited night work and heavy lifting, and stipulated the number of hours worked per week was used to bar women wholesale from certain job categories and from union membership. Today, only 16 percent of U.S. working women belong to unions (as opposed to 28 percent of men). Without union protection these women are extremely vulnerable.

Second, most of these jobs belong to the sector of the economy known as the service sector. The service sector (more accurately, the non-goods-producing sector) includes government, wholesale and retail trade, and such services as hotels, restaurants, health care, and repair shops, and is the sector of the economy that has been growing, while the manufacturing sector has declined. Since 1973 more people *started* new jobs flipping hamburgers and waiting on tables than the total number of people building cars and working in steel. By 1980 69 percent of *all* employment was in the non-goods-producing sector, and only 31 percent of jobs held in the United States were in industry.

Service sector jobs differ from those in productive industry in several noteworthy ways. They rely heavily on women (in contrast to manufacturing, where women account for only 31 percent of all employment). They have short weekly hours, low hourly pay, and limited opportunities for promotion or advancement.[4]

But while service sector jobs differ from industrial jobs, their specific characteristics have remained largely unexamined. Many men have not been that interested in conditions affecting women and many women have colluded in this silence. Women have been reluctant to draw attention to their own needs because doing so has often backfired against them. For example, because discrimination against women workers has been justified on the ground that their primary role is as reproducers and tenders of the hearth, women have been afraid to insist on needs related to these activities. Instead, they have become caught up in trying to meet male standards, to prove that they function no differently from men. This emphasis on "sameness" has led to the creation of false parallels between conditions affecting women and those affecting men. For example, pregnancy is legitimated by comparing it to an illness (which might befall a man), while a similar analogy is made between the hazardous conditions of the service sector and those of the industrial sector. The problem with these male-female parallels is that they distort the reality of women's situations. Hospital workers' conditions are different from those of factory workers, even though both face threatening physical environments. The environmental hazards in offices are not as catastrophically health threatening as those in coal mines or steel plants, but they are still legitimate problems. One purpose of this book is to call attention to conditions in the service sector *on their own terms.*

The third noteworthy feature of women's jobs is that, as all of the writers in Part 1 (as well as Harriet Rosenberg in Part 3) emphasize, stress on the job is a prime health hazard. Whether the origins are in the overwhelming demands of the task and the contrast between expectations and reality (as for nurses—see Linda Colemen and Cindy Dickinson, chapter 2), the lack of respect and nerve-frazzling environment (as for office workers—see Jane Fleishman, chapter 3), speed-ups and exacting and tedious fine work (as for electronics assemblers—see Robin Baker and Sharon Woodrow, chapter 1), the burden of trying to protect your children from the harsh work environment (as for farmworkers—see Sonia Jasso and Maria Mazorra, chapter 4), an invasion of bodily privacy and dignity (as with sexual harassment—see Peggy Crull, chapter 5), or the combined assaults of racial and sexual discrimination (as for minority women—see Leith Mullings, chapter 6)—in all these cases it is *stress* that emerges as a common thread.

Stress affects male workers too. In fact, it is the contemporary catch-all term to describe how life in advanced industrial capitalist societies makes people sick. There is an extensive medical literature documenting changes in blood pressure, heart rate, gastric acid secretion, and other physiological conditions in response to stress.[5]

Industry also understands that stress contributes to worker illness, absenteeism, and decreased productivity. However, it refuses to accept responsibility for creating work environments that stress workers. Instead it insists that the problem is located within the individual, and offers remedies that focus on the individual rather than the work situation. Many corporations offer on-the-job meditation and exercise programs to offset the physiological stress responses experienced by their employees.[6] (An important exception occurred in New York City when police and firefighters won the right to compensation for heart attacks—the stressful conditions of the job were acknowledged to contribute to heart disease.)[7]

Both men and women may undergo stress, but there are sex-based differences between how their experiences are perceived and treated. The concept of "mass hysteria" is indicative of this. "Mass hysteria," or, in more high technical jargon, "mass psychogenic illness," is poorly understood. The term has been used to describe various kinds of outbreaks among predominantly female workforces: outbreaks of fainting, of nausea and dizziness, of such diffuse symptoms as headaches, irritated eyes and throat, rashes, and menstrual irregularities. Discussion of one such outbreak among Malaysian electronics workers in a scientific journal reveals the bias of this approach to investigating these situations: "There was a total of 24 spells of hysteria involving 22 employees [all females] . . . the affected subjects seemed to have higher neuroticism and extroversion and lower intelligence scores [than the unaffected]."[8] It is probable that several different phenomena are subsumed under the label mass hysteria. In some circumstances these episodes may be underground wildcat attempts at resistance; in others they may result from physical responses to low levels of chemicals present in the workplace environment, or even to a lack of sunlight and air. We know very little about the health consequences of these conditions.

In fact, one consequence of trivializing women's work is that we continue to learn very little about the impact on health, for both men and women, of low level exposure to any number of substances. Many "women's jobs" are characterized by chronic low levels of exposure to ambient solvents, plastics, low dose radiation (i.e., from visual display terminals, or VDTs), fluorescent lighting, and so on, rather than the high-level exposures to carcinogens or other toxins which occur all too often in "heavy industry." (Many women also work in conditions where they face high dose exposures to toxic substances and risk serious illnesses, e.g., textile workers and Brown Lung disease, but that is another issue.)

We have isolated or anecdotal reports of illness associated with work in these conditions. One study reports higher than expected rates of melanoma in women working in offices with fluorescent lighting.[9] Several clusters of adverse reproductive outcomes (miscarriages, birth defects) have been reported among VDT workers, although further research has not as yet corroborated this link (see Mary Sue Henifin, chapter 3).[10] There have been numerous incidents of "tight building syndrome" around the country, in which workers in new or renovated offices that have no direct lighting or ventilation and many synthetic fabrics have complained of irritated eyes and throat, rashes, menstrual irregularities, and lethargy (see Wendy Chavkin, chapter 3).[11] That so little is known about these phenomena should provoke more and intensified research, not a dismissal of the problem as inconsequential or hysterical.

In the second section of this book, "Damned If You Do, Damned If You Don't: Work and Reproduction," we turn our attention to reproduction. These chapters examine the ramifications of identifying women solely with their role in reproduction and then punishing them for it.

There are also adverse consequences for the health of men that arise from ignoring their role in reproduction—Maureen Hatch reviews these in chapter 8. The refusal to temporarily modify jobs to accommodate the changes of pregnancy can be harmful to women's health (see Wendy Chavkin, chapter 10). Judy Scott in chapter 9 and Wendy Chavkin in chapter 10 describe discriminatory corporate policies related to reproduction, such as coercive sterilization, inadequate infant care leave or provision for breastfeeding, and the further economic hardship they create for working women. Some of these policies pose such a threat to both women and unions that the two are undertaking new alliances in order to combat them.

Job modifications are too rarely made to accommodate workers' temporary physical needs related to conception, pregnancy, or breastfeeding. Simultaneously, the assumption is made that *only* women perform the nurturant tasks involved in child*rearing*. This cultural assignment of child care to women has drastic consequences for their performance on the job: it is generally women who miss work to stay home with sick children, take a child to the doctor, attend parent-teacher conferences, and so forth. They are then labelled less responsible workers and this tag in turn serves as a pretext to justify lower salaries, limited advancement options, and other discriminatory measures.

Two examples that encapsulate many of these issues are that of garment sweatshop workers and the related question of home piecework. Unorganized sweatshop workers, who are often undocumented immigrants from Latin America and Asia, work in appalling turn-of-the-century conditions, as a report in the *New York Times* noted:

> While sweatshop conditions vary, there is a grim sameness to the basic appearance: rows of women bent over sewing machines, separated by narrow aisles often made impassable by dress racks and piles of piece goods. Fire exits and windows, too, are often blocked or even padlocked, reducing emergency escapes to a rickety freight elevator and unlit stairs.[12]

Often the workers have to bring their children to work. They earn far less than the minimum wage. Unions tackle a difficult task here, since language barriers, extreme poverty, and fear of deportation make organizing extremely difficult.

It is nevertheless critical that some approach be developed—not only for the sake of these women, but also because of the threat this kind of work represents to unions. And a further threat comes from the move to promote at-home piecework as a "solution." Recent newspaper articles have extolled the virtues of such work for mothers with children, and the Reagan administration has deliberately promoted it. A *New York Times* article stated:

> Working at her knitting machine in a quiet room looking out on snow-covered fields, tall trees and craggy hills, Audrey P. does not feel the least bit exploited. In fact she thinks that her job knitting ski hats in her own pleasant log home at her own pace is a pretty good deal. . . . At the same time [she] can keep an eye on her two young children and keep the woodburning stove stoked and the house spotless.

This blissful image contrasts sharply with realities experienced by most at-home pieceworkers, which the same article goes on to describe:

> In that single room, an Ecuadorian woman named Rosa, who is in this country illegally, lives with her two children, one of whom is brain damaged. She . . . works 12 or more hours a day making skirts at 20 cents each. By working seven days a week at her sewing machine, she can make $120 a week or even a little more. But sometimes, too, the contractors cheat her out of her wages, knowing there's nothing she can do about it.[13]

At-home piecework is a fundamental slap in the face to unions. It capitalizes on the bind in which so many workers who are mothers find themselves. Responsibility for the children is assumed to be solely the task of the mother, and yet our society has refused to accommodate her need for child care, leave time to take care of sick children, etc. It is not surprising that some women have opted to juggle both by working at home, but these women too need the protection of unions—while unions need to protect themselves by addressing their concerns.

The final section, "On the Homefront," turns the spotlight on the unacknowledged work women do in the domestic sphere. Employers often try to justify lower female salaries by claiming that women are unskilled workers. This exposes the fundamental disrespect and lack of recognition of the work women do in the home. The skills transmitted from mother to daughter are privatized and invisible. They are thus classified as "natural," or unskilled.

The women's movement has made a major contribution by bringing this hidden knowledge to light. On the homefront, we can see these unrecognized skills at work. Housework, as Harriet Rosenberg tells us in Chapter 11, depends upon them. Nick Freudenberg and Ellen Zaltzberg demonstrate in chapter 12 how women also draw upon this accumulated experience when they organize within their own communities. They explore the neighborhood networks, social sensitivity, informal contacts that are included in the arsenal of some of these activists. Women have played prominent roles in community struggles against local environmental problems, in part because the homefront is perceived as their domain.

Another consequence of the failure to acknowledge work at home is that its hazards are equally ignored. Industrial products do not respect the sanctity of the home and enter through air pollution; through contamination of the skin, hair, and clothes of industrial workers when they return home; by leaching into the water supply or soil when dumped nearby; and in the form of household cleaning agents bought in the supermarket. Once the inseparability of workplace and community is understood, many new alliances become possible: between community residents and workers in the neighborhood, between those who do paid work and those who work in the home. Let us hope that we do not remain so easily divided.

There is a grim message that runs through the articles in this book: that serious health hazards threaten us at work, at home, and in the community at large. Yet the contributors also document the growing resistance to this situation. In some ways this is a difficult moment, in other ways a promising one, to assert the needs of women workers. The anti-labor, anti-regulatory stance of the Reagan administration has already succeeded in demolishing the union of air traffic controllers, and has devastated those federal agencies (EPA, OSHA, NIOSH) designated to protect the environment and the workplace.[14] These same reactionary forces have made the changing role of women a major focus of their crusade. Under the guise of defending the sanctity of the "traditional family," they are attempting to drastically curtail women's ability to move freely on every front—sexuality, physical self-protection, property, work, and wages.[15] On the other hand, the faltering economy and the growth of the service and the hi-tech manufacturing sectors mean that women workers cannot be so easily ignored. The stigmatization and low salaries characterizing "women's" jobs means that men, despite high unemployment and a declining industrial sector, have not readily taken them on. Thus, if women working in traditional female jobs make demands, men will not easily replace them (although other women, and teenagers, may). If these demands are met, women will no longer be a cheaper, more exploitable, labor force. The struggle for "comparable worth" is critical here. If women were paid on the same scale as men, then a major incentive for maintaining sex segregation in the workplace would disappear.

Thus, organized labor and women workers need each other badly. As the industrial sector dwindles, unions are losing members and power. They need to recruit the women workers of the service sector in order to maintain their strength. Does the fact that the Teamsters are now trying to organize officeworkers, and the American Federation of Teachers is trying to organize nurses, indicate an understanding of the new shape of the economy?

We should recognize, then, that this may be a golden moment for a collaboration between feminists and labor. The Right has made its joint interests clear by targeting both women's rights *and* workers' rights. Feminists can expand their own vision and their base of support if they address the needs of women workers while forging a cooperative alliance with labor; labor can maintain itself as a force in the changing economy if it seriously defends the interests of women workers.

At the same time, women workers need to challenge the enormous domestic load they also shoulder. If women do not do this, they will never undermine the material basis for women's secondary status in the labor force. Women will remain second class citizens in the work world, unable to fully participate in union activities as long as they remain responsible for the entire second job of household and children. It is time to insist that the needs of the 51 percent be met.

Notes

1. "Four Women Assert Jobs Were Linked to Sterilization," *New York Times*, 5 January 1979; William Serrin, "200 Mississippi Women Carry on a Lonely, Bitter Strike," *New York Times*, 27 February 1980; Adeline Gordon Levine, *Love Canal: Science, Politics, and People* (Lexington, MA: Lex Books, 1982).
2. Daniel M. Berman, *Death on the Job: Occupational Health and Safety Struggles in the United States* (New York: Monthly Review Press, 1978).
3. Claudia Dreifus, ed., *Seizing Our Bodies: The Politics of Women's Health* (New York: Vintage Books, 1978). See also The Boston Women's Health collective, *Our Bodies, Ourselves*, 2nd ed. rev. (New York: Simon & Schuster, 1979).
4. Emma Rothschild, "Reagan and the Real America," *New York Review of Books*, 5 February 1981, pp. 12-18; "Shifting Sands: A Long View of the U.S. Economy," *Dollars and Sense* 78 (July-August 1982).
5. J. Mason, "A Historical View of the Stress Field," *Journal of Human Stress* 1 (1976): 6-12; G. E. Schwartz and S. M. Weiss, *Proceedings of the Yale Conference on Behavioral Medicine*, DHEW Publication No. (NIH)78-1414 (Washington, D.C.: U.S. Government Printing Office, 1978); Hans Selye, *Stress in Health and Disease* (Wolburn, ME: Butterworths Publishers, 1976).
6. Gary E. Schwartz, "Stress Management in Occupational Settings," *Public Health Reports* 95 (1980): 99-108; Andrew J. J. Brennan, ed., "Worksite Health Promotion," *Health Education Quarterly*, special supplement 9 (1982).
7. 207K General Municipal Law. See also Samuel G. Freedman, "Officers Get Choice: Pounds or Dollars," *New York Times*, 19 February 1983, p. 25.
8. Chan Oi Yoke, Zee Kok Onn, and Wong Chai Kee, "Epidemic Hysteria: High Risk Factors in Singapore Factory Workers," *Occupational Health and Safety* (October 1979): 58-60.
9. Valerie Beral et al., "Malignant Melanoma and Exposure to Fluorescent Lighting at Work," *Lancet* 2 (1982): 290-93.
10. For a summary of reported clusters of adverse reproductive outcomes among VDT users, see 9 TO 5, Campaign on VDT Risks Technical Memorandum, Appendix A, "Summary of Adverse Pregnancy Clusters Involving VDT's in Canada and the United States."
11. Michael J. Colligan, "Mass Psychogenic Illness in Organizations: An Overview," *Journal of Occupational Psychology* 52 (1979): 77-90.
12. Sandra Salmans, "Resurgence of Sweat Shops Reported in New York," *New York Times*, 26 February 1981, p. A1.
13. Philip Shabecoff, "Dispute Rises on Working at Home for Pay," *New York Times*, 10 March 1981, pp. A1, B8.
14. The Conservation Foundation, *State of the Environment 1982* (Washington, D.C.: The Conservation Foundation, 1982); Urban Environment Conference, National Resources Defense Council and Sierra

Club, *Poisons on the Job* (San Francisco: Sierra Club Natural Heritage Report No. 4, 1982).

15. Center for Constitutional Rights, *Fact Sheet on the Family Protection Act* (New York: Center for Constitutional Rights, 1982).

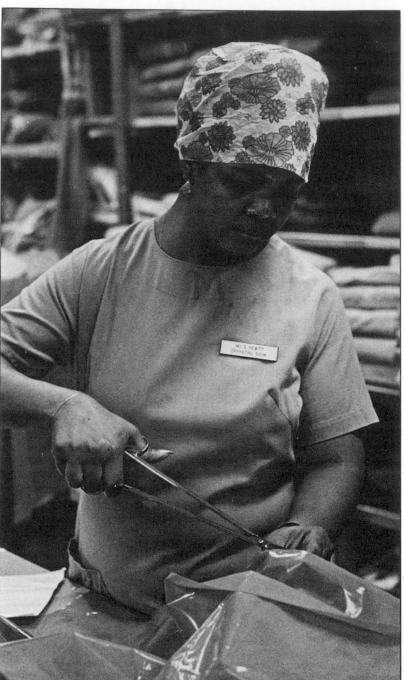

Part 1
Women at Work

Introduction

In the United States, and much of the world as well, jobs are generally segregated by sex. Consequently, women workers face hazards that are specific to the jobs they hold. This section examines the health consequences of working in a few of these job categories: office work, electronics, nursing, and farmwork. There is no attempt to be comprehensive; many volumes are needed to adequately describe the occupational hazards of laundry workers, teachers and child care workers, food handlers, waitresses, garment and textile workers, seamstresses, meatpackers, and the other low-paying, low-status jobs performed by women. The Bureau of Labor Statistics, Women's Bureau, informs us that in 1980 about 43 million women worked—or more than 40 percent of the workforce. The average women worker earns less than two-thirds of what the average working man earns. Full-time women workers with college degrees earn less than men with only eighth grade educations; women high school graduates earn less than men who have not completed elementary school. Most women work because of economic need: nearly two-thirds are single, widowed, divorced, separated, or have husbands who earn less than $10,000.[1]

In this section, we look at three jobs that employ significant proportions of the female workforce. Electronics is a burgeoning field. Both in the United States and the third world, the labor-intensive, tedious, and debilitating part of this work is performed by women. Robin Baker and Sharon Woodrow tell us of the many health hazards facing these workers in chapter 1.

Eighty percent of *all* hospital workers are women, who work in such diverse jobs as aides, technicians, laundry workers, kitchen workers, and in housekeeping. Chapter 2 focuses only on the subcategory of nurses—over 95 percent of whom are women—because their jobs are such that it is possible to explore both health-threatening work conditions and the impact of the mystique of professionalism. As Linda Coleman and Cindy Dickinson show, the "professional" label offers seductive promises of status, salary, and skill which it fails to deliver, obscures exploitative work conditions, and impedes alliances with sister workers.

Eighty percent of all clerical workers, and 99 percent of secretaries, are women. The average annual wage of full-time women clerical workers in 1979 was $8,814. Jane Fleishman describes their work conditions in chapter 3.

Sonia Jasso and Maria Mazorra's article on farmworkers (chapter 4) describes the conditions under which farmworking women labor. The highly exploitative and unsafe conditions facing male farmworkers are experienced by the women as well. Yet the women are also restricted to the lower paying jobs and simultaneously carry the huge load of responsibility for home and children.

All of these jobs are characterized by lower salaries and limited opportunities for advancement. The assumption that women's primary vocation is in the home underlies job segregation by sex and low pay for women within the workforce. In order to bolster this framework, certain jobs are designated as "women's jobs," and described in terms contrived to demonstrate their similarity to home tasks:

> In Morocco, in six weeks, girls (who may not be literate) are taught the assembly under magnification of memory planes for computers—this is virtually darning with copper wire. . . . In the electrical field the equivalent of sewing is putting together wiring harnesses.[2]

Such forced analogies not only obscure the true nature of the work done, both in these jobs and at home, but also foster assumptions that work conditions are comfortable, safe, and pleasant (just like home [see chapter 11]). As a result, the occupational hazards of women's jobs do not receive attention. The articles on officeworkers, electronics assemblers, and nurses all puncture these images by revealing the rough edges beneath the pink frill—the discomforting, stressful, and health-damaging effects of these jobs.

Minority women workers are in double jeopardy as they also face the discrimination arising from racism. These women are the very last hired and first fired. When we arrange wages in a hierarchy by sex and race, we come up with the following:

Wages for full-time workers	Earnings as percent of white male earnings
White men	100
Black men	71
Hispanic men	71
White women	60
Black women	54
Hispanic women	52

If we arrange unemployment rates in a similar hierarchy, we get this, however:

Unemployment rates	Percent
White women	7.8
White men	7.4
Hispanic men and women	14.0
Black women	17.0
Black men	19.2

Sex, then, appears to be the most important factor in determining wages, while race is more significant in determining employment status.[3] Leith Mullings provides an overview of the work conditions experienced by minority women workers in chapter 6. She shows that job categories such as "clerical worker" may be over-broad and obscure the different experiences of certain subgroups within the whole. A woman's status in terms of the three parameters of race, class, and sex locates her in a particular spot in U.S. life and defines a specific experience. While Mullings' chapter concentrates on the experience of black women, it is clear that other racial and ethnic groups face their own particular conditions. And most of these result in higher rates of health problems.

Another way in which women are informed that they are considered unwelcome interlopers in the workplace is through sexual harassment, a crude reminder of female sexual vulnerability in a society where men dominate. It serves to intimidate, terrorize, and—because it is experienced in the privatized and shameful realm of sex—to isolate the women victims. It has further consequences, such as economic loss. Peggy Crull's focus in chapter 5 is on the effects of sexual harassment on health: she argues that attempts to maneuver within conflicting constraints actually make some women sick.

Protection against occupational hazards comes primarily from unions, enforced through collective bargaining. The small proportion of women workers who are organized (16 percent) is widely bemoaned,[4] but male workers and male-dominated unions have at times actively sought to restrict the employment options of women.[5] Protective labor legislation was one device for achieving such restrictions. In chapter 7, Alice Kessler-Harris traces the historical relationship between the U.S. women's movement and the labor movement, and shows the way in which concern for women's health became a terrain of battle between them. While the two groups originally shared the goal of safeguarding female health—although for divergent reasons—this concern and the protective legislation in which it was embodied later became the pretext for discrimination against women workers. The feminist movement and women's trade union movement were torn asunder, as each concentrated on the different benefits and repercussions of these laws. In fact, both sides' criticisms were accurate, since the laws never represented more than half a loaf—that is, they never offered both health protection *and* full employment opportunities for women workers.

Unionization is vital for women, as it is for all workers. Without organization women remain highly vulnerable and exploited in their ghettoized jobs. The jobs described in this section are all in a sector of the economy that is growing, and organized labor needs these workers in order to maintain a meaningful presence on the political scene. But to gain their adherence it must demonstrate that it takes women workers seriously: through organizing efforts, through support for "women's issues," and through concern about the conditions women face on their jobs. These chapters provide evidence that this potential may be realized. Simultaneously, feminists, if they wish to play a meaningful political role, must address themselves to the working conditions dominating the lives of so many American women.

Notes

1. U.S. Department of Labor, Office of the Secretary, Women's Bureau, *20 Facts on Women Workers* (Washington, D.C.: U.S. Government Printing Office, 1980). See also U.S. Department of Labor, Bureau of Labor Statistics, *1981 Weekly Earnings of Men and Women Compared in 100 Occupations* (Washington, D.C.: Government Printing Office, 1981); Janet Norwood, "The Female-Male Earnings Gap: A Review of Employment and Earnings Issues," U.S. Department of Labor, *Bureau of Labor Statistics Report 673* (September 1982); Nanay F. Rytina, "Earnings of Men and Women: A Look at Specific Occupations," *Monthly Labor Review* (April 1982): 25-30.
2. M. Sharpston, "International Subcontracting," *World Development* 4 (1976): 334.
3. Bureau of Labor Statistics, "The Employment Situation," press release, 8 July 1983. See also *20 Facts on Women Workers*, and Terri Leyton, "Civil Rights Report Shows Feminization of Poverty Worsening," *National NOW Times* (May 1983), p. 4.
4. Linda H. LeGrande, "Women in Labor Organizations: Their Ranks Are Increasing," *Monthly Labor Review* (August 1978): 8-14.
5. See Philip S. Foner, *Women and the American Labor Movement* (New York: The Free Press, 1979); Heidi Hartmann, "Capitalism, Patriarchy, and Job Segregation by Sex," in *Capitalist Patriarchy and the Case for*

Socialist Feminism, ed. Zillah R. Eisenstein (New York: Monthly Review Press, 1979); Ann C. Hill, "Protection of Women Workers and the Courts: A Legal Case History," *Feminist Studies* 5 (1979): 347-73; Meredith Tax, *The Rising of the Women* (New York: Monthly Review Press, 1980).

1
The Clean, Light Image
of the Electronics Industry:
Miracle or Mirage?

Robin Baker and Sharon Woodrow

The electronic revolution, the miracle of modern microcircuitry, is ushering in the biggest transformation of our society since the Industrial Revolution. Since its inception just over twenty-five years ago, the electronics industry has introduced a plethora of technological innovations, from pocket calculators and PacMan to intricate scientific equipment and sophisticated military weaponry.

This new industrial giant is touted as the "clean" and "light" industry of the future. U.S. cities compete to become the newest home for microprocessor manufacturing. The industry promises economic salvation without sacrificing environment, low-slung modern industrial parks without the smokestacks of older industry, antiseptic laboratory conditions, "clean rooms" for the manufacture of the delicate microcircuitry-on-a-chip. "Colorado Springs wants electronics companies because they're stable and don't pollute," says one city developer, echoing the national sentiment.[1]

It is no wonder, then, that few people want to hear the health complaints of electronics workers—not managers, not government officials, at times not even the workers themselves. No one wants to spoil the pipedream. Yet this reluctance to dispel the myth of America's clean, light industry has been at the expense of the hundreds of thousands of women working in electronics around the world.

Women form the backbone of the production process in this $100 billion worldwide industry. In third world countries, where the most labor-intensive, tedious, and low-skilled production is concentrated, the electronics workforce is almost entirely female. For instance, in Southeast Asia, an estimated 200,000 to 300,000 women are employed in electronics production. In a typical plant, women make up 90 percent of the assembly workforce.[2] In Silicon Valley, California, where the silicon-chip manufacturing industry makes its home, women also fill the majority of assembly jobs. The valley, which lies just south of San Francisco, sports more than 500 electronics companies, employing nearly 200,000 people—over a quarter of the area's labor force. According to Santa Clara County employment statistics, more than 75 percent of the production workers are women, and at least 40 percent of these are minorities, primarily Hispanic and Asian. (This last is an undercount as the percentage of minorities is growing rapidly due to the recent influx of Southeast Asian immigrants.) The production workforce stands in sharp contrast to the large managerial and professional upper echelon, which is almost entirely (90 percent) white and male.[3]

Wage differentials and job segregation are obvious reasons for the creation of a women's ghetto in the electronics manufacturing workforce. The average female production worker (an assembler) is paid $5.07/hour by a Silicon Valley employer; the average male (a technician) is paid $6.60/hour.[4] These female semiconductor production workers are among the most poorly paid industrial workers in the United States today. The advantage of using women is enormously magnified when the production work is shipped overseas where—in Southeast Asia for instance—women are paid between 17¢ and 55¢ an hour for equivalent work.[5]

A variety of alternative rationales have been put forth by the industry to explain the number of women in microcircuitry production. Some suggest that clean and light plant conditions make them particularly suitable places for women to work. "It's a high quality workplace. You're not going to come home covered with dirt and grease and god knows what else," explains a representative of the American Electronics Association.[6] Others postulate that women are simply better equipped to do such detailed work. According to a spokesman for the National Semiconductor Corporation, "Experience has shown that women seem to be more dextrous and generally better suited for this kind of work. The young men tend to get antsy."[7] This is particularly believed to be the advantage of Southeast Asian women. As the industry puts it, its "secret weapon" in the "competitive field of sophisticated electronics devices is the 'FFM'—or 'fast-fingered Malaysian.'"[8]

Whatever the reason, the fact is that the industry has used the disadvantaged economic position of women and minorities to obtain a cheap and cooperative labor force. Adding insult to injury, these workers have also been used as scapegoats for the industry's health and safety problems. Workers' complaints have been conveniently written off, using the age-old stereotype of the hysterical female.

The first reports of health problems among electronics workers in the United States began to surface in the 1970s. For example, within a period of two months in 1976, four electronics plants in different parts of the country reported "mystery illnesses" among large numbers of workers.[9] Complaints included headaches, dizziness, and nausea. When government scientists were brought in to investigate worker complaints, they were baffled. Because the industry was new, had a clean image and no unions to demand that research be conducted, investigators found no data accumulated to substantiate the workers' claims that their jobs were making them sick. In addition, when they monitored these workplaces, they found that the air levels of individual chemicals did not exceed the existing OSHA limits. No specific cause was ever identified for any of these incidents, although government investigators did recommend that the ventilation systems be improved. For lack of a better answer, investigators began to draw on the diagnosis of "mass psychogenic illness," an up-dated label for "female hysteria."

Despite the lack of industry, scientific, or government legitimation of their health complaints, increasing numbers of workers were becoming concerned. Based on their own experiences, workers began to doubt that electronics plants provided the safe work environment they advertised. In September 1977, a small article appeared in the San Jose *Mercury News* announcing that a pilot study at the University of California Medical Center in San Francisco was looking for volunteer research subjects from the electronics industry in order to examine the possibility of a link between solvents such as TCE (trichloroethylene) and breast cancer, and asked that volunteers contact a local community organization. The local group was flooded with calls from electronics workers with a vast array of job-related health concerns. A common complaint was that their symptoms had not been taken seriously in the workplace and had often been dismissed as personal problems or hypochondria.

While the breast cancer study itself never got off the ground, it was an important catalyst, providing the first official recognition for many workers that the world's cleanest, safest, most modern industry might not provide the most sophisticated protection against on-the-job hazards. The outpouring of concern following the announcement of the study launched a grass roots community effort to uncover the secrets of Silicon Valley. The clean image of the electronics industry has never been the same.

An organization was established in 1977 that came to be known as ECOSH, the Electronics Committee on Safety and Health. It was composed of representatives of diverse community groups, from the Commission on the Status of Women and the American Friends Service Committee to the United Electrical Workers' Union Organizing Committee. With help from a grant from the federal

Occupational Safety and Health Administration (OSHA), the group set out to unravel the complexities of the electronics manufacturing process and to get the story directly from the electronics workers about the health problems they were confronting in the industry.

The Hidden Hazards

The committee's first and most significant realization was that electronics is not a sterile, clean industry but relies on the use of hundreds of potentially dangerous substances for the production of its miracle chips. The manufacture of semiconductor components starts by growing long cylindrical crystals from molten silicon, the basic raw material, and sawing them into thin slices called wafers. They are then baked in "diffusion furnaces," and the heated wafers are treated with a variety of gases to improve their conductivity. Next, a photochemical process is used to create complex circuitry on hundreds of tiny squares, or "chips," on the wafers. After testing and sorting for defective wafers, the final product is typically shipped overseas for the more labor-intensive assembly processes. The wafers are split into individual chips, each with the identical integrated circuit pattern on its surface, bonded to microscopic wire leads, and encapsulated in protective casings. The assembled integrated circuits are then returned to the United States for testing and finishing. The semiconductors and other components are next soldered into printed circuit boards, which are assembled into every kind of electronic device, from computers to elevators.

Contrary to the popular image of wires and vacuum tubes, the real tools of the electronics trade are a wide variety of chemicals. Organic solvents, such as xylene, chloroform, trichloroethylene (TCE), freons, methyl ethyl ketone (MEK), and numerous others are used extensively throughout the industry for cleaning, stripping, and degreasing operations. They are known to cause a range of health problems, including dermatitis; central nervous system effects such as nausea, dizziness, and headaches; liver and kidney damage; and even cancer. Corrosive acids are also commonly used and can cause serious burns when splashed on the skin and eyes, as well as lung damage when inhaled. (Acid burns are the most commonly reported occupational health problem in the industry.) Other toxic substances, including gases such as arsine and phosphine, metals such as lead and other solders, and epoxies, pose additional threats.

Few of the hundreds of different chemicals used in the industry have been adequately tested for their safety. Some substances, such as arsenic, benzene, cadmium, carbon tetrachloride ("carbon tet"), and trichloroethylene are either known or suspected to cause cancer, and a report to the National Institute for Occupational Safety and Health (NIOSH) in 1977 concluded that the scientific instruments industry and electrical equipment manufacturers rank as the first and third most hazardous among industries exposing workers to carcinogens.[10] Further, reproductive hazards include radiation and various chemicals, such as methyl ethyl ketone (MEK), xylene, antimony, and lead. These can affect the reproductive systems of both men and women by causing changes in the reproductive organs, sexual drive, menstruation, and pregnancy. For instance, some believe that xylene, one of the most widely used solvents throughout the industry, causes menstrual irregularities, toxemia in pregnant women, and sterility.[11]

Every step of the production process requires the use of these corrosive and toxic chemicals, often in combinations that are not found in any other setting. Yet the scientific community has done very little to research the synergistic, or combined, effects of these chemicals, and the state of the art is just not keeping pace with workplace realities. The technology changes at a lightning pace, as fierce competition within the industry dictates constant growth and innovation—one major chemical supplier for the electronics industry predicts an annual growth rate of 25 percent a year, resulting in a $3 billion domestic market for semiconductor chemicals by 1985.[12]

The chemical hazards present in electronics manufacturing are often compounded by stressful working conditions. Production work is fraught with the pressures of speed-ups, mandatory overtime, and detailed, monotonous tasks, including hours spent over the microscope. Stress is also caused by shiftwork, which requires adaptation to new schedules. Such irregularity can be extremely difficult for women with children, particularly for the many electronics workers who are single mothers. These pressures, sometimes combined with sexual and racial discrimination, add up to significant occupational stress.

The hidden hazards present in electronics manufacturing are leading to the development of new patterns of illness in the workforce. Chemical sensitization is a syndrome that has recently gained increased recognition in the medical community. While the exact mechanism is not fully understood, it is believed to be the result of a breakdown of the body's immune response system. For instance, one worker who now reacts to everything from laundry detergent to copying machines as a result of chronic exposure to chemicals on the job, says the job has made her "allergic to the twentieth century."

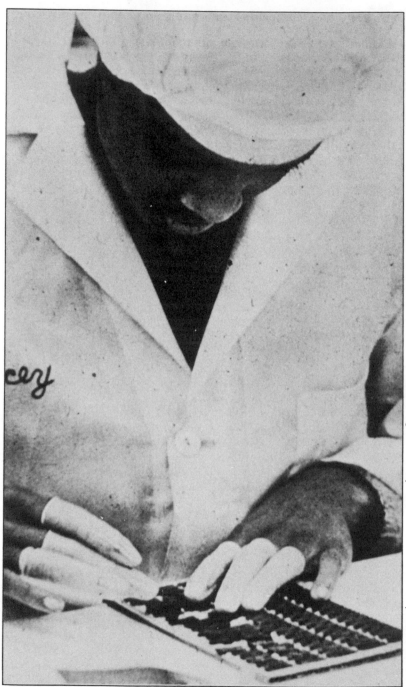

Not surprisingly, the approach that the electronics industry has taken to occupational health considerations has been one of righteous indignation. It has attempted to maintain its professed clean bill of health through self-policing and denial. It declares itself to be innocent until proven otherwise, and the burden of proof has fallen largely upon the workers. According to industry spokesmen, the "clean rooms," which are specially ventilated to protect the delicate electronic circuitry against dust particles, also serve to protect workers against harmful exposure. Thus unexplained symptoms plaguing workers are once again neatly put in the category of "mass psychogenic illness." Since the majority of the victims are women, this diagnosis allows researchers to invoke the Victorian attitude that women are hysterical, while couching such sexism in scientific jargon. It diverts attention away from the possibility that these symptoms are directly related to the hazards and stressful conditions encountered on the job. Rather than focusing on improving environmental monitoring and controls and reducing stressful conditions, research efforts are directed toward identifying the "hysteria-prone worker"—another case of blaming the worker rather than fixing the workplace.

While using the label "mass hysteria" may be a way for the companies to sidestep scientific ignorance and avoid research into the real causes of the symptoms, the symptoms at times may also be a form of wildcat resistance. This has been particularly true among electronics workers in Southeast Asia. For example, in Malaysia, a center of the overseas global electronics industry, over fifty workplace "hysteria" episodes were reported in the media during the 1970s.[13] Such an episode would typically begin with one young woman sighting an evil spirit and reacting by falling to the floor, screaming and convulsing. The spirits would move quickly down the production line, until the bulk of the workforce was thoroughly possessed. These outbreaks often resulted in plant shutdowns that lasted a week or more. Traditional ceremonies, such as sacrificing a lamb, would have to be undertaken to clear out the spirits before the women would return to work. The women, of course, were turning traditional beliefs to new uses—their revolt against the disruptive influence of modern U.S. plants on Malaysian culture. The attacks are likely to follow production speedups or a tightening of plant discipline. Some academics speculate that these episodes represent a form of "covert industrial conflict" in a country where labor unions are not permitted.[14]

The Signetics Three

Perhaps the greatest contribution to exploding the myths and uncovering the hazards of the electronics industry in Silicon Valley was made by three courageous women who have been dubbed the "Signetics Three." By 1977 many problems in the industry had been publicized through community investigation: the extensive use of hazardous chemicals, the high rates of illness in general, and the extent to which protection was being geared to the product rather than the worker. Yet industry, government, and the media continued to ask, "Where are the bodies? Has anyone really been hurt?"[15]

In a nonunionized workforce with no job protection, it is not surprising that workers did not want to make examples of themselves. But in 1977 Cathy Bauerle, Cathi Hee, and Marta Rojas, three disabled employees from a large Silicon Valley firm, decided that they had had enough and came forward with their story. They had worked in the research and development department of the Signetics Corporation, a subsidiary of the multinational Phillips Corporation, which manufactures semiconductors in one of its plants in Sunnyvale, California. In 1977 they began to compare notes and found that they were all experiencing similar symptoms, including nausea, headaches, along with blisters and a metallic taste in their mouths. Cathy, who had worked in the department the longest of the three, had been experiencing her symptoms for some time, but she did not realize that they might be work-related until her co-workers began to talk about their own problems.

For several months the three women complained to their supervisor about their health and sought assistance from company medical personnel. According to Cathy, "They [management] said, 'We've heard of this before; we think it might be mass hysteria.' We had to fight them tooth and nail to convince them that it wasn't. The overtone was always that we were hysterical women."[16] Finally, what was first referred to in company memos as the "female problem in R & D" suddenly changed to the "fume problem in R & D." Why the switch? The women's male supervisor had started to exhibit related symptoms—and the company began to investigate the problem seriously for the first time. In 1978 it brought in an outside private consulting firm which found "significant quantities of trichloroethylene, butyl acetate, and xylene" in the filters of the building's air conditioning inlets. In addition, the consultants suggested that the "problem appears to be one of ventilation."

While never agreeing that the three women's problems were work related, the company assigned them to different work stations and undertook a $500,000 project to revamp the ventilation system in the R & D area. These measures proved to be too little too late—Cathy, Cathi, and Marta all found that they had become so sensitized to chemical environments that there was no work area that did not elicit an allergic reaction. Even after the ventilation was overhauled in the R & D area, the women continued to react there too. The three were then assigned to simply sit in the cafeteria. Like canaries in coal mines, they were used by management to "sniff the air"—if they got sick, that would indicate contamination. They waited in the cafeteria for over a year while the company promised to find them a chemical-free environment in which to work.

When the boredom and humiliation of sitting uselessly in the cafeteria all day, every day, all week, every week became too much and it appeared that the company was not going to find them suitable work, the three women sought outside assistance. In 1979, with the help of ECOSH and their attorney, Cathy, Cathi, and Marta filed a request with the National Institute for Occupational Safety and Health (NIOSH) for a "health hazard evaluation" of their workplace. They knew that they might be risking their jobs by "going outside," but they felt that they had exhausted every internal channel and were getting nowhere.

The NIOSH investigation substantiated the workers' claims that their jobs were making them seriously ill. The two doctors sent in by NIOSH concluded that "a significant occupationally related health problem" existed at Signetics, confirmed the consulting firm's recommendation for better ventilation, and urged an in-depth study of the entire plant. At the same time, the three women, along with several of their co-workers, filed claims for Workers' Compensation benefits. They argued that their hypersensitivity to chemicals was not only affecting their ability to work in the plant, but was extending beyond the workplace. They were now reacting to everyday chemicals found in almost every modern environment, from factories and offices to the detergent section of grocery stores. While the doctor to whom they were sent by the company found that there was no basis for their claims, an independent physician came up with different findings. In late 1979 the head of the occupational medicine program at the University of California Medical Center in San Francisco diagnosed the three women as "super-sensitive" to chemicals as a result of their overexposure in the workplace.

Shortly after NIOSH initiated its investigation of Signetics, the three women were fired. The company said that they had no place for them to work. The following week, Signetics officials refused to allow NIOSH to continue their investigation by denying the government agency access to employee medical records. The NIOSH evaluation has never been completed. Nonetheless, the initial findings of the NIOSH team and the story of the "Signetics Three," who spoke out publicly about their plight, were important steps in revealing and documenting the hazards in the electronics industry. This effort led the way for thousands of other workers to question their own working conditions and to seek information and protection. It also provided the impetus for various government agencies and the companies themselves to begin to take a serious look at problems that they had previously written off as female hysteria.

Fairchild or My Child?

Following close on the heels of the "Signetics Three" case came the next milestone in the investigation of hazardous chemicals used in the electronics industry. This time the catalyst came from outside the plants, and revealed the dramatic impact the industry could have on the environment.[17]

In January 1982, as a result of a confidential tip to the media, the Fairchild Camera and Instrument Corporation, a subsidiary of another multinational company, was forced to acknowledge publicly that one of its underground solvent storage tanks had been leaking into a public water well (Well 13) for an undetermined length of time. The tank contained 1,1,1 trichloroethane, a potentially hazardous solvent that is widely used as a degreasing agent in electronics manufacturing, as well as smaller amounts of other solvents, including trichloroethylene and xylene. Well 13, the largest of an interconnected well system supplying drinking water to approximately 16,500 households in San Jose, California, was shut down after the discovery of the leak and contamination.

When residents in the San Jose neighborhood surrounding the offending plant read reports of the leak, they began their own informal "epidemiological" investigation, only to uncover an apparent clustering of birth defects, miscarriages, and stillbirths during the preceding three years. By mid-February over seventy parents in the area had reported having children with birth disorders. One baby was born with a heart defect in which her pulmonary artery and aorta were transposed, two had died from congenital defects in the heart and urinary tract, and yet another had multiple heart operations and remains under observation.

These reports touched off a series of industry and governmental investigations, which have yielded conflicting, and sometimes questionable, results. The Great Oaks Water Company delayed public acknowledgment of the well contamination and shutdown for six weeks after being notified by Fairchild officials (on December 4, 1981). Although the concentration of 1,1,1 trichloroethane in the well water was as much as twenty-nine times the level recommended by the state Department of Health Services, the department did not at that time consider the contamination to be a "major threat to public health." In addition, a Fairchild spokesman all but admitted that the company had been negligent in not maintaining closer control of the solvent tank. As he put it, "We would have known about the leak sooner if we had, but that duty had been transferred to another division, and the responsibility was just forgotten."[18]

To further complicate the picture, a mysterious so-called "sampling error" may also have been responsible for delaying the discovery of the contaminated drinking water: in the summer of 1980 the state Department of Health Services had collected 150 samples from major domestic wells in Santa Clara Valley to test for two industrial chemicals—trichloroethylene and perchloroethylene—and then announced that no significant contamination was found. Nothing was said about "losing" any of the samples. However, when the "bad news" about Well 13 surfaced in January 1982, the health department announced that the sample taken from Well 13 had been "lost" before it had been analyzed and that somehow no resampling had been done. The Well 13 sample was the only one that met such a convenient fate.

Without this kind of evidence, it is all that much harder to determine the precise time at which public drinking water became contaminated. Fairchild scientists maintain that the leak started no more than eighteen months prior to its discovery and that it took sixteen months to migrate to the wellhead. Others say that the leak could have begun much earlier and taken a much shorter time to reach the well. Obviously, Fairchild hopes to show that its apparent role in contaminating the water supply could not conceivably have affected the pregnancies of the women who have come forward since learning of the leak and its effect on water quality. The issue is still being litigated.

There is also the question of whether or not there is in fact a clustering of birth defects in the area. The Santa Clara County Health Department has performed an initial review of birth certificates, infant-death and fetal-death records. It has reported that the check reveals no significant difference between the county birth-disorder rate and that in the affected South San Jose neighborhood. However, the department's statistics department recently conceded the inadequacy of a review based on birth certificate data, as many birth defects, particularly those involving the heart, are not found at birth and hence are not recorded on birth certificates. Yet there are no reporting requirements for birth defects discovered after a baby leaves the hospital, and birth certificates are the only official record of congenital defects that the authorities have been keeping to date. An advisory committee of state and local health experts, appointed by the health department, thus concluded that further study is needed to determine whether the incidence of birth disorders in the South San Jose neighborhood is actually higher than in other areas of the county.

Such a study was never completed. In the meantime, the controversy over the relationship of the chemical leak to the incidence of birth defects rages on. Fairchild is presently being sued for millions of dollars by residents who claim that they and their children have been harmed. Predictably, the company—relying mainly on reports commissioned by the chemical industry—is contending that 1,1,1 trichloroethane, the principal contaminant found in the well, is not capable of affecting birth outcomes.

Amidst this tangled web of information, residents are left asking why no one has been monitoring the public water supply for industrial chemical contamination. Their outcry has opened up a virtual Pandora's box of previously unreported problems. For instance, when the Santa Clara County health department ordered testing of all public water wells in the county, it quickly became evident that many semiconductor firms have been releasing toxic chemicals into the public water supply via underground storage tanks. Other chemicals found in the ground water and/or in public wells included xylene, acetone, 1,1 dichloroethylene, isopropyl alcohol, and trichloroethylene, which is a suspected carcinogen. The list of offending companies reads like a Who's Who in semiconductor manufacturing: Intel, Hewlett-Packard, IBM, Memorex, and Signetics. Ironically, these are the large multinational corporations with "good guy" images, not the small, unsophisticated plants usually believed to be the worst health and safety culprits.

All in all, water officials estimate that there are probably hundreds of underground storage tanks in Silicon Valley, but there is no way of knowing precisely how many there are, where they are located, or what they contain. A report issued by the State Regional Water Quality Control Board in February 1982 revealed leaks from chemical storage tanks at some three dozen Bay Area locations in the previous two years alone. Though not all of these leaks contaminated public water supplies, their mere existence has underscored the lack of design standards for storage tanks, the absence of monitoring requirements, and the need to determine a coordinated response to the problem.

As is so often the case, this need is only being identified in response to a crisis situation. This can create the illusion that such problems only came into existence recently. In reality, the short history of the electronics industry in Silicon Valley has been punctuated by a series of environmental incidents, including leaks, spills, fires, and explosions. A few examples from the past three years include:

- May 1978: scores of fish were poisoned by the dumping of toxic waste chemicals in a local creek.
- January 1980: a fire gutted an electronics firm, causing a round of explosions from chemicals used in the plant.
- August 1981: 1,200 gallons of silicon tetrachloride spilled from a truck, creating a mushrooming white cloud of gas over the Bay area.
- September 1981: improper lining of a tank truck destined for a waste site resulted in a leak of acid fumes which forced evacuation of 4,000 students and the closing of an eight-mile stretch of highway.
- November 1981: arsine, a poisonous gas, was found leaking inside an electronics plant and forced the evacuation of the building, sending several firefighters to the hospital.

Even under a constant barrage of such horror stories, Silicon Valley residents have found it difficult to admit that perhaps the electronics industry is not as clean as it was cracked up to be. Reality does not live up to the industry's image, and the public may finally be catching on. San Jose Mayor Janet Gray Hayes reacted to the recent groundwater contamination by saying, "I remember being so happy that we were having clean industry come to our community. I remember thinking about the smokestacks of other industries around the country. I didn't expect this problem to erupt in my own community."[19]

Community and Worker Response

Disclosure of environmental contamination by industry has forced the issue of social responsibility to surface in the valley. Industry has traditionally withheld information regarding toxic chemicals from workers and residents of surrounding communities on the basis of protecting trade secrets. Data compiled by Santa Clara County indicates that county residents died from cancer at a rate that increased *20 percent* from 1970 to 1978.[20] Local communities are coming to realize that they can no longer afford to take an out-of-sight–out-of-mind approach to industrial chemical contamination: outraged residents are demanding the right to know.

Inside the plants, the predominantly female production workforce has become equally vocal. Following the example set by the "Signetics Three," numerous other electronics workers have filed complaints and insisted on investigations in their workplaces. These demands for protection, unprecedented in a nonunionized workforce, have resulted in the first two major studies of electronics hazards, one by the California OSHA office, and the other by the NIOSH. Unfortunately, however, these studies have not provided objective scientific information. The Cal/OSHA study was converted to a "joint government-industry effort" to quell the fears and outrage of industry at the prospect of having its hazards researched. Only cooperating companies—presumably those with exceptionally good hazard controls in place—were investigated, and no worker input was obtained. Not surprisingly, the study gave the industry a clean bill of health and documented few industry hazards. Upon its completion, the author of the study was promptly hired by a major electronics company in Silicon Valley. The NIOSH study, which was recently completed, is more comprehensive than the California effort, but it suffers from some of the same problems. Despite attempts by labor and community groups to get the researchers to take a balanced approach, no method was developed for obtaining input from electronics workers themselves about the hazards they face on the job.

Another result of the outpouring of worker concern about health and safety has been a rejuvenation of the effort to organize the electronics workforce. Union organizing has been an uphill struggle in Silicon Valley. There are a variety of explanations offered for this, including ethnic and language barriers between workers, the ardent union-busting activities of employers, what some believe to be the failure of the union movement to adequately address the needs of a female and ethnically diverse workforce, the industry's ability to automate, and its high mobility—its ability to take its work elsewhere, overseas or to less developed areas within the United States. (Some experts even predict that Silicon Valley will become a corporate administration and research center, with few or no production facilities.)

Electronics firms often go to great lengths to divert attention away from the need for a union, attempting to create a family-like atmosphere and a sense that "we're all in this together." Fancy recreation centers, stock option plans, and paid educational leave are just part of the laundry list of benefits offered by firms to prove that the quality of work life is unbeatable. One company even held a raffle called the "American Dream" which granted an employee chosen at random $1000 every month for the next twenty years. At the extreme end of the paternalistic approach are the U.S. electronics firms that sponsor Miss America-style beauty contests and "guess whose legs these are" contests in their foreign plants as a means to cultivate there the sexist roles that keep women tied to their employers.

Despite the multitude of barriers, a number of labor groups in the United States see new organizing potential in relation to health and safety issues. Unions, in particular, have vital protection to offer in the health and safety area. Addressing such concerns and offering protection against discrimination for workers who exercise their rights, the local AFL-CIO Organizing Committee in Santa Clara County has recently been attempting to breathe new life into their union's outreach programs. Labor and community groups have also begun to join together with local firefighters to address common concerns about industrial pollution. A recently formed Silicon Valley Toxics Coalition has won a battle for a community "Right to Know" ordinance. Part of a model code for regulating the handling and storage of toxic materials, this measure requires disclosure of hazardous material information to firefighters as well as to the community at large. The effort to develop such a model code was initiated by the firefighters, who face dangerous and unknown hazards while fighting fires and cleaning up spills in the electronics plants. The need for an ordinance became clearer with the discoveries of drinking water contamination and the high frequency of hazardous situations faced by workers and firefighters alike.

From the battles of the "Signetics Three" and the San Jose neighborhood contaminated by Well 13, to labor organizing efforts in Silicon Valley, a move is afoot to challenge the clean, light image of the United States number one new-age industry. While it is nothing less than a David versus Goliath proposition, the struggle is off to an impressive start.

Notes

The authors wish to thank Patricia Lamborn, Amanda Hawes, Gayle Southworth, and other members of Santa Clara Center for Occupational Safety and Health for their contributions to this chapter and their continued efforts to promote decent conditions for the workers of Silicon Valley.

1. H. P. Burstyn, "Colorado Springs Attracts Firms that Need Engineers," *Electronic Business* (June 1980): 124.
2. Rachel Grossman, "Women's Place in the Integrated Circuit," *Southeast Asia Chronicle* 66 and *Pacific Research* 9, no. 5-6 (Special Joint Issue): 3.

3. Marcie Axelrad, *Profile of the Electronics Industry Workforce in the Santa Clara Valley: A Preliminary Report from the Project on Health and Safety in Electronics.* San Jose, CA: Santa Clara Center for Occupational Safety and Health, 1979, p. 23.
4. Ibid., p. 25.
5. B. Ehrenreich and A. Fuentes, "Life on the Global Assembly Line," *Ms. Magazine* (January 1981): 54.
6. Robert Howard, "Second Class in Silicon Valley," *Working Papers* (September-October 1981): 21.
7. Bill Waller, "Tucson Hits the Industrial Big Time," *Tucson Weekly News*, 20-26 February 1980, p. 7.
8. Linda Y. C. Lim, "Women Workers in Multinational Corporations: The Case of the Electronics Industry in Malaysia and Singapore," *Michigan Occasional Paper* 9 (Fall 1978): 7.
9. C. Talbot and A. Hricko, "Special on Electronics Hazards," Labor Occupational Health Program *Monitor* (August-September 1977): 2E.
10. Congressional Record, September 26, 1977, reprinted from *Science* (September 1977).
11. Roberta N. Hipolito, "Xylene Poisoning in Laboratory Workers: Case Reports and Discussion," *Laboratory Medicine* 11, no. 9 (September 1980): 594.
12. Alan S. Brown, "Silicon Valley: Fertile Ground for Chemical Suppliers," *Chemical Business*, 16 November 1981, p. 10.
13. Barry Newman, "Spooks Stir Up Mass Hysteria in Women in Factories: A Way of Raising the Pay?," *Wall Street Journal*, 7 March 1980.
14. Ibid.
15. An account of the Signetics story was featured in the *San Jose Mercury News*, 6–8 April 1980, in a series called "The Chemical Handlers."
16. Robert Howard, "Second Class in Silicon Valley," *Working Papers* (September-October 1981): 29.
17. An account of the Fairchild story appeared in the *San Jose Mercury News*, 3 February 1982, "Birth Disorders Near Plant Now Total 18," p. 1.
18. For the Department of Health Services report, see Susan Yoachum, "Water Contaminated by Leak," *San Jose Mercury News*, 20 January 1982; for the quote from the Fairchild spokesperson, see Susan Yoachum and Tom Harris, "Flood of Conflicting Facts Confuses Residents After Leak," in ibid., 6 February 1982.
19. Susan Yoachum, "Chemical Spills Tarnish Industry's Image," ibid., 21 February 1982.
20. Karen Klinger, "Santa Clara County Cancer Death Rate Jumps, Experts Puzzled by 20% Increase in 8 Years," ibid., July 31, 1980.

2
The Risks of Healing: The Hazards of the Nursing Profession

Linda Coleman and Cindy Dickinson

Personal Testimony

My first nursing job was on a forty-bed medical ward in one of New York City's municipal hospitals. I had a lot of responsibility for my patients. The doctors were rarely on the floor. I was always assigned between eight and sixteen patients, depending on our staffing that day. My orientation to the floor lasted two days (preceded by ten days in the classroom learning hospital rules and regulations). By the end of my first week I was fully responsible for the nursing care of eight patients. In the middle of my second week I was assigned seventeen patients to care for unassisted. I quickly learned that unless my day was organized with clockwork routine and precise time allotments, I would soon fall behind. Then I would feel panic set in as things began to go wrong—an intravenous line that went dry, a medication error or omission, a forgotten promise to a patient. . . . I'd begin to cut corners, hoping there would be no serious repercussions, that no one would die, that no one would find out. I would ignore patients in pain so as to take care of other patients in more pain. I would pass by one foul-smelling body in order to clean up another more infected one. At any given time, at least one-half of my patients were comatose or totally senile stroke victims. Because of the shortage of beds in nursing homes, these patients would remain on our floor for months at a time; bodies to clean and then clean again, bodies to turn every three hours to slow the inevitable deepening of bed ulcers, bodies with eyes that watched you and maybe did or didn't feel pain, maybe could hear, maybe could feel. . . . Often I left them for hours for other more "critical" patients. Few people would contest the morality of choosing to give priority to living viable patients, but many might pass judgment on a system that forces us to make those decisions alone. I had months of outrage and anxiety and nightmares before I stopped feeling.

Then patients became bed numbers with diseases whose eyes in *the bed you avoid, and then you avoid the bed altogether. You stop making the connection between what you're expected to do each day that you can't possibly accomplish the way it should be done, and the increasingly cold and distant attitude you take toward people in pain, people that need, the increasingly difficult time you have getting up in the morning, getting to the factory on time.*

Introduction

Probably most women in our society fantasized at some point in their childhood about becoming a nurse. Their images promised to fulfill the ultimate identity of sacrificial mothering and nurturing—an image that women have, until recently, been conditioned to believe is their only truly valid role in life.

The nurse (in the child's mind) masters a certain saintliness to be revered by all, and eventually her efforts trap the affection of the most handsome of successful doctors—a few prime fish in the pool might be Dr. Hudson in the 1950s, Ben Casey or Dr. Kildare in the 1960s, or Joe Gannon, Marcus Welby, or Hawkeye in the 1970s.

Television and other media have contributed to and reflect the common popular assumptions about—and images of—nurses. A recent comprehensive review of nurses' image on prime time television and in novels over the past thirty years showed that, at best, these nurses are portrayed as competent at unidentifiable tasks but always need their doctor's assistance in the resolution of hospital and personal problems. At worst, they are portrayed as a group of mindless sex objects fawning over any man who would make a "good catch."[1] In this chapter we point out that the reality of contemporary nursing practice has little connection to these fictional dramas. Nor does the reality correspond with the image that many nurses and most nursing leaders currently advocate and perpetrate, i.e., that nurses are professional, autonomous, valued, and respected members of the health care "team." While such assurances of their "professional" identity serve to divide nurses from other hospital workers, the reality is that bitter struggles for recognition continue and that true professional status by and large does not exist. In fact, the daily reality is that nurses have more in common, task-by-task, with other hospital workers—who have even lower salaries, less recognition, and similar or greater workplace hazards to contend with—than they do with doctors or administrators. Further, the most striking dividing lines occur on the basis of sex and race: most health care workers, including nurses, are female (72 percent) and nonwhite (69 percent), while most doctors and administrators are male and white.[2]

This chapter, then, will discuss the major occupational health and mental health hazards of nursing in the hope of clarifying the current contradiction between the benign public image and the rougher realities of current hospital nursing practice.

Though statistics vary, it has been estimated that between 25 and 55 percent of all qualified nurses do not work at their profession.[3] Of those who do, approximately 20 percent work part-time. In 1970, 70 percent of staff nurses in hospitals across the country resigned, and the average nurse under 44 years of age changes jobs every 2-4 years.[4]

These statistics reveal some of the causes of today's highly publicized nursing shortage. It is due to the complex cycle of events that are a direct consequence of a health care system regulated by profit, and it is both the cause and effect of many of the health hazards to be described. Simply put, hospitals are tremendous industries with ever increasing fixed costs that must be met by patient fees (including private insurance, Medicaid, and Medicare payments). Hospitals compete for patients by competing for physicians (who bring in the patients), and they do this by attempting to provide the most complete, up-to-date services and the latest medical technology. All other concerns, including those of the patients, nurses, and other hospital personnel, are secondary. Excessive construction and redundant purchases of equipment lead to further increases in costs.[5]

Hospital directors attempt to cut the budget in what they perceive as the only flexible area: staffing. As nurses tend not to be unionized, they lack protection against administratively imposed staffing cuts.[6] Thus nurses, even in the most prestigious medical centers across the country, work under dangerously low-staff/high-patient ratios. At Bellevue Hospital Center in New York City, for example, the psychiatric hospital is periodically between 68 percent and 93 percent short of nurses on any given shift.[7] Hospitals across the country estimate that they are at least 100,000 nurses short of what they need to maintain adequate patient care standards.

Traditionally, hospitals have explained their failure to recruit adequate numbers of nurses by admitting that salaries are too low, or by blaming the nurses' family responsibilities for the high rate of turnover and dropping out. Recent studies have shown, however, that neither of these are the primary explanations for nursing job dissatisfaction. Instead, it is the *nature of the work itself,* as well as the degree of role conflict experienced, that are the principle causes of nursing job dissatisfaction, turnover, and dropping out.

Stress Among Nurses

Although articles abound identifying potentially stressful stimuli in nursing jobs, there is a startling paucity of research quantifying the effects of these stimuli in any scientific way. Not surprisingly, stress research has focused on male-dominated occupations: air traffic controller, policeman, and accountant and executive,[9] and what statistical evidence there is focuses on the incidence of coronary artery disease, peptic ulcer disease, and hypertension. Any discussion of stress among nurses is thus limited largely to conjecture and hypothesis, to making analogies between nursing and the few studied occupations.

A recent study by the National Institute for Occupational Safety and Health (NIOSH), however, provides concrete evidence that nursing and other health-related occupations may be among the most stressful of all occupations.[10] NIOSH researched the incidence of mental health disorders in 130 major occupational categories. Nursing-related occupations (including nursing aides, Licensed Practical Nurses, and Registered Nurses) ranked 3, 10, and 27 respectively in terms of the relative incidence of mental health disorders, and seven of the top 27 highest incidence occupations were in health-related occupations.

Substance abuse among health professionals (including alcoholism, narcotics addiction, etc.) is another barometer of stress experienced on the job. One study found nurses and doctors to be almost identical in both rate of addiction and type of drugs chosen.[11] Several studies estimate that doctors use sedatives, alcohol, and narcotics between thirty and one hundred times more frequently than the general public.[12] Further, the rate of suicide attempts among one group of one hundred alcoholic nurses was twice that of a similar group of MD abusers.[13]

What is so particularly stressful about working in a hospital environment?

In one of the few studies on occupational stress and the pathogenesis of disease, a research group from Michigan provides evidence that workers who have "ultimate responsibility for the destinies of people" experience greater stress than workers whose tasks focus on material concerns (i.e., monetary transactions, production of goods, etc.).[14] They also show that *role conflict, work overload,* and *underutilization of skills* are common and significant stressors among working populations. Workers who report these problems, as well as overall job dissatisfaction, are more likely to experience somatic complaints, are more accident prone, and are less productive. These are exactly the stressors that nurses identify in their working situations, and it is therefore important that we look at them in more detail.

Role conflict

There is no shortage of letters and articles in the nursing journals from angry and disillusioned new graduates experiencing the "reality shock" of trying to fulfill their roles as hospital staff nurses. The phrase "reality shock" has been coined to describe the experiences of nurses adjusting to the task-oriented routine of hospital nursing after the anticipation of "professionalism and autonomy in practice" that they had been taught to expect during their training programs. Not surprisingly, role stress has been shown to increase with the amount of professional training received, with graduates of Bachelor's programs experiencing the greatest amount of stress from role conflict.[15] The new graduate finds that as a staff nurse she is forced to perform as a wage laborer in any industry would perform: giving the minimum service to the maximum number of people, performing routine and repetitive tasks at a hectic pace with little opportunity for concern for the "whole patient," and so on.

Nurses often reject this sort of working environment—as shown by rapid job turnover, and by the number of nurses who leave the profession. But nurses have also struggled to implement new working arrangements: for instance, the recent introduction of the concept of "primary nursing" care is an attempt to restore the professional role of the nurse by giving her full responsibility (in conjunction with the doctor) for the planning and implementation of care for a few "primary" patients. The problem is that this is rarely practiced as intended. Instead, it has become a way for hospitals to further cut corners on staffing—and therefore costs. As nurses' wage increases have lagged behind other hospital workers over the past decade,[16] hospitals have found it to their fiscal advantage to use nurses in jobs previously done by others. There has been a dramatic increase in the proportion of RNs to other hospital nursing personnel.[17] Thus under the primary nursing model nurses find themselves manipulated into caring for many patients instead of a few, without the support of auxiliary staff. This might be a cost-effective solution for the hospital if the nurses complied, but they leave instead, so that in fact more money is spent recruiting and orienting new nurses, and hiring more expensive temporary nursing staff.

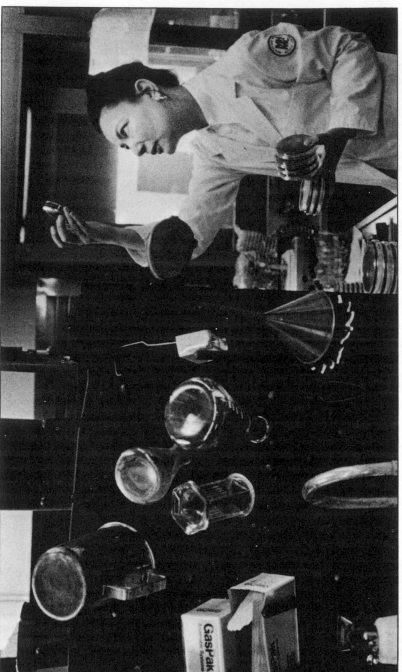

In the few cases where primary nursing has been practiced as originally conceptualized, reports show a significant decrease in illness/absenteeism and job turnover, with a corresponding increase in reported job satisfaction.[18] More importantly, patients recover more quickly with less medically induced complications (due to hospital-acquired infections, accidents, medication errors, etc.) and with greater reported satisfaction with their nursing care.

Unfortunately, the struggle to secure a professional image often undermines more concrete organizing drives for better working conditions in hospitals, and nurses have long resisted any form of organized representation or collective action. Nurses seduced by the professional mystique often reject alliances with hospital workers who fall into "nonprofessional" categories.

It was not until 1968 that the American Nurses' Association, for almost seventy years the nursing profession's most powerful representative organization, rescinded its "no strike" policy. It has recently given high priority to a program of its own to organize nurses—spurred on by organizing drives led by national labor organizations and independent unions. Even so, of the more than 1 million employed registered nurses in 1978, less than 15 percent were represented by a bargaining agent in their place of employment.[19] (Of these, 105,000 were in state nurses' associations, 30,000 in national labor organizations and 6,000 in independent unions.)[20] Despite this low participation, collective action has won higher salaries and greater satisfaction with material aspects of nursing work, although it has not as yet significantly reduced other aspects of job dissatisfaction, i.e., by redefining the nurse's work role or increasing her access to decision-making processes. As these are crucial areas of interest, there is little doubt that as the collective action movement continues to grow, there will be stronger demands for such participation.

Burnout

One of the most serious consequences of role-conflict for nurses is a syndrome recently identified by Herbert Freudenberger as "burnout."[21] Frances Storlie has described this as a "highly personal happening inside the nurse—the literal collapse of the human spirit."[22] Patients become diseases or bed numbers, less and less time is spent at the bedside, "by-the-book" treatment is substituted for more personalized and creative patient care, and jokes are increasingly at the patient's expense. Alternatively, the nurse finds she cannot leave her work behind; she "brings her patients home with her." She frequently works long overtime hours or volunteers for double shifts. In her attempt to live up to an ideal image, she continually confronts failure and exhaustion and moves rapidly into guilt, self-hate, and then on to "total disgust, a sour attitude toward humanity and self, resulting in terminal burnout."[23]

The burnout syndrome can occur in any working environment where dedicated people work under high pressure at tasks that become monotonous and routine and where they have no voice in making decisions and policies that affect them. As Storlie puts it, "Burnout is the resignation to a lack of power—the perception that no matter what you do or how hard you try, you cannot make a difference in the situation."[24] A nurse's priorities, such as patient comfort, emotional support, patient education, and a holistic approach to patient care, often conflict with those of the administration and the doctors and become impossible to implement. It is the conflict between the two that produces incredible anxiety and conflict within the nurse and leads to burnout.

Many nurses are developing strategies to control and/or treat victims of burnout. Most are "stop-gap" measures—peer group counseling, exercise and meditation, assertiveness training—in which the individual nurse takes responsibility for the prevention or treatment of her own problem. At the same time, new strategies for patient care are being developed. But although these measures may well provide relief and may even prevent burnout among some nurses, they neither address nor alter the greater systemic illness. The essential problem is the development of industrialized medical care, with its technology, specialization, bureaucracy, and fragmented care. Burnout will not disappear until we treat the source of the problem instead of its symptoms.

Hazards of the Hospital Environment

Injuries and Accidents

Much has changed since the 1930s. However, while mines and construction sites are more dangerous workplaces than hospitals, hospital workers nevertheless have more on-the-job accidents than workers who produce alkali, chlorine, explosives, guided missiles and space vehicles.[25] The U.S. Department of Labor reports that the incidence of occupational injury and illness per 100 full-time employees is 55 percent higher among hospital workers than among those in other service industries.[26]

Several hospital surveys have reported that nursing is a particularly high risk occupation in terms of injuries, outpacing all other hospital work. For example, in 1973 a Veterans Administration Hospital in California reported that although nurses represented only 24.9 percent of all hospital personnel, they experienced 42.1 percent of total workdays lost due to injury.[27] Similar results have been described in a survey of 232 California hospitals, one New York City hospital, and several others across the country.[28]

Although accident profiles differ among hospitals, there are a number of similarities. Handling equipment and supplies accounts for the largest percentage of injuries. (This includes puncture wounds and injuries from moving heavy equipment.) Injuries relating to direct bedside assistance rank second, and back injuries caused by lifting patients are the most expensive in terms of hospital cost per employee;[29] they also account for the majority of accident-related lost work time.[30]

It is often difficult to quantify the health effects of the general wear and tear of the work nurses do—of long hours of standing, running, lifting, and transporting patients and equipment, and constant bed making. However, a French research team recently reported that the effects of such a work pattern may be reflected, among other things, in poor obstetrical prospects for the nurses: they found that long hours of work without a break and a high patient-to-nurse ratio were associated with increased rates of premature delivery among hospital nurses.[31] Furthermore, two other studies suggest that nursing work predisposes the nurse to develop blood clots in the veins of the legs.[32]

Chemical Hazards

As in an industrial workplace, exposure to chemical hazards in the hospital is frequent, often difficult to isolate, and constantly changing as new and "better" substances are introduced. Many of the chemical hazards that hospital nurses encounter are familiar: skin sensitivity to drugs is frequently reported, particularly to antibiotics and disinfectants (formaldehyde in particular). Methylmethacrylate, a cement used in orthopedics and dental work, can also cause skin rashes and has been associated with liver disease in nurses following long-term exposure. Mercury, which is highly toxic in small quantities, is released as a vapor from broken thermometers, blood pressure machines, and infant incubators, and may in this form be a health hazard.[33] The following paragraphs will highlight a few of the more common hazards that health workers encounter in their day-to-day work.

Cytotoxic drugs: Many of the cytotoxic (cell-damaging) anti-cancer drugs can also cause local toxic or allergic reactions. Many are themselves cancer-causing and are teratogenic—they interfere with the development of the fetus. In 1979, for instance, a group in Finland reported finding "mutagenic activity" (a change in the genetic material of living cells) in the urine of 66 nurses administering anti-cancer drugs.[34] Another study, also from Finland, demonstrated chromosome damage in the blood cells of nurses handling cytotoxic drugs.[35] Whether such changes will affect the nurses' health over the long term is not yet known, but some experts are advising that nurses avoid contact with these drugs by wearing protective gloves, goggles, and masks (to prevent inhalation of the powder),[36] and that hospitals provide instruction on the proper precautions to be taken and handling techniques to be used with these substances. Recently, a group of oncology nurses in a New York hospital refused to mix anti-cancer drugs because the conditions for on-site mixing were unsafe. Interns and residents were then required to mix the drugs, and when they too refused a special satellite pharmacy was established on the floor, with trained pharmacists who would mix the drugs under more controlled conditions.

Anesthetic gases: Controversy continues to rage over the possible hazardous effects of anesthetic gases on health workers.[37] Although many studies have been criticized on methodological grounds, the findings are consistent: the reported effects of such anesthetics as nitrous oxide, halothane, and trichloroethylene include impairment of perceptual, cognitive, and motor skills, headaches, irritability, and depression.[38] There are also less well-documented responses reported to halothane, such as liver toxicity and hypersensitivity reactions.[39]

Much of the controversy has focused on those findings related to pregnancy: a doubling in the rate of spontaneous abortion and perinatal death among women employed in the anesthesia service,[40] a 30 percent spontaneous abortion rate among operating room nurses, compared to a 9 percent rate among general duty nurses;[41] three times as many birth defects among children of nurse anesthetists working during pregnancy than among their nonworking colleagues;[42] and triple the cancer rate among female anesthesia personnel (compared to age-adjusted rates from the Connecticut Tumor Registry).[43]

Fortunately, there are anesthetic scavenging devices that can eliminate so-called waste gases from the air; they are easily available, efficient, and inexpensive,[44] but hospitals are not as yet mandated to install them. (Those air-conditioning systems that involve the recirculation of air, although they may save energy, will not make operating rooms safe from the build up of anesthetic gases.)[45] Instead, some hospitals place the burden of protection on the operating room staff: one designed a consent form that describes the risks of exposure and releases the hospital from liability for the hazards of the environment.[46] The message is clear: work here at your own risk.

Hexachlorophene: In 1972 the Food and Drug Administration restricted the use of hexachlorophene detergents after studies revealed that they caused damage to the nervous system, especially among newborns. Their use in neonatal units was then discontinued, but they are still used on many general wards and in operating rooms. Yet a Swedish researcher has reported that children of pregnant nurses who washed their hands frequently with hexachlorophene may have five times as many birth defects, compared both to the general population and to a control group of nurses who did not wash with hexachlorophene.[47] The researcher found that nurses who washed frequently with hexachlorophene-containing detergents had measurable levels of hexachlorophene in the blood, and it is known to cross the placenta. Until further research clarifies the nature of this potential occupational hazard, it would seem reasonable to eliminate it from the hospital stock room.

Infectious Hazards

Of all the occupational health problems experienced by nurses, infectious diseases have received the most attention. Direct contact with patients with tuberculosis, pertussis, meningitis, and hepatitis, such infectious agents as streptococcus, staphylococcus, and a myriad of other viruses and bacteria continue to pose significant health risks to the working nurse. Infections during pregnancy may endanger the fetus. Tuberculosis and Hepatitis-B are two of the most commonly reported infectious diseases to which nurses are exposed and they will be highlighted here.

Tuberculosis: The incidence of active tuberculosis infection among nurses has greatly diminished since the development of specific anti-TB medications in the early 1950s. Before 1950 two-thirds of registered nurses exhibited exposure to tuberculosis; by 1964 this figure had decreased to less than 5 percent.[48] Nonetheless, the story of the struggle to control this health risk is illustrative of the negligence and lack of concern hospitals classically exhibit toward the safety and health of their employees.

Many nurses who trained before the antibiotic era lost classmates and colleagues to tuberculosis infection acquired on the job.[49] Before the 1950s, between 3 and 10 percent of nursing students could be expected to fall ill with tuberculosis during their period of training.[50] During this time there was public acknowledgment of, and protest against, this great human loss and effective methods were developed—but not widely employed—to contain the problem. In the end, monetary penalties and legal action were required to force hospitals to comply with tuberculosis control regulations.[51]

Inadequate ward ventilation and poor communication among staff members play important roles in the remaining risk of tuberculosis contamination for nurses and other hospital workers. In addition, undiagnosed cases of active tuberculosis expose an average of thirty-five hospital personnel per patient before diagnosis and isolation.[52] Measurable exposure on a properly ventilated ward has been shown to be half that of a poorly ventilated ward.[53] The frustrating lack of communication between doctors and other hospital workers, particularly nurses, is exemplified in the following interview: "I had been taking care of Mr. X for five days. I noticed all the doctors on rounds that morning wore masks as they entered his room. When I asked what the precautions were for, I was told that Mr. X might have tuberculosis, although there was no conclusive evidence as yet. Still, not one of the nurses or aides had been let in on this secret, even though they had been discussing the possibility for five days."

Hepatitis-B: Hepatitis-B is a viral infection that primarily affects the liver. Because the virus is generally transmitted through blood products, it is commonly known as "serum hepatitis." Besides crowding due to poverty, one setting that favors the transmission of Hepatitis-B is the hospital. Surveys have shown that twice as many health-care workers carry the immunologic marker for Hepatitis-B (indicating exposure) as non-health-care workers, and nurses with exposure to infectious materials have shown a significantly higher rate of infection than a control group of nurses who lack such exposure.[54] Hospital workers associated with kidney dialysis appear to be at particularly high risk. Infected patients with chronic kidney disease may remain carriers of Hepatitis-B and infect others who come into contact with their blood.

As any ward nurse can tell you, short staffing has been statistically linked to higher rates of exposure.[55] Most nurses will admit to taking shortcuts when working under high pressure, often to their own detriment. As one said, "If I filled out incident reports every time I stuck myself with a needle, I'd spend more time at the employee health service than with my patients. I just don't have that kind of time."

As health care funding is increasingly reduced, there will be a rise in health problems directly correlated to understaffing. As a result, some nurses are trying to specify safe staffing levels in their contract negotiations; others are logging and filing separate incident reports with their supervisors as accidents due to inadequate staffing occur.

Infections and Pregnancy

For the pregnant nurse, occupational exposure to infections not only endangers her own health but also that of the fetus. Pediatric outpatient clinics attract children with the normal assortment of childhood diseases: rubella on the fetus (German measles), measles, mumps, and chickenpox. Nurses working in neonatal intensive care units care for premature and sick newborns who may shed a variety of viruses, including rubella, cytomegalo-virus, and toxoplasma gondii, all of which are especially hazardous to the fetus. Medical and surgical wards expose nurses to hepatitis, herpes, and influenza. Many of these viruses (i.e., rubella) are particularly dangerous to the fetus during the first trimester, thus creating a problem for nurses who don't yet know that they are pregnant. The terrible affects of maternal rubella on the fetus (including deafness, cataracts, and cardiac lesions) have been well-documented, and outbreaks of rubella in hospitals, some involving nurses, have been recently reported.[56] Other viruses, such as toxoplasma and hepatitis, are more dangerous to the fetus later in pregnancy. Many of these infections have been associated with subsequent birth defects and other adverse effects, such as premature delivery.[57]

Specific research linking the effect of infection to pregnancy outcome among nurses is sparse. One 1968 Canadian study of 1,568 nurses with a total of 4,173 pregnancies assessed the comparative incidence of congenital defects among children of nurses who could be considered a "high risk" group due to their exposure to viral infection during pregnancy.[58] It found that nurses who took care of babies with congenital defects and of prematurely born infants (many of whom might be shedding viruses) gave birth themselves to infants with a high rate of birth defects. In addition, nurses who reported having overt infections during pregnancy had twice the incidence of congenital defects in their offspring as compared to those reporting no illness. The researchers concluded with a strong recommendation that nurses who work during their pregnancies should be protected as far as possible from contact with patients with viral infections, and that virological screening of potentially high risk infants would help to reduce the hazards to those who nurse them. Despite these disturbing results, no further work in this area has followed.

Physical Hazards: Noise, Electricity, and Radiation

Technological advances in the medical field have provided real benefits. They have also provided a more hazardous environment for both staff and patients. The level of noise in the recovery room, intensive care unit, and emergency room are known to adversely affect a nurse's performance.[59] At the same time, the new, complicated diagnostic and therapeutic procedures involve increased use of electricity and radiation. Electrical burns, fires, and explosions are frequent by-products of improperly functioning and poorly grounded equipment. There have been reports of faulty design in new medical devices. For instance, the Emergency Care Research Institute in Philadelphia has reported a poorly designed defibrillator paddle that simultaneously shocked patient and staff.[60]

Almost half of all U.S. workers who are exposed to ionizing radiation on the job are health workers.[61] Exposure outside of the X-ray department is often the most hazardous because protection is not as complete or awareness of the danger as acute. The amount of radiation received depends on the amount of radiation being given off, the exposure time, the distance from the source, and the type of shielding used.[62] Nurses are regularly exposed from the scattering of X-rays from portable machines, while positioning X-ray patients, and from cobalt and radium implants. The maximum permissible exposure to radiation is 5 rems/year, or less than 100 millirems per week. This allows for less than one hour per week for the bedside care of patients with radium implants![63] Some hospitals also require pre-employment chest X-rays, followed by yearly re-tests. This only adds to exposure, because unless other tuberculosis screening tests (the PPD or tine test) are positive, it is unnecessary.

There is a growing debate about the long-term effects of low doses of radiation.[64] It is known that ionizing radiation damages the skin, eyes, gonads, and bone marrow, leading to an increased risk of skin cancer, sterility, genetic damage, and leukemia.[65] The greatest danger is to the embryo and fetus, and women of childbearing age need to be particularly careful. Some cities have recognized this particular danger and have passed protective legislation regarding the exposure of these women. The New York City Health Code—which specifically provides that fertile women and individuals under eighteen years cannot position patients during X-ray procedures—is an example of this, but some hospitals have complied reluctantly.

Conclusion

Despite the proliferation of technological innovations and advancements in hospitals, occupational hazards continue to abound, and even increase. Nurses must recognize that the safety and health of employees are not usually seen as a priority by hospital administrators. It is important, therefore, for every nurse to know her legal right to protection and to be aware of the tactics used, and victories won, by other nurses and hospital workers.

There is a long history of resistance on the part of administrators to compliance with safety and health measures for hospital workers. Without the strength of a union or strong independent organization, nurses have little hope that a hospital will voluntarily make costly renovations, increase staffing, or make job improvements that will be a financial drain on the hospital budget. The importance of organized bargaining power is therefore paramount for on-the-job protection.

Indeed, organized nurses have begun to win protection clauses in their contracts. Nurses in Ashland, Wisconsin, for example, represented by 1199 National Union for Hospital and Health Care Employees, recently won a provision that assured adequate staffing and were able to correct a dangerous nursing shortage in a center for the severely retarded, where there had been 1 RN for every 128 patients.[66] Because of their contractual clause, which states that any condition that is unsafe for workers or patients is legally objectionable, the state had to remedy the situation.

In another example of effective organized action, nurses and orderlies in Waterbury Hospital in Connecticut combined forces to clean up diesel fumes that were leaking into their work area, causing headaches, dizziness, and nausea. With union backing, they forced the hospital to change saturated (and thus ineffective) charcoal filters and to clean the coils in the air vents.

There has also been some activity at the national level. At the 1982 national convention of the American Nurses' Association, a resolution was passed that the organization would assist nurses in identifying and reporting health hazards, and encourage research into occupational risks and hazards encountered by nurses in the workplace. In addition, a national organization called Nurses Environmental Health Watch has recently been established. It is dedicated to educating both nurses and the public about general threats to human and environmental health. It produces a quarterly newsletter and runs a nationwide speakers' bureau on a wide variety of topics. Finally, despite the severe cutbacks instituted by the Reagan administration, statewide Occupational Safety and Health committees are increasingly involved in programs for educating hospital workers in on-the-job hazard detection and correction.

Over the last ten years a number of independent nursing groups have emerged that address theoretical and political issues in nursing, and also provide services not traditionally offered by unions or professional associations. Such groups as Nurses Unite in Philadelphia and Nurses' Network in New York City work to bring together all levels of nursing personnel to discuss mutual working concerns, act as resource and network groups for other nurses, and provide alternative research on nursing problems. One of their most important functions is to encourage positive feelings about nursing, reinstilling a sense of self-worth and pride for work that is so essential to society and yet is not respected by most of the public.

Finding a solution to the negative attitudes people in this country have always held about *all* helping and caretaking occupations (including motherhood) is beyond the scope of this chapter. But at long last changes are coming to nursing, as nurses unite in independent groups, unions, and professional organizations. And as a nurse's self-image grows, partly as a result of these groups, she will begin to feel able to pursue the changes so desperately needed to ensure the safety and health of herself, her patients, and her working colleagues.

Notes

1. Phillip A. Kalisch and Beatrice J. Kalisch, "Nurses on Prime-Time Television," *American Journal of Nursing* (February 1982).
2. U.S. Department of Labor, *Handbook of Labor Statistics*, Bureau of Labor Statistics Bulletin No. 2070, December 1980.
3. Linda H. Aiken, Robert J. Blenden, and David E. Rogers, "The Shortage of Hospital Nurses: A New Perspective," *American Journal of Nursing* (September 1981): 1615; Arthur P. Brief, "Turnover Among Hospital Nurses: A Suggested Model," *Journal of Nursing Administration* (October 1976): 55.
4. Lynn Donovan, RN, "What Nurses Want (And What They're Getting)," *RN* (April 1980): 27-28; Jane Fairbanks, "Primary Nursing: More Data," *Nursing Administration* 5 (Spring 1981): 51-52.
5. Leonard Rodberg and Gelvin Stevenson, "The Health Care Industry in Advanced Capitalism," *Review of Radical Political Economics* 9, no. 1 (Spring 1977): 107.
6. Aiken et al., "The Shortage of Hospital Nurses," p. 1613.
7. Ronald Sullivan, "Nurse Scarcity Forces Cut in Care in New York Municipal Hospitals," *New York Times*, 6 August 1981, p. A1.
8. Brief, "Turnover Among Hospital Nurses," p. 56; J. L. Krueger, "The Education and Utilization of Nurses: A Paradox," *Nursing Outlook* 9, no. 10 (1971): 676-79; L. G. Corwin, "Role Conception and Career Aspirations: A Study of Identity in Nursing," *Sociology Quarterly* 2, no. 2 (1961): 69-80; W. A. Rushing, "Social Influence and Social-Psychology Function of Defense: A Study of Psychiatric Nursing," *Social Forces* 41, no. 2 (1962): 142-48.

9. John Ivancevich and Michael Matteson, "Nurses and Stress: Time to Examine the Potential Problem," *Supervisor Nurse* (June 1980): 18.
10. M. J. Colligan et al., "Occupational Incidence Rates of Mental Health Disorders," *Journal of Human Stress* 3, no. 34 (September 1977).
11. LeClair Bissell and Robert W. Jones, "The Alcoholic Nurse," *Nursing Outlook* (February 1981): 98.
12. Thomas M. Canfield, "Drug Addiction of Health Professionals," *AORN Journal* 24, no. 4 (October 1976): 667; see also Solomon Garb, "Narcotic Addiction Among Nurses and Doctors," *Nursing Outlook* (November 1965): 30-34.
13. Bissell and Jones, "The Alcoholic Nurse," p. 98.
14. Clinton G. Weiman, "A Study of Occupational Stresses and the Incidence of Disease/Risk," *Journal of Occupational Medicine* 19, no. 2 (February 1977): 119.
15. Arthur Brief, Mary Van Sell, Raymon Aldag, and Nancy Melone, "Anticipatory Socialization and Role Stress Among Registered Nurses," *Journal of Health and Social Behavior* 20 (May 1979): 161.
16. Aiken et al., "The Shortage of Hospital Nurses," p. 1615.
17. Ibid., p. 1616.
18. Jane Fairbanks, "Primary Nursing: What's So Exciting About It?" *Nursing 80* (November 1980): 54-57; Fairbanks, "Primary Nursing: More Data," pp. 51-62; T. Corpus, "Primary Nursing Meets Needs, Expectations of Patients and Staff," *Hospitals JAHA* 51 (November 1977): 95.
19. Eleanor Feldbaum, *Public Policy and Planning for Nurse Education and Practice* (College Park: Program of Health Services Delivery, Bureau of Governmental Research, The University of Maryland, 1980), p. 84.
20. Ibid.
21. Herbert J. Freudenberger, "Staff Burn-Out," *Journal of Social Issues* 30, no. 1 (1974): 159-66.
22. Frances J. Storlie, "Burnout: The Elaboration of a Concept," *American Journal of Nursing* (December 1979): 2108.
23. Seymour Shubin, "The Professional Hazard You Face in Nursing," *Nursing 78*, no. 8 (1978): 22-27.
24. Storlie, "Burnout," p. 2109.
25. Mary F. Foley and Matilda A. Babbitz, "Hospitals: Neglecting the Need for Employer Health Programs," *Occupational Health and Safety* 49 (1980): 46-48.
26. U.S. Department of Labor, *Handbook of Labor Statistics*, Bureau of Labor Statistics Bulletin no. 1905, 1976, p. 327.
27. Elizabeth A. Hefferen and Betty J. Hill, "Analyzing Nursing's Work-Related Injuries," *American Journal of Nursing* 76 (1976): 924-27.
28. Frank A. Gohr, "Spotlighting Hospital Safety: Safety Is Everybody's Business, Part II," *Hospital Management* 100 (1965): 44-48; Robert Lewy, "Preventive Strategies in Hospital Occupational Medicine," *Journal of Occupational Medicine* 23 (1981): 109-11; R. D. Gordon, "Study of Nurse Injuries Shows Need for Better Safety Training," *Hospitals* 41 (1967): 70-74.

29. Sally A. Hoover, "Job-Related Back Injuries," *American Journal of Nursing* 73 (1973): 2978-79.
30. H. W. Mammren, "The Need for Employee Health Services in Hospitals," *Archives of Environmental Health* 9 (1964): 750-57.
31. M. Estryn, M. Kaminski et al., "Grossesse et conditions de travail en milieu hospitalier," *Revue Française Gynécologia* 73 (1978): 625-31.
32. L. E. Ramsey and N. A. MacLeod, "Incidence of Idiopathic Venous Thromboembolism in Nurses," *British Medical Journal* 2 (1973): 446-48; P. E. Sartwell et al., "Thromboembolism and Oral Contraceptives: An Epidemiological Case Control Study," *American Journal of Epidemiology* 90 (1969): 365-80.
33. E. Rudzhi, "Occupational Dermatitis Among Health Service Workers," *Dermatosen in Beruf and Umwelt* 27 (1979): 112-15; K. Kaplan and L. Weinstein, "Anaphylaxis to Cephaloridine in a Nurse Who Prepared Solutions of the Drug," *Journal of the American Medical Association* 200 (1967): 75-76; D. J. Hendrick and L. J. Lane, "Occupational Formalin Asthma," *British Journal of Industrial Medicine* 34 (1977): 11-18. On methylmethacrylate, see Ralph Milliken et al., "Hospital Environmental Pollution and Employee Health Hazards," *Hospital Topics* 55 (1977): 22-26; *Project Module: Hazards to Hospital Workers* (Tucson: Arizona Center for Occupational Safety and Health, University of Arizona, February 1980).
34. K. Falk et al., "Mutagenicity in Urine of Nurses Handling Cytostatic Drugs," *Lancet* 1 (1979): 1250-51.
35. H. Norppa, M. Sorsa, H. Vainio, P. Grohn et al., "Increased Sister Chromatid Exchange Frequency in Lymphocytes of Nurses Handling Cystostatic Drugs," *Scandinavian Journal of Work and Environmental Health* 6 (1980): 299-301.
36. R. S. Knowles and J. E. Verden, "Handling of Injectable Anti-Neoplastic Agents," *British Medical Journal* 281 (1980): 589-91.
37. Askrof, Cohen, and Corbitt have all reported adverse effects of anesthesia. The following are references which critique these findings: P. Rosenberg and A. Kivves, "Miscarriages Among Operating Theatre Staff," *Acta Anaesthesiologica Scandinavia* 53, Suppl. (1973): 37-42; and C. J. Cote, "Criticism of Corbett's Birth Defects Among Infants of Nurse Anesthetists," *Anesthesiology* 42 (1975): 514-15. See also Maureen Hatch's chapter in this volume.
38. H. J. Seufert, "A Review of Occupational Health Hazards Associated with Anesthetic Waste Gases," *Association of Operating Room Nurses Journal* 24 (1976): 744-52; K. Korttlila, P. Pfäfei et al., "Operating-Room Nurses Psychomotor and Driving Skills after Occupational Exposure to Halothane and Nitrous Oxide," *Acta Anaesthesiologica Scandinavia* 22 (1978): 33-39.
39. L. W. Chang and K. Z. Jordan, "Pathologic Effects of Chronic Halothane Inhalation: An Overview," *Anesthesiology* 45 (1976): 640-43.
40. Vagn Askrog and Bent Harvald, "Teratogen effekt af inhalations anaestetika," *Nordisk Medicin* 83 (1970): 498-500.
41. E. N. Cohen, J. W. Belville, and B. W. Brown, "Anesthesia, Pregnancy

and Miscarriage: A Study of O.R. Nurses and Anesthetists," *Anesthesiology* 35 (1971): 343-47.

42. T. H. Corbett, R. G. Cornell et al., "Birth Defects Among Children of Nurse Anesthetists," *Anesthesiology* 41 (1974): 341-44; E. W. Cohen et al., "Occupational Disease Among Operating Room Personnel: A National Study," *Anesthesiology* 41 (1974): 317-40.

43. T. H. Corbett, R. G. Cornell et al., "Incidence of Cancer Among Michigan Nurse-Anesthetists," *Anesthesiology* 38 (1973): 260-63.

44. J. H. Lecky, "The Mechanical Aspects of Anesthetic Pollution Control," *Anesthesia and Analgesia* 56 (1977): 769-76.

45. "Air Recirculation Causes Anesthetic Gas Build-Up," *Association of Operating Room Nurses* 20 (1974): 756.

46. R. M. McWilliams, "Nurses Concerned with Hazards of Waste Gases," *Association of Operating Room Nurses* 21 (1975): 857-58.

47. H. Halling, "Suspected Link Between Exposure to Hexachlorophene and Birth of Malformed Infants," *Lakartidningen* 74 (1977): 542-46; see also B. Baltzar, A. Ericson, and B. Kallen, "Pregnancy Outcome Among Women Working in Swedish Hospitals," *New England Journal of Medicine* 300 (1979): 627-28.

48. Ada Levine, "TB Risk in Students of Nursing," *Archives of Internal Medicine* 121 (1968): 545-48; W. Weiss, "TB in Student Nurses at Philadelphia General Hospital," *American Review of Respiratory Diseases* 107 (1973): 136-39.

49. Elizabeth Barrett, "The Epidemiology of TB in Physicians," *Journal of the American Medical Association* 241 (1979): 31-38.

50. See Levine, "TB Risk in Students of Nursing."

51. A. J. Myers, R. E. Boynton, and H. S. Diehl, "TB Among Nurses," *Disease of the Chest* 28 (1955): 610-32.

52. N. J. Ehrenkranz and J. L. Kicklighter, "TB Outbreak in A General Hospital: Evidence for Airborne Spread of Infection," *Annals of Internal Medicine* 77 (1972): 377-82.

53. R. R. MacGregor, "A Year's Experience with TB in a Private Urban Teaching Hospital in the Post-Sanatorium Era," *American Journal of Medicine* 58 (1975): 221-28.

54. T. L. Lewis et al., "A Comparison of the Frequency of Hepatitis-B Antigen and Antibody in Hospital and Non-Hospital Personnel," *New England Journal of Medicine* 289 (1973): 647-51; B. Janzen, "Epidemiology of Hepatitis-B Surface Antigen (HB-SAG) and Antibody to HB-SAG in Hospital Personnel," *Journal of Infectious Disease* 137 (1978): 261-65.

55. B. S. Levy, J. C. Harris, J. L. Smith et al., "Hepatitis-B in Ward and Clinical Lab Employees of a General Hospital," *American Journal of Epidemiology* 106 (1979): 330-35.

56. J. L. Gladstone and S. J. Million, "Rubella Exposure in an Obstetric Clinic," *Obstetrics and Gynecology* 57 (1981): 1822-26.

57. Charles A. Alford and Robert F. Pass, "Epidemiology of Clinic Congenital and Perinatal Infections of Man," *Clinics in Perinatology* 8 (1981): 397-414; M. Siegel, "Congenital Malformations Following

Chickenpox, Measles, Mumps, and Hepatitis: Results of a Cohort Study," *Journal of the American Medical Association* 226 (1973): 1521-24.
58. E. U. Haldane, C. E. Van Rooyen, J. A. Embel et al., "A Search for Transmissible Birth Defects of Virologic Origin in Members of the Nursing Profession," *American Journal of Obstetrics and Gynecology* 105 (1969): 1032-40.
59. S. A. Falk and N. F. Woods, "Hospital Noise Levels and Potential Health Hazards," *New England Journal of Medicine* 289 (1973): 774-81.
60. E. A. Trought, "Equipment Hazards," *American Journal of Nursing* 73 (1973): 858-62; J. A. H. Williamson, "The Hazards of Electrical Apparatus in the Operating Room Theatre," *Australian and New Zealand Journal of Surgery* 41 (1971): 101-107.
61. "Radiation on the Job Is a Concern for at Least One Million Americans," *New York Times*, 3 July 1979, p. 1.
62. "Occupational Radiation: Fact Sheet for Nurses," Nurses Environmental Health Watch, Room 215, 655 Sixth Avenue, New York, NY 10010.
63. Vilma Hunt, "Occupational Radiation Exposure of Women Workers," *Preventive Medicine* 7 (1978): 294-310.
64. I. D. J. Bross, M. Ball, and S. Falen, "A Dosage Response Curve for the One Rad Range: Adult Risks from Diagnostic Radiation," *American Journal of Public Health* 69 (1979): 130-36; J. D. Boise and C. E. Land, "Adult Leukemia Following Diagnostic X-Rays?" *American Journal of Public Health* 69 (1979): 137-45.
65. Hunt, "Occupational Radiation Exposure," pp. 294-310.
66. *1199 News*, March 1982, p. 27.

3
I Like My Job, It's the Work
that Makes Me Sick

The Health Hazards of Office Work
Jane Fleishman

In order to understand the health risks associated with office
work, we must first understand the economic and social position of
office workers—most of whom are women—and the historical
forces that brought this situation about. For while there are few
working women today who haven't had some association with
clerical work, either as office "temps"—temporary clerical workers—or as permanent employees, this has not always been the case.
Few women worked as clerks in the nineteenth century. Before the
corporation became large and centralized, and before typewriters
were developed and offices bureaucratized, clerks were usually
middle- or upper-class young men who were expected to rise to the
tops of their companies—especially if these were owned by their
fathers or fathers-in-law.[1]

In the late nineteenth century, however, business functions
began to expand rapidly, and there was an increasing demand for
staff to keep up with the growing amount of correspondence,
record-keeping, and office managing. At the same time there was
an increasing "rationalization" of office work—its division into
smaller and less skilled tasks. The typewriter keyboard became
standardized and its use in the office was accepted by the late
1890s. The new occupation of typist, which replaced that of hand
copyist, promised higher pay for its practitioners, as well as to
allow more time for tasks requiring greater thought and skill. But
these promises were never realized—at least, not by clerical workers. Typing was considered to be more suitable for women than for
men because women's fingers were believed to be more dextrous.[2]
Women became typists, while men, relieved of copying, took on
the less tedious work. Women, who were by this time receiving
more public education than in the past—in 1900 more women than

men received high school diplomas[3]—also took on such additional clerical tasks as stenography, bookkeeping, and "salesmanship."[4] But they were paid half the wages of their male predecessors, and they were not considered apprentices "clerking" their way to the top. By 1920 they had been clearly confined to the lower ranks of office work: they made up the majority of low-level, low-status, low-paid stenographers, typists, secretaries, shipping and receiving clerks, office machine operators, and other clerical workers.[5] And in the increasingly hierarchically organized and male-dominated offices, where the bosses were almost always men, a subservient relationship went along with the job. There were strict dress and behavior codes and traditional views of female sexual roles. Office duties paralleled the housekeeping duties of the traditional wife. The small size of the typical office fostered an identification with the employer, rather than with the work itself.

Clerical work has grown enormously since the 1920s, but the lowly position of the clerical worker has changed very little. There are 19 million clerical workers in the United States today:[6] 4 out of every 10 workers is a clerical worker, and 8 out of 10 are women. For women, clerical work is the largest occupational category: it now includes such jobs as typing, bookkeeping, filing, stenography, machine operating, accounting, answering telephones, key punching, and switchboard work. As has been the case since the beginning, women are still confined to the lower paying clerical jobs, and the average annual wage for a woman clerical worker in the United States is $8,814.[7] Many live at or below the poverty level, and many are even eligible for food stamps, despite the fact that they are full-time employees. Clerical workers who are black, Puerto Rican, Asian, or members of other racial or ethnic minorities face the additional pressure of racial discrimination. Black women, for instance, are hired into—and remain in—lower paying jobs than white women. Minority women make up only 6 percent of all secretaries, who are considered relatively "high status" clerical workers, but 22 percent of all key punchers. Minority women are usually confined to the lower paid, lower skilled "back office" jobs, and do the majority of night shift work.

The Hazards of the Office Environment

It is widely assumed, by office workers and non-office workers alike, that the office is a relatively clean and safe place to work. After all, an office worker doesn't have to get dirty as a factory worker does, or have to change from a uniform at the end of the day. But during the past few years this assumption has increasingly

Carla Katz

come into question as a growing body of literature has begun to show that the office may in fact be unsafe. Occupational health experts, health professionals, working women's organizations, unions, and, most important, clerical workers themselves have begun to pay close attention to the health hazards of the office workplace. They have begun to question the safety of low-level exposure to various office chemicals, including those used in office machinery, to artificial lighting, to inadequate ventilation, to high noise levels, and to low-level radiation. They have begun to ask why office work is so unsatisfying and stressful, and to examine the way technological change affects office organization and layout.

There is as yet very little research on many of the hazards of office work. What follows will summarize what is known about the potential dangers of various aspects of office work, and outline the research that exists. Two more detailed sections—on VDTs (by Mary Sue Henifin) and "closed office-building syndrome" (by Wendy Chavkin)—will look at these issues in more detail.

The most common hazards of the office environment are so common that their danger can all too easily be ignored. But as any office worker knows, slippery floors, poorly made office furniture, swinging doors, and open file drawers can cause injuries ranging from the minor to the serious; while less obvious hazards—blocked hallways, doorways, and exits, faulty electrical wiring, overloaded circuits—can be even more dangerous. Dim, harsh, or flickering lights can lead to eyestrain and irritation, and can affect overall efficiency. Artificial lighting may interfere with our circadian rhythms, leading to unnecessary weariness (and may affect ovulatory cycles), and may also contribute to the creation of indoor photochemical smog, another irritant.

Noise can be another hazard. One secretary in a retail company described the number of different noises she was subjected to in her office: "Calculators, typewriters, piped-in music—loud—a Mag-Card memory typewriter, air conditioning fans—all of the above in an office with four secretaries answering telephones, placing calls, taking orders, all in an open-type area."[8] The Occupational Safety and Health Administration standard for noise exposure in an industrial setting is 90 decibels over an eight-hour period—while for the office the acceptable level ranges from 55 to 70 decibels.[9] This may avoid the most severe health effects, such as hearing loss, but it ignores the potential behavioral and nervous system disorders that have been associated with low levels of noise,[10] including circulatory, digestive, and neurological disorders.[11]

Even low levels of noise can be lowered. Some employers mask noise by using "white noise," or prerecorded music, to mask the office noise; but noise reduction can be better accomplished by using carpeting, enclosures, drapery, and acoustical ceiling tiles. Significant noise reduction can even be accomplished at the source, inexpensively and simply. One typewriter manufacturer has suggested that the cost of reducing typewriter noise would be no more than 60 cents a machine.[12]

Office work has another type of hazard, one associated with the repetitive nature of the work, and therefore directly related to the work environment. Constant keyboard work, whether at a typewriter, VDT terminal, keypunch machine, or calculator, is part of many a clerical worker's day. This type of repetitive lower arm, wrist, and finger motion, when combined with limited back movement, has been found to be associated with musculoskeletal pain in the neck, arms, hands, and back.[13] The chart lists the three most common disorders, their causes, and their symptoms:

Disorder	Causes	Symptoms
Carpal tunnel syndrome	Repetitive flexing of wrist combined with pulling and grasping with the finger(s).	Damage to the median nerve. Symptoms: tingling of thumb, fingers after work, sharp pain, weakening of thumb.
Tenosynovitis	Rapid repetitive motions.	Inflammation of tendon and tendon sheaths of hand, arm. Symptoms: pain, swelling, numbness, tingling of hand, wrist, forearm; muscle, shoulder pain.
Occupational cervico-brachial syndrome	Rapid work pacing.	Muscle pain in the arm, neck, shoulders.

Some of these nerve disorders—especially carpal tunnel syndrome—are so common among women workers that some researchers have claimed that they are women's disorders—that women are more "prone" to them than are men. Yet they fail to mention that this may be because of the sex-segregated nature of keyboard work. One company has gone so far as to claim that "word processing operators won't be getting much exercise in the office anymore," since

automated equipment will deliver, retrieve, and process information. But constant sitting can lead to a number of disorders,
including varicose veins, hemorrhoids, and other signs of circulatory sluggishness, as well as such musculo-skeletal strains as stiff
necks and lower back pain. All these are exacerbated by poorly
designed chairs and work areas.

The modern office employs a number of chemicals, many of
which are known to be hazardous and others of which are suspected of being so. The chart on the following page lists some of the
many chemicals which have been used in the office and the health
problems they may cause. The harmful effects of these chemicals
can be minimized if exposure is reduced or other less toxic chemicals substituted. The most damaging of the effects listed in the
chart will result only after high dosages and long-term exposure,
but an individual's level of sensitization varies and what will affect
one worker may affect another differently.

As if this list were not enough, there is the additional possibility
that some of these hazardous chemicals will not be confined to the
area in which they are supposed to be used, but will circulate
throughout the office. In an effort to reduce energy costs, recently
constructed buildings are often "sealed," or build with windows
that do not open. Such buildings rely on air filtration and circulation systems that recirculate some of the old air, so that vapors,
fumes, dust, and other airborne particles find their way into parts of
the building far from their place of origin. Even nearby laboratories, industrial production areas, and parking garages may become a
source of pollutants in the office.

In addition, without adequate air circulation, irritating and toxic
chemicals can build up. One office worker described her company
duplicating room:

> The once-large room has been halved, and the xerox room is
> now the size of a small closet—big enough for a small xerox
> machine, one small table, and one person. Not until someone
> fainted . . . did they install a fan in the wall. However, every-
> one keeps the door to the room open. The fan blows out into the
> hall, not to an outside vent. There are fumes in the room, and in
> the hallway, although more dispersed than before.[24]

This is not an uncommon situation. And it is compounded by poor
temperature and humidity control. In a survey of approximately
1000 women office workers in Boston and Cleveland, preliminary
results showed that 90 percent complained that their offices were
too hot, too cold, or both. A survey of 1100 office workers in New
York City had similar results: 75 percent complained of too little air

Chemical	Where used	Potential damaging effects
Ozone	Photocopiers; emitted in exhaust fumes.	Nervous system, lung, and genetic damage. A suspected carcinogen in humans.[14]
Nitropyrenes	Are often contaminants in the toner used in photocopying machines.	Known mutagen in animals and a suspected carcinogen in humans.[15]
Ultraviolet radiation	The main light source in photocopiers.	May cause conjunctivitis and cataracts.[16]
Trinitroflourenone	Used in computer printout machines.	Causes cancer in mice.[17]
Methanol (methyl alcohol)	Contained in duplicating-machine fluid.	An irritant to the skin, eyes, lungs, and central nervous system. Can lead to liver damage.
Ethanol (ethyl alcohol)	An alternative in duplicating-machine fluid.	Causes intoxication, dizziness, headaches, and dry skin. Can lead to liver damage.
Ammonia	Contained in duplicating-machine fluid.	Causes burning, swelling of the eyes, nose, throat, and chest.
Formaldehyde	An insulator in building materials; used in carbonless copying paper, coatings for automatic signature machines, particle board, fire retardants, desk furniture sealants. Released from disintegrating carpets.	Causes eye irritation, skin rashes, and lung problems. May be a carcinogen in humans.[18]
Trichloroethylene, tetrachloroethylene, trichloroethane	Used in liquid eraser products.	Causes drowsiness, giddiness, dizziness. Is suspected of being carcinogenic.[19]
Benzene, toluene	Trace amounts are found as impurities in other solvents.	Benzene is a known carcinogen; toluene is a narcotic and causes drowsiness.
Polychlorinated biphenyls (PCBs)	Used in electrical transformers in buildings, adhesives, plastics, carbonless carbon paper.	Damages skin, eyes, nose, throat, and liver. Suspected carcinogen.[20] Particularly hazardous in case of fire.
Abietic acid	Contained in office paper.	Causes dermatitis.
Sodium sulfonated napthalene condensate	Used in multilith paper.	Causes allergic reactions.[21]
Colophony	A resin used in sizing for paper products.	Causes allergic reactions.[22]
Oxalic acid	Used in making blueprints.	Causes burning, skin ulcers, loss of fingernails.
Potassium hydroxide	Used in papermaking.	Causes burning, skin ulcers, loss of fingernails.[23]

movement and of stuffiness; over 70 percent reported that the temperature was too hot or too cold; and 65 percent said that the air was too dry.

Stress: It's Not Just in Your Head

It's the lack of respect that gets me the most. Being called a girl. I'm forty years old! . . . They can make you feel, if you're doing a low-skilled job, then you must not be very bright and being a woman you don't need to work. And then it's the "hurry up" routine. I only get 45 minutes for lunch, and the cafeteria is fourteen floors down.[25]

In one of the offices I worked in the supply cabinet was filled with all of our office supplies, including a huge bottle of Mylanta—for ulcer relief. Every two hours the head secretary would rush down the hall and take a slug from the bottle. Tales of ulcer medicine in the supply cabinet, blood pressure testers in the bathroom, and company-dispensed "aspirin for your nerves" are common among office workers. AT&T, for instance, has been known to prescribe "two weeks' rest" at a company-owned retreat.[26] Scientists, unions, and office worker organizations are increasingly concerned about a "stress epidemic" among women clerical workers. This is recent: for a long time the only office jobs that were considered stressful were those held by men at the top, who suffered from a malady labeled "executive stress." But recent research indicates that job stress may be much more frequent among women at lower levels than was originally believed. One woman who works at a major Hartford insurance company summed up her stress ailments this way: "After spending fifteen years there, I now have a nervous stomach, diarrhea, indigestion, I drink a lot of milk, I can't sleep, I can't eat certain foods, I get backaches—my health is a mess."[27]

The Framingham Heart and Hypertension Study, a long-term epidemiological investigation, included a section on the correlation between coronary heart disease and women workers. Researchers found that women clerical workers develop coronary heart disease at almost two times the rate of all other working women, including housewives. (None of the women had heart disease before the eight-year study began.) The women at greatest risk were clerical workers whose husbands were blue-collar workers: 21 percent of these women developed coronary heart disease. There were three key factors that were predictors of the disease: a non-supportive boss, the lack of job changes over a ten-year period, and difficulty in expressing anger.[28]

In 1977 National Institute for Occupational Safety and Health

(NIOSH) researchers found that out of 130 occupations covered in a long-term longitudinal study, secretaries were second only to laborers in the incidence of stress-related diseases.[29] NIOSH researchers also found that people who work on VDTs face higher stress than any other occupational group, including air traffic controllers.[30]

The commonly held belief that certain individuals are more prone to stress and thus bring their problems on *themselves* has recently been re-evaluated. In a study conducted by Robert Karasek it was found that typical female jobs offer the women much less control over decision-making than do typical male jobs. And since many of the jobs associated with high levels of psychological stress are clerical—office machine operator, file clerk, keypunch operator, receptionist—Karasek concluded that the concentration of women in these jobs, rather than the women's frailties or hysteria, may account for the higher rates of mental strain among them.[31]

Creating a Healthy Office Environment: The Role of Trade Unions

Organizations representing women began to organize clerical workers in the 1970s—the first attempt to do so since the 1930s when the CIO launched a major organizing drive and won major contracts with insurance and financial institutions, particularly on the East Coast. Unionized clerical workers struck the New York Cotton Exchange, *Parents'* magazine, and the Westinghouse Corporation.[32] But the red baiting of the CIO leadership in the late 1940s destroyed the organizing drive, and between 1950 and 1970 office workers were not on the agenda for the labor movement.

In 1973 the National Organization for Women (NOW) and the Coalition of Labor Union Women (CLUW) decided to make organizing clerical workers a priority. In the same year, Women Office Workers (WOW) was born in New York City, the result of the combined efforts of feminists and trade unionists. Other organizations followed: Women Employed (WE) in Chicago, 9 TO 5 in Boston, and Union W.A.G.E. in San Francisco. These working women's organizations began to campaign for equal and better pay for clerical workers, and for affirmative action programs in the office; they also conducted research about the inequities of clerical work. They became the models for 9 to 5's national organization, which emerged in 1979 as a unifying force in this growing movement.

With the rise of these organizations the clerical worker has finally found a movement concerned with her welfare, and the larger labor movement has begun to take the recruitment of clerical

workers seriously, abandoning its long-held notion that these workers too often identify with their bosses to be willing to join unions.
Major campaigns to organize clerical workers in both the public
and private sectors have been begun by several major unions.[33]
Women now represent one in every five union members, and
account for much of the recent growth in total union membership.

One of the results of this has been an increased emphasis on
correcting the conditions that clerical workers face by negotiating
contractual language in collective bargaining agreements. For
instance, contracts have been negotiated that cover such items as
sexual harassment, layoffs due to the introduction of new technology, discriminatory wage and promotion policies, inequitable
benefit plans, and work overload. District 65 of the United Auto
Workers negotiated an agreement at Boston University that con-
tains a path-breaking provision on sexual harassment and sex
discrimination (see Peggy Crull, chapter 5, for more on this issue).
And Local 3 of the Office and Professional Employees International
Union bargained successfully with Blue Cross/Blue Shield in
California for protections for VDT workers. Some workers have
also filed and won workers' compensation claims for stress-related
diseases suffered while on the job.[34] But very few states have
workers' compensation statutes that cover mental or emotional
illnesses that result from events on the job,[35] and the law governing
stress is far from uniform and cannot be relied upon by workers
suffering from acute or chronic disorders that are the result of
such stress.

In addition, only 14.8 percent of the clerical workforce is unionized, so that clauses in union contracts are only a partial solution to
the problems of work hazards for women clerical workers. One result has been the growth of self-help groups that have helped some
non-unionized office workers to organize for better conditions.[36]

Conclusion

The health problems associated with clerical work can be controlled and prevented, and the growing unionization of women
clerical workers—if it is accompanied by a concern for their specific problems—will help in the creation of office environments
that are healthier, more comfortable, and less stressful. At the same
time, women must demand that more research be carried out,
especially on the effects of new technology on health and of
automation on their work. In addition, women clerical workers—
whether unionized or not—must form alliances with other workers
and with other women. The labor movement has much to gain from

the success of clerical organizing drives. And clerical workers have much to gain from the successes of all workers who struggle for better, healthier, and safer working conditions.

Notes

I am indebted to the many women I have worked with while completing this chapter, to the women I worked with as a typist, who shared their lives and stories with me; for the research and encouragement I received from 9 TO 5, most especially Judith Gregory, whose insights, intelligence, and perseverance were invaluable, to Gloria Gordon, Mary Sue Henifin, Lee Schore, Marsha Love, Mikki Karotkin, and Jackie Zachary for their critical help reading drafts and suggesting revisions.

1. Margery Davies, "A Woman's Place Is at the Typewriter: The Feminization of the Clerical Labor Force," in *Capitalist Patriarchy and the Case for Socialist Feminism*, ed. Zillah R. Eisenstein (New York: Monthly Review Press, 1979), p. 252. See also Evelyn Nakano Glenn and Roslyn L. Feldberg, "Clerical Work: The Female Occupation," in *Women: A Feminist Perspective*, ed. Jo Freeman (Palo Alto: Mayfield Publishing Co., 1979), pp. 313-38.
2. Davies, "A Woman's Place Is at the Typewriter," p. 252.
3. Office of Education figures, as cited in ibid., p. 251.
4. Edith Abbott, *Women in Industry: A Study in American Economic History* (New York: Arno Press, 1969), p. 2.
5. Davies, "A Woman's Place Is at the Typewriter," p. 252.
6. Max L. Carey, "Occupational Employment Growth Through 1990," *Monthly Labor Review* (August 1981): 46.
7. The most recent data available is for 1979; see U.S. Department of Labor, "Employment in Perspective: Women Workers," *Bureau of Labor Statistics Report No. 653* (1979).
8. Working Women Education Fund, *Warning: Health Hazards for Office Workers: An Overview of Problems and Solutions in Occupational Health in the Office* (Cleveland, 1981), p. 43.
9. Susan Mackenzie, *Noise and Office Work* (Ithaca: Cornell University NYSSILR, 1975).
10. Ibid.
11. Dan Macleod, *Noise Control—A Worker's Manual* (Detroit: UAW Social Security Department, 1978), p. 48.
12. *The Economic Impact of Noise*, prepared by the National Bureau of Standards for the U.S. Environmental Protection Agency, Office of Noise Abatement and Control, 1971.
13. Working Women's Education Fund, *Warning*.
14. R. E. Zelac et al., "Inhaled Ozone as a Mutagen," *Environmental Research* 4 (1971): 262; R. R. Guerrerro et al., "Mutagenic Effects of Ozone on Human Cells," *Environmental Research* 18 (1979): 336.

15. AFSCME District Council 37, *Nitropyrene Fact Sheet.*
16. Joel Makower, *Office Hazards* (Washington, D.C.: Tilden Press, 1981), pp. 73-79.
17. "Hazard Profiles for 33 Chemicals Drafted, Dispositions Still Pending," *Chemical Regulation Reporter,* 4 September 1981, p. 507.
18. The State of Massachusetts has banned urea formaldehyde foam from use in that state. The Chemical Industry Institute of Toxicology found that formaldehyde caused cancer in rats and mice. Following publication of their report, the Formaldehyde Institute, an industry-based group, urged postponement of any restrictions pending outcome of further study. It claims that preliminary studies have shown no unusual number of cancers. Dr. Peter Infante, director of OSHA's Office of Carcinogen Identification, recently came under fire over this controversial issue. He was charged with insubordination and misrepresentation of OSHA policy concerning the carcinogenicity of formaldehyde. Infante based his interpretation on the industry study, but was under fire by the Formaldehyde Institute when he determined that formaldehyde should be classified as a carcinogen in humans. Infante was reinstated after tremendous pressure regarding OSHA's handling of the controversy. See *Occupational Safety and Health Reporter* 11, no. 6 (July 1981): 108-109, and *WORRC News* 3, no. 2 (March/April 1981).
19. Liquid erasers such as Liquid Paper are nearly 100 percent trichloroethylene. In 1979 a teenager in Oregon died from sniffing Liquid Paper. Three deaths in the past seven years have been attributed to the product in Dallas, where the product is made. The causes of death were cardiac arrest. Since then the company replaced trichloroethylene with trichloroethane, but it has since been linked to cancer. Information on the cause of death was obtained by Working Women through interviews with Dallas County Medical Examiners Office, Oregon Medical Examiners Office, and representatives from Liquid Paper Corp. as reported in Working Women Education Fund, *Warning.*
20. See numerous articles in *Public Sector,* the official publication of the Civil Service Employees' Association, including 18 February 1981, 4 March 1981, 11 March 1981, 16 September 1981; and see the *New York Times,* 23 October 1981, p. B5.
21. "Occupational Dermatitis," *National Safety News,* Data Sheet I-510-81 (January 1981): 48-56.
22. Kjell Wikstrom, "Allergic Contact Dermatitis Caused by Paper," *Acta Dermato-venereologica* 49 (1969): 547-57.
23. "Occupational Dermatitis."
24. Working Women's Education Fund, *Warning,* p. 34.
25. Personnel communication from Michelle Karotkin.
26. Personal communication from a female AT&T employee.
27. Personal communication from Michelle Karotkin.
28. Suzanne G. Haines and Manning Feinlieb, "Women, Work, and Coronary Heart Disease: Prospective Findings from the Framingham Heart Study," *American Journal of Public Health* 70 (February 1980): 133.

29. NIOSH, Conference on Occupational Stress, *Proceedings*, NIOSH Publication #78-156 (Cincinnati, March 1978).
30. NIOSH, *An Investigation of Health Complaints and Job Stress in Video Viewing* (Cincinnati, February 1981).
31. *WOHRC News* (September/October 1981): 3.
32. Vera Shlakman, "The Status of Clerical and Professional Workers," in Colston E. Warne, *Labor in Post-War America* (Brooklyn, N.Y.: Remsen Press, 1949), p. 574.
33. By official AFL-CIO count, twelve AFL-CIO affiliates are now engaged in clerical organizing drives.
34. Joann S. Lublin, "On-the-Job Stress Leads Many Workers to File—and Win—Compensation Awards," *Wall Street Journal,* 17 September 1980, p. 33.
35. Stephen S. Leavitt, "Determining Compensable Workplace Stressors," *Occupational Health and Safety* (September 1980): 38.
36. The Institute for Labor and Mental Health in Oakland, CA, has been facilitating occupational stress groups for various unions since 1980. I am indebted to Lee Schore of the institute for explaining the functions and purpose of these groups.

The Particular Problems of Video Display Terminals
Mary Sue Henifin

Introduction to a Processed World[1]

Computers are revolutionizing the workplace. So far the impact has been greatest in offices where video display terminals—known as VDTs—are replacing pencils and paper, typewriters, and adding machines. A VDT is a keyboard attached to a television-like screen. Computer memory may be incorporated into the unit itself or the VDT may be connected via telephone or electrical lines to a computer many miles away.[2] When attached to printers, VDTs are used as "word processors," producing reports and letters. They are also used to manipulate, store, and transmit textual, numerical, and graphic information.

There are currently 10 million VDTs in use in the United States. Experts predict that by 1990 40 to 50 percent of all U.S. workers will be using them daily and that there will be more than 38 million terminal workstations in factories, schools, and offices across the country.[3]

VDTs are doing more than replacing the traditional tools of office work: they are also changing the very organization of work itself. Secretarial and blue collar jobs are being eliminated and office work is taking on aspects of the assembly line for the workers who perform highly routinized data-entry jobs eight hours a day.[4] Jobs that once required higher paying skills are being redefined as clerical and downgraded, or even eliminated. For example, in the newspaper industry reporters are now directly inputting stories into VDTs, editors are editing them on the VDTs, and the material is then set into type by a computer-managed process, completely eliminating the need for typesetters. VDTs are also being used to control computer-managed functions that used to be the province of skilled blue-collar workers. For example, telephone repair technicians now monitor system malfunctions by staring at VDT screens rather than inspecting underground cables. VDTs can be used to control computerized robots, whether they are used to build cars in Detroit or sheer sheep in Australia.[5]

In 1982, for the first time in the United States, the consumer, financial, and service industries employed more workers than did manufacturing.[6] IBM predicts that by 1985 40 percent of the total workforce will be employed in jobs primarily involved in information processing. While we can only speculate on the long-term social implications of this shift away from labor-intensive goods production, workers and health professionals have already begun to document some of the immediate health effects of VDT use. This section briefly describes the types of health hazards frequently encountered by VDT operators and outlines some solutions to these problems. The notes contain references to more detailed books and articles, as well as to groups that can provide resources for further exploration of this topic.

As more workers are spending longer periods of time using VDTs, complaints about discomfort and other health effects are mounting. The majority have centered around eye problems, including visual strain and fatigue, and sore, itching, tingling, and tearing eyes. Back and neck aches, sore arms, and other strains due to uncomfortable work positions are also prevalent, and there are complaints about stress and job dissatisfaction. In addition, there has been a growing concern over the issue of radiation emissions from VDTs. In the face of these complaints, a number of unions and organizations have taken positive steps to address the short- and long-term problems workplace automation has engendered.

Eyestrain

One group of researchers found a temporary reduction in the visual ability to discriminate fine details and a lengthening of the time it takes the eyes to accomodate to different focal distances after intensive VDT use;[7] another group found a higher incidence of eyestrain in VDT users compared to other office workers.[8] Reducing the glare from VDT screens, being able to adjust brightness and contrast, designing machines that eliminate flicker, and having screen characters that are large enough can all reduce visual problems (see Table 1 for specific suggestions).[9] In addition, appropriate corrective glasses or contact lenses may be needed for those with bifocals, lenses ground for inappropriate focal distances, or uncorrected visual problems. Overall office lighting, if too bright or placed so that it produces glare on the screen, may make viewing especially difficult and fatiguing. Blinds and shades on the windows, appropriate positioning of the VDT screen, and adjustable office lighting can all reduce glare and help prevent eyestrain.[10]

Biomechanical Strains

Biomechanical strains occur when the human body is forced to conform to a machine rather than having the machine designed to fit the wide range of human shapes and sizes. Working at a VDT can cause a variety of aches and pains. A poorly designed workstation forces the operator to sit for long periods in a position where the muscles and joints are in an awkward or unnatural position. Even in a carefully designed workstation, a job that requires long periods of sitting will be tiring to the muscular system (not to mention the mind). A VDT user who holds her or his neck and head in the same position for an extended period will be particularly prone to muscular fatigue. One researcher reported that "almost daily" pains in the neck, shoulder, and arm were experienced by about 15 percent of VDT operators working at data-entry tasks, by about 5 percent of other VDT operators and non-VDT typists, and by only 1 percent of traditional office workers.[11] Medical examinations of the muscles, tendons, and joints of these workers confirmed the verbal complaints. Researchers at the National Institute for Occupational Safety and Health (NIOSH) found significantly higher levels of at least fifteen different musculoskeletal complaints, including arm pain, swollen joints, stiff arms or legs, sore shoulders, hand cramps, and sore wrists in clerical workers using VDTs compared to those who were not.[12]

Adjustable equipment and workstations can greatly reduce these problems. VDTs with thin, detachable keyboards; rotating, tilting screens; task-oriented and adjustable lighting; and adequate work space allows the operator to move about and adjust the equipment to fit her or his particular needs. Adjustable chairs, document holders, and footrests also reduce biomechanical strains.

VDTs and Radiation

VDTs can theoretically emit both non-ionizing and ionizing (X-ray) radiation.[13] The machines have been designed to safeguard against emissions of ionizing radiation and most researchers have found that they do not emit X-rays in levels higher than natural background radiation.[14] However, one study, conducted by the Bureau of Radiological Health, found that some older models emitted X-rays when the screen was filled with characters and a special protective device was disconnected.[15]

The concern about the possibility of radiation emissions has grown as reports of problem pregnancies among VDT users have appeared in the newspapers. The few studies that have been conducted have not confirmed an association between birth defects or miscarriages and VDT use, however, although a large-scale study is needed before we can be sure that there is no such relationship.[16] In the meantime, some unions and 9 TO 5, the National Association of Office Workers, recommend prudence as the best policy, and suggest that pregnant workers should have the right to transfer from VDT work to other work within the company during the course of pregnancy if they wish, without loss of pay, seniority, or benefits.[17] Unfortunately, these recommendations ignore the established vulnerability of sperm to both ionizing and non-ionizing radiation,[18] as well as the potential risk of miscarriages and birth defects through paternal exposures.[19] For this reason, any recommendations regarding voluntary job transfers for pregnant women should include such options for men who are planning paternity. If there is a problem, to single out pregnant women may leave the offspring of men at risk while inviting management to discriminate against fertile women, a practice that has become all too common in chemical and manufacturing industries.[20]

VDTs also produce several forms of non-ionizing radiation. Some researchers are particularly concerned about the very low frequency (VLF) and extremely low frequency (ELF) radiation produced by VDTs because no one is sure what the biological effects of exposure to these types of radiation may be.[21] Research results have so far been inconclusive and contradictory.

Shielding VDTs with thin metal strips can eliminate or reduce VLF and ELF non-ionizing radiation emissions—as well as "electronic spying" on sensitive computer information.[22] Manufacturers can install inexpensive shields, and some unions have negotiated with management that only shielded VDTs be purchased.[23]

If you are concerned about the problem of radiation, you or management can request the results of radiation emission testing from the manufacturer before deciding what model to purchase.

Responsible manufacturers make this information available to consumers. Some unions have negotiated periodic radiation testing of the terminals in their offices.

Stress and VDTs

Researchers and writers who use VDTs as an adjunct to creative and self-supervised work may appreciate the greater ease with which VDTs allow them to manipulate data or make corrections, even if they experience some of the physical symptoms described in this chapter. But VDT operators who work all day performing data-entry tasks often find their work psychologically debilitating. Both the physical stresses of poorly designed work environments and equipment, and the emotional stresses of timed, often boring and repetitive work can and do combine to make many jobs that routinely use VDTs both stressful and dissatisfying. Research done by NIOSH found high levels of psychological distress among VDT operators. The problems were most severe in jobs with heavy work loads and time pressures. Symptoms included anxiety, depression, irritability, monotony, fatigue, and lack of inner security.[24]

Many VDT operators are "machine supervised," with a computer program monitoring both their speed and their error rate. Some jobs are machine paced, so that the operator has no control over the rhythm of the work. For example, long distance telephone operators spend their days under such control. A computer automatically assigns incoming calls needing operator assistance. The computer generates a "beep beep" signal into the operator's headset, signalling that a new call has come in, and such information as the number dialed by the customer is displayed on the VDT; the operator obtains any necessary additional information from the customer and types it into the terminal. Operators have no control over the rate at which calls are assigned to them by the computer, and the time it takes to complete each call is closely monitored.[25] Researchers have shown that jobs like these, with high demands and low control, are extremely stressful and linked with the development of coronary heart disease.[26]

Solutions to this kind of job stress include rest breaks and job rotation. NIOSH has recommended fifteen-minute breaks every two hours for operators with moderate visual demands and work loads, and fifteen minute breaks every hour for operators under high visual demands, high workloads, and/or for those engaged in repetitive tasks.[27] The Association of Scientific, Technical, and Managerial Staffs (ASTMS), a union in Great Britain, has recommended that for work requiring day-long VDT operation, "operators should work a maximum of two hours followed by a thirty minute break. No more than four hours should be worked in any one day."[28] Unfortunately, such a recommendation, if implemented, might encourage management to create part-time jobs—of four hours a day—without employee benefits.

Another way to reduce stress is to allow the operator to adjust the work situation and to control the work flow. As noted earlier, there are a number of ways in which the equipment can be made adjustable and the overall work situation made more comfortable. In addition, however, the work itself can be organized differently, so that the worker has some variety and relief from a physically demanding pace and a psychologically enervating routine.

Computerization of the office is expected, in the long run, to lead to a decrease in the number of clerical jobs. For example, although the number of office jobs is now expanding, a European study predicts a 30 percent reduction in clerical jobs in the finance industries in France by 1990.[29] Similar projections have not been made for the United States because the Department of Labor has not developed methods for making such predictions, but it is clear that older workers are often replaced rather than retrained when management computerizes an office.

9 TO 5 has closely monitored another avenue of job-loss: the export of data-entry jobs, via satellite, to developing countries where people work for lower wages than their U.S. counterparts. Companies have also been touting "home work," encouraging women to do data-entry work part time at home—for low wages and no fringe benefits. One computer company recently picked up on this theme in a *New York Times* ad that pictured a woman sitting at a VDT in her living room with one eye on her work and the other on her baby in a playpen. The kitchen loomed in the background, implying that the woman could work at the VDT, watch her baby, and cook at the same time. Not only do part-time workers cost less, but they also reduce the threat of unionization because workers are isolated from each other. Without the strength of numbers, homeworkers do not have the power to change the conditions of their work.

Controlling VDTs

The steps already discussed may involve more than one individual's efforts to institute changes that will avoid the health hazards of VDTs. If you are part of a union that has an active health and safety committee, you can use it to help negotiate specific contract language governing VDT work. If your workplace is not unionized, a good way to begin is to develop a worker health and safety committee. Try to win the right to have a say in purchasing and work organization decisions *before* large-scale computerization takes place in your workplace.[30] Companies sometimes encourage such involvement because they feel it will help the workers accept the new technology. Health and safety committees can turn to some of the resources listed in the notes to gain expertise in VDT health and safety issues and strengthen their bargaining positions.[31]

Many states have committees for occupational safety and health with active VDT committees. Such COSH groups have organized conferences to inform workers and develop strategies for improving workplace conditions. MassCOSH has developed sample VDT contract language to use as a model.[32] A number of COSH groups have worked to sponsor legislation governing health and safety on the job at the state level; at least eight states are considering such legislation regarding VDTs.[33] Union representatives and legislators in the Scandinavian countries, where some of the earliest research was conducted documenting the physical and psychological hazards associated with VDT use, have developed comprehensive rules to control VDT hazards. For example, proposed legislation in Norway seeks to prohibit the creation of new data-entry jobs that are monotonous, repetitive, and highly monitored.[34] Yet in the United States, the prestigious National Academy of Sciences recently released a report, *Video Displays: Work and Vision*,[35] branding VDT health and safety legislation and regulations premature as long as the technology is changing so rapidly. An eloquent dissent by Lawrence Stark chastises the academy for not "condemning the poor quality and legibility of current VDTs" and for "supporting the status quo of no standards or guidelines for VDT workplaces and no clear concern with unacceptable levels of ocular discomfort and visual fatigue."[36]

The office of the future depends on our actions today. We can passively stand by and let new technologies control us, or we can take active steps to develop work environments that enhance our health and improve the quality of our lives.

Appendix 1
9 to 5 Bill of Rights for the Safe Use of VDTs

9 TO 5 recommends the following protections while research to determine the causes of problem pregnancies is conducted and long-term solutions are developed:

—Workers should have the right to transfer away from VDT work to other work within the company during the course of pregnancy, without loss of pay, seniority, or benefits.
—VDT equipment should be made safe for all workers by the manufacturer through the use of inexpensive metal shielding. Machines already in use should be retrofitted with shields in order to eliminate any possible radiation emissions.

For the safety of all workers, including pregnant workers, 9 TO 5 recommends the following standards:

—All workers should have a minimum rest break of 15 minutes for every 2 hours of VDT work, or 15 minutes for every hour of intense VDT work.
—Continuous use of VDTs should be limited to 4 hours each day.
—All VDT equipment should have adjustable screens, keyboards, and glare-reduction devices; and furniture, lighting, and work environments should be designed for the comfort and safety of the operator. Employers should provide regular eye examinations for all VDT workers.
—Stress-inducing features of automated jobs such as machine pacing or computer monitoring should be eliminated.
—All VDTs should undergo periodic thorough testing for X-ray emissions, and a regular maintenance schedule is a must.
—Further research into all potential health hazards of VDTs should be conducted without delay.

Appendix 2
Summary of Recommended Characteristics
for VDTs and Workstations

Screen color and contrast	Dark green with lighter green or yellow characters; or black with white characters; the machine should also have contrast adjustability since user preferences differ
Letter size	A 5 x 7 or 7 x 9 dot matrix; minimum height—3.1–4.2 mm; maximum height—4.5 mm; width : height ratio, 3 : 4 to 4 : 5
Character refresh rate (to reduce flicker)	40 to 60 hertz minimum for low to medium persistence phosphor, with higher level preferable
Spacing	Between words: 1/2 character height; between lines: 1 character height

Lighting	Overall office lighting should generally be at the lower end of the recommended scale of 30 to 150 footcandles
Artificial lighting	Shielded or indirect; concealed lighting reflected from upper walls preferred; local desk lighting should be shielded and fitted with a dimmer, so that individuals can adjust to their own preference
Windows	Fitted with adjustable blinds or curtains; VDTs placed at right angles to (not facing) windows
VDT and other surfaces	Matte to avoid reflection
Screens	Coated by fine-grained, anti-reflection materials
Keyboard	Thin and adjustable
Screen	Adjustable tilt and rotation
Document holder	Adjustable and stable
Desk	Adequate surface and storage space for work and personal materials
Keyboard, chair, footrest	Arranged to allow 90 degree bend between upper and lower arms; body trunk and thighs, and calves and thighs; footrest may be needed

Adapted from tables in Jeanne M. Stellman and Mary Sue Henifin, *Office Work Can Be Dangerous to Your Health* (New York: Pantheon Books, forthcoming).

Notes

This chapter is adapted from a longer chapter, "Video Display Terminals: The Computer Connection," in Jeanne M. Stellman and Mary Sue Henifin, *Office Work Can Be Dangerous to Your Health* (New York: Pantheon Press, forthcoming).

1. This subheading is inspired by a stimulating magazine, *Processed World*, that explores the impact of computerization on office workers through graphics, articles, and "fantasies." Available from Processed World, 55 Sutter Street #829, San Francisco, CA 94104. Creative ideas for "scandalizing industry-sponsored events with costume picket lines and leaflets" and overcoming worker isolation are also included.
2. A thorough description of how VDTs work, as well as comprehensive information on their health hazards, can be found in A. Cakir, D. J. Hart, and T. F. M. Steward, *The VDT Manual* (New York: John Wiley, 1979). The most up-to-date information on VDT risks is available from the 9 TO 5 VDT hotline at 1-800-521-VDTS (in Ohio only, 1-800-522-

VDTS). You can get copies of 9 TO 5's VDT Bill of Rights to circulate to your co-workers and friends.

3. Vincent E. Giuliano predicts the future of computerized offices in "The Mechanization of Office Work," *Scientific American* 247, no. 3 (September 1982): 148-65. The entire issue is devoted to the mechanization of work, including an article by Joan Wallach Scott, "The Mechanization of Women's Work."

4. *Race Against Time: Automation of the Office* (Cleveland: 9 TO 5, 1980) documents the assembly-line nature of many office jobs.

5. A *New York Times* report on "The Manless Factory" (13 December 1981, pp. F1, F27) notes that there are 14,000 programmable robots in operation in Japan, 4,100 in the United States, and 2,300 in West Germany.

6. *New York Times*, 6 July 1982, p. A11.

7. R. R. Mourant, R. Lakshmanan, and R. Chantadisal, "Visual Fatigue and Cathode Ray Tube Display Terminals," *Human Factors* 23 (1981): 529-40.

8. See articles referenced in R. Matula, "Effects of Visual Display Units on the Eyes: A Bibliography (1972-1980)," *Human Factors* 23 (1981): 581-86.

9. See *VDT Manual* for detailed descriptions of the causes of visual fatigue and their solution.

10. Chapter 5, "Shedding Some Light on the Issue," in *Office Work Can Be Dangerous to Your Health*, describes how to evaluate and improve office lighting, including the lighting of VDT work stations.

11. W. Hunting, T. Laubli, and E. Grandjean, "Constrained Postures of VDT Operators," in *Ergonomic Aspects of Visual Display Terminals*, ed. E. Grandjean and E. Vigliana (London: Taylor and Francis, 1980), pp. 175-84.

12. M. J. Smith et al., "Job Stress in Video Display Operations," in *Ergonomic Aspects of Video Display Terminals*, pp. 201-10.

13. See *VDT Manual*. A thorough and understandable technical memorandum on VDTs and radiation is available from 9 TO 5, 1224 Huron Road, Cleveland, OH 44115.

14. See, for example, W. E. Murray et al., "Potential Health Hazards of Video Display Terminals" (June 1981), NIOSH Publication No. 81-129 (available from NIOSH, 4679 Columbia Parkway, Cincinnati, OH 45226); "Potential Health Effects of Video Display Terminals and Radio Frequency Heaters and Sealers," U.S. House of Representatives, *Hearings Before the Subcommittee on Investigations and Oversight of the Committee on Science and Technology*, May 12-13, 1981; and E. A. Cox, "Radiation Emissions from Visual Display Units," *Proceedings of Conference on Health Hazards of VDUs*, Loughborough University, December 11, 1980, available from Human Sciences and Advanced Technology (HUSAT) Research Group, Department of Human Sciences, Loughborough University of Technology, Leicestershire, LE11 3TU England.

15. Bureau of Radiological Health, "An Evaluation of Radiation Emissions from Video Display Terminals (1981)," HHS Publication FDA 81-

8153, available from U.S. Department of Health and Human Services, Public Health Services, Food and Drug Administration, Bureau of Radiological Health, Rockville, MD 20857.

16. See 9 TO 5's technical memorandum on VDTs and radiation for more information on problem pregnancies.

17. For a union response, see R. DeMatteo, *The Hazards of VDTs*, published by Ontario Public Service Employees Union, Department of Special Operations, 1901 Younge Street, Toronto, Ontario M45 2Z4 Canada.

18. See the following reports for references to the literature on male reproductive damage due to exposure to ionizing and non-ionizing radiation: J. Manson and N. Simons, "Influence of Environmental Agents on Male Reproductive Failure," in *Work and the Health of Women*, ed. Vilma Hunt (Boca Raton, FL: CRC Press, 1979); Arthur Bloom, ed., *Guidelines for Studies of Human Populations Exposed to Mutagenic and Reproductive Hazards* (New York: March of Dimes Birth Defects Foundation, 1981), p. 98; and United Nations Scientific Committee on the Effects of Atomic Radiation (UNSCEAR), *Sources and Effects of Ionizing Radiation, 1977 Report to the General Assembly* (New York: U.N. Publications, 1977).

19. For information on adverse reproductive outcomes following paternal exposure to physical and chemical hazards see: G. R. Strobino, J. Klein, and Z. Stein, "Chemical and Physical Exposure of Parents: Effects on Human Reproduction in Offspring," *Journal of Early Human Development* 1 (1978): 371; and Wendy Chavkin and Laurie Welch, *Occupational Hazards to Reproduction: An Annotated Bibliography*, published by the Program in Occupational Health, Montefiore Medical Center (111 E. 210th St., Bronx, NY 10467), 1980.

20. For accounts of the exclusion of fertile women from nontraditional jobs in chemical and manufacturing industries, see Jeanne Stellman and Mary Sue Henifin, "No Fertile Women Need Apply: Employment Discrimination and Reproductive Hazards in the Workplace," in *Biological Woman—The Convenient Myth* (Cambridge, MA: Schenkman Publishing Co., 1982); and Joan E. Bertin, "Discrimination Against Women of Childbearing Capacity," an address presented at the Hastings Center, 8 January 1982, and available from the Women's Rights Project, American Civil Liberties Union Foundation, 132 West 43rd Street, New York, NY 10036. See also Judy Scott's chapter in this volume.

21. See K. Marha, "The State of Knowledge Concerning Radiation from Video Display Terminals" (October 1982), available from Canadian Centre for Occupational Health and Safety, 250 Main Street East, Hamilton, Ontario L8N 1H6, Canada. *Microwave News*, a monthly report on non-ionizing radiation edited by Louis Slessin, has published *VDTs: Health and Safety*, a compilation of reports on pregnancy problems, PCBs and VDTs, skin rashes, radiation surveys, government actions, and worker compensation claims (available from P.O. Box 1799, Grand Central Station, N.Y., NY 10163).

22. See "Every Computer 'Whispers' Its Secrets," *New York Times*, 5 April

1983, p. C1, for discussion of "electronic leakage" from computers and espionage concerns.

23. See *The VDT Workplace Manual,* available from The Newspaper Guild, Research Department, 1125 15th St. N.W., Rm. 835, Washington, D.C. 20005.

24. Murray, *Potential Health Hazards of Video Display Terminals.*

25. For a vivid description of telephone operator stress see "Strung Out at the Phone Company," *Mother Jones* (August 1981). The Canadian Labour Congress's Labour Education and Studies Centre has documented stress-related symptoms as well as other health problems associated with VDT use in "Towards a More Humanized Technology: Exploring the Impact of Video Display Terminals on the Health and Working Conditions of Canadian Office Workers" (1982), available from 2841 Riverside Drive, Suite 301, Ottawa, Ontario K1V 8N4, Canada.

26. See R. Karasek et al., "Job Decision Latitude, Job Demands, and Cardiovascular Disease," *American Journal of Public Health* 71 (1981): 694-705, and references cited therein.

27. Murray, *Potential Health Hazards of Video Display Terminals.*

28. ASTMS, *Guide to Health Hazards of VDUs,* (1980), available from 10-26a Jamestown Rd., London.

29. See Karen Nussbaum, "Office High Tech Is Not Here for Good," *In These Times,* 24-30 May 1983, p. 12. *Office Automation: Jekyll or Hyde,* eds. Daniel Marshall and Judith Gregory (Cleveland: Working Women Education Fund, 1983), provides an international perspective on the impact of computerization on office work.

30. A useful guide to consult before purchasing machines is *The Human Factor, 9 TO 5's Consumer Guide to Word Processors,* available from 9 TO 5.

31. NYCOSH maintains an updated listing of VDT resources including slide shows and films. See "VDT Answer Source," available from NYCOSH, 32 Union Square, Rm. 404, N.Y., NY 10003.

32. "Health and Safety Contract Language for Operators of VDTs/CRTs," available from the Massachusetts Coalition for Occupational Safety and Health, 120 Boylston St. #206, Boston, MA 02116. *VDT Newsletter* is a quarterly publication updating information on medical problems, collective bargaining, and legislation related to VDTs in Canada, the United States, and Europe, and is available from VDT Committee, Labour Council of Metropolitan Toronto, 15 Gervais Drive, Rm. 407, Don Mills, Ontario, Canada.

33. *Microwave News* covers proposed VDT legislation on a state-by-state basis.

34. For information on Scandinavian research, legislation, and union contracts, see: Olov Ostberg, "Office Computerization: Research Then and Now," and Lisbet Hjort, "Labor Legislation in Norway: Its Application to the Introduction of New Technology," in *Office Automation.*

35. National Academy of Sciences, *Video Displays: Work and Vision* (Washington, D.C.: National Academy Press, 1983).

36. Ibid., pp. 235–36.

Closed Office-Building Syndrome
Wendy Chavkin

In the last five years or so many groups of office workers have reported "outbreaks" of irritated eyes, nose, and throat, skin rashes, dizziness, and fatigue. These are very disturbing to those involved: the affected workers are uncomfortable and alarmed; their employers are worried about lowered efficiency and morale; and researchers are only able to shrug their shoulders in puzzlement.

In order to understand how to proceed when confronted with such outbreaks, office workers and union activists need to understand the current state of knowledge about "building-related illness." This section provides such a summary.

Since 1977 nearly 200 investigations of "building-related" health complaints have been undertaken by government agencies, research institutions, and private consultants. Rarely has a cause been pinpointed. While this failure may in part reflect the complex nature of the problem, the investigations have also suffered from several methodological flaws: lack of a uniform or consistent approach; no comparable information from control buildings whose occupants have not complained; lack of follow-up; and the use of inappropriate environmental measurements (ventilation often excluded). Nevertheless, those working on the subject generally agree that the symptoms can be divided into four categories: irritative, neurophysiologic, infectious, and allergic or hypersensitivity.

Irritative and Neurophysiologic Symptoms

The most frequently raised complaints in building-related outbreaks are eye, nose, and throat (mucous membrane) irritations. The recent drive to conserve energy has prompted the construction of "tight" or "closed" office buildings whose windows do not open and whose central air conditioning recirculates filtered air. There are many possible sources of irritation in such an office environment. They include:
—dirt, glue, and detergent residues in carpets; these can occur in older, "unsealed" buildings, as well as in newly constructed ones;
—"outgassing" from synthetic fabrics and construction materials (room dividers, caulking, glues, sealant, and so forth);
—office machinery and its associated chemicals (duplicating chemicals, printing chemicals, carbonless copy paper, whiteout, etc.).

Sometimes imbalances in the ventilation system can lead to the creation of "micro-environments." For example, inadequate ventilation in an area where many office machines are concentrated may lead to irritative symptoms only among those workers who spend much of their time there.

Chemical measurements made in these cases usually reveal low levels of organic hydrocarbons in the air. Since these levels are far below OSHA standards, most investigators have dismissed the possibility that they are the cause of the problem. However, OSHA standards at best reflect what we now know about the serious health damage that can result from occupational exposures (i.e., cancer, chronic lung disease), and do not address less catastrophic health consequences, including discomfort or mucous membrane irritation. Lack of information does not mean that there is no potential problem. In addition, nothing is known about the possible additive or synergistic effects of exposure to many low-level airborne organic substances at the same time.

Headaches, lightheadedness, fatigue, lethargy, and a reduced ability to concentrate are also frequently reported in building-related outbreaks. They often accompany irritative symptoms, leading some researchers to ascribe the whole syndrome to indoor air pollution and inadequate ventilation, humidity, and temperature regulation. Others believe the symptoms result from carbon monoxide levels that are too high for comfort (although below the level considered dangerous)—either from cigarette smoke in a sealed building with a high percentage of recirculated air, or from air intake ducts placed too close to exhaust vents or near an external contaminated source, such as a garage.

Still other investigators have concluded that the complaints are psychogenic in origin. Since no specific causal agent can be found, it is assumed that no physical basis exists for the complaints. Some researchers have even elaborated a theory that worker-management strife underlies many of these outbreaks. According to this view, a precipitating factor (like an unusual odor or illness in an individual) triggers mass symptomology, which is therefore psychogenic (or stress-based) in origin. These theoreticians insist that theirs is not a victim-blaming approach but that worker stress resulting from poor worker-management relations must be seen as a legitimate problem and confronted head-on. Nevertheless, supportive evidence for this theory is lacking. Failure to implicate a physical/chemical/allergenic/infectious agent is more likely to reflect inadequate industrial standards, inadequate sampling or detection methods, or failure to look in the right place or consider the appropriate diagnosis.

Most investigations to date have not been able to identify a specific agent which is causing the symptoms. Even without pinpointing the cause, many of these outbreaks have abated following improvements in ventilation, temperature, and humidity regulation.

Infections, and Hypersensitivity Pneumonitis or Humidifier Fever

Here the term "infectious" refers to a disease that is not usually contagious but spreads in an environment generally thought to be nonhazardous. Examples include Legionnaire's Disease in a hotel, Pontiac fever in a county health department, and Q fever in a research laboratory. It does not refer to the rapid transmission of a known infectious disease (like a cold) among people crowded together in a confined space like an office. While infectious and hypersensitivity syndromes represent the most serious of the building-related illnesses, they occur infrequently and yet have received the most research resources. They are the easiest type of building-related diseases to deal with conceptually, since they are caused by an identifiable organism and thus lend themselves to "objective" laboratory documentation (growth of the micro-organism in environmental samples, antibody titres in the affected people). On the other hand, these illnesses have also been the most serious. For example, Legionnaire's Disease has a case fatality rate of approximately 15 percent.

Cough, chest tightness or shortness of breath, fever, and a flu-like syndrome can result when certain sensitive workers are exposed to such allergy-causing substances as mold, fungus, or bacteria in humidifiers, air cooling systems, ductwork, and air filters. If the exposure continues, this humidifier fever (hypersensitivity pneumonitis) may lead to a chronic lung impairment called interstitial lung disease.

These categories are not mutually exclusive. Irritative and allergic symptoms can overlap. Chemical "out-gassing" is heaviest immediately after construction or renovation. After an initial peak of complaints among workers in a newly constructed or remodelled office, these complaints dwindle as time and air dilution reduce the ambient levels of irritating, noxious substances. On the other hand, some workers may develop allergic responses with repeated exposure to sensitizing substances in the workplace. Other skin problems reported by office workers, like itching and dryness, are thought to reflect inadequate humidification.

In addition, menstrual irregularities (changes in length of cycle, flow pattern, cramps, bleeding between periods) have also been

84 / Wendy Chavkin

reported during these outbreaks. Because no association between menstrual dysfunction and chemical exposure has yet been documented, most investigators have dismissed it as implausible. Yet medical science knows very little about menstrual patterns, so the final word is not yet in on this question.

Summary

The evidence so far suggests that the majority of these outbreaks (excluding infectious and hypersensitivity illnesses) result from the increasing use of chemicals in the office, accompanied by a reduction in fresh air. The upswing in the number of outbreaks has coincided with the redesigning of offices to conserve energy. Increasing the percentage of fresh air and adjusting temperature and humidity have most often solved the problem.

Therefore, office workers and activists who find themselves involved in a building-related outbreak may want to demand that the investigation focus on the building's ventilation. Given the sparse and disorganized data on the subject, they may also want to insist that the investigation use a standardized systematic approach and follow-up. And worker education should be integrated into the process. Those experiencing symptoms and anxiety will feel less victimized if they understand the potential and limitations of any such research.

I would like to thank Andy Goodman, Andy Rowland, Stephen Schultz, and especially Diana Hartel for their help in thinking about this new topic.

Selected Bibliography

There is an extensive literature on indoor air pollution and building-related illness. The following have been selected because they are especially useful and/or represent particular viewpoints and approaches.

American Society of Heating, Refrigerating, and Air Conditioning Engineers. *Ventilation for Acceptable Indoor Air Quality*, ASHRAE Standard 62-1981. Atlanta, 1981.
Colligan, M.J., and Murphy, L.R. "Mass Psychogenic Illness in Organizations: An Overview." *Journal of Occupational Psychology* 52 (1979): 77.
Keenlyside, R.A. "Recent NIOSH Indoor Air Quality Investigations." *Proceedings of an Overview NIOSH Conference on Occupational Health Issues Affecting Clerical/Secretarial Personnel at Cincinnati* (July 1981).
Kreiss, K., and Hodgson, M.J. "Building-Associated Epidemics." In *Indoor Air Quality*, ed. Walsh and Dudney. Boca Raton, FL: CRC Press, 1983.

Levy, B.S. "Investigation of Menstrual and Systemic Symptoms Among Research Workers at the University of Massachusetts (Amherst)." Occupational Health Service, University of Massachusetts Medical Center (Worcester), 24 October 1981.

Messite, J., and Baker, D. "Occupational Health Problems in Offices: A Mixed Bag." In *Proceedings of an Overview NIOSH Conference on Occupational Health Issues Affecting Clerical/Secretarial Personnel at Cincinnati* (July 1981).

Report to the Congress of the United States: "Indoor Air Pollution: An Emerging Health Problem." CED 80-111. Washington, DC: U.S. Government Printing Office, September 1980.

Seppalainen A. *et al.* "Neurophysiological and Psychological Picture of Solvent Poisoning." *American Journal of Industrial Medicine* 1 (1980): 31–42.

Sterling, E., and Sterling, T. "The Impact of Different Ventilation and Lighting Levels on Building Illness: An Experimental Study." Paper presented at the International Symposium on Indoor Air Pollution, Health and Energy Conservation, Amherst, MA, October 13–16, 1981.

Sterling, E., Sterling, T., and McIntyre, D. "New Health Hazards in Sealed Buildings." *Journal of the American Institute of Architects* (April 1983): 64–67.

Sterling, T., and Kobayashi, D. "Exposure to Pollution in Enclosed 'Living Spaces.'" *Environmental Research* 13 (1977): 1–35.

"Symposium on Health Aspects of Indoor Air Pollution." *Bulletin of the New York Academy of Medicine* 57 (10) (1981).

Working Women Education Fund. *Health Hazards for Office Workers.* Cleveland: WWEF, April 1981.

World Health Organization Working Group. *Health Aspects Related to Indoor Air Quality.* EURO Reports & Studies no. 21 (Copenhagen: WHO, Regional Office for Europe, 1979).

4
Following the Harvest:
The Health Hazards of Migrant
and Seasonal Farmworking Women
Sonia Jasso and Maria Mazorra

Introduction

The issues of work, living conditions, and family life are generally acknowledged to be integrally related to each other. For migrant and seasonal farmworkers this is particularly so, in part because these workers rely heavily on family teamwork and on each member's ability to earn a wage, and in part because they often live in close proximity to the fields in which they work. Many of the health-damaging conditions of this grueling type of labor overlap into the nonworking hours: overexposure to heat, sun, and the elements; direct exposure to pesticides as well as to the spray-drift from the application of these; and other occupationally related safety and health problems, including inadequate field sanitation, which increases the risk of parasitic infections; poorly designed equipment, which can result in the mutilation of limbs and even death; and, in the case of migrant workers, substandard labor-camp housing. In fact, agriculture is the third most dangerous industry in the United States after mining and construction.

The sociological and economic factors affecting many migrant and seasonal farmworkers—such as minority status, substandard income and educational levels, and linguistic barriers—exacerbate their occupational health problems. The role of women who engage in migrant and seasonal farmwork is particularly important because of the additional stress these women undergo. Migrant and seasonal farmworking women raise their children under very harsh conditions, and often shoulder the major responsibility, and consequently the additional stress, of maintaining family life as the family moves about to follow the harvest; they are responsible for home chores and child-raising in addition to physically grueling work outside the home. They are also segregated into certain jobs and often receive even lower pay than the substandard wages received by farmworking men.

Who Are the Farmworkers?

Farmwork involves the various tasks connected with planting and harvesting, including irrigation, fertilizing, pruning, weeding, pest control, and harvesting. Nevertheless, the term "farmworker" or "farm laborer" is defined differently by various governmental agencies, and sometimes includes landowners, growers, and employers. Here it will be used to apply to the men, women, and children who are hired to perform some aspect of farm labor in return for a wage. Seasonal farmworkers are generally people who live and harvest crops in their own communities. Migrant farmworkers can also be considered seasonal workers if they work in their home states, but when such work is not available they travel various distances to find employment.

There are no precise figures on the general magnitude of the agricultural workforce in the United States or the percentage of migrant and seasonal farmworkers; nor is it known how many of these workers are women. Both the Department of Labor (DOL) and the Department of Agriculture (USDA) estimate the total farm workforce at 1.7 million, while the USDA has further determined that 22 percent of all hired farmworkers are women.[1] Of this 22 percent, 9 percent are classified as migrant workers.[2] Estimates by farmworker advocates, including the National Association of Farmworker Organizations (NAFO), Rural America, Inc., and the Legal Services Corporation put the total number of migrant and seasonal farmworkers and their dependents at between 4.8 and 5.8 million. Analyses of DOL and USDA data reveal that these numbers were collected to facilitate the agricultural economists' projections of the number of workers needed to meet future agricultural production goals, and thus are probably an undercount. The data enumerate jobs not people, and so fail to account for the number of workers who are unemployed, for job turnover (many migrants may fill the same job over one season), for illegal immigrant status ("undocumented" workers are not reported as wage earners), and for workers employed by labor contractors—where only the crew leader/contractor's name appears on the payroll, while he or she actually provides the grower with as many as 100 workers.[3] This underestimation and misrepresentation is crucial to the lives of farmworkers because it translates into a reduced amount of money allocated for social services by federal and state agencies—and thus with lower levels of health care, education, and other services.

The predominant ethnic composition of the migrant workforce varies according to the "stream" in which it travels—the path the migrant workers take from one region to another. There are three main migrant streams, as well as many minor ones. One originates in Florida, one in Texas, and one in southern California. The one that originates in Florida includes black and white Americans, Puerto Ricans, Haitian refugees, and Jamaican and other West Indian "guest workers." It moves from the Florida citrus regions up to Appalachia and into New England, harvesting apples, cranberries, and shade-growing tobacco.[4] The stream originating in Texas is composed mostly of Mexicans and Mexican-Americans, as is the stream that originates in southern California, although the latter also has a large component of U.S. whites, blacks, and some Asians.

Whereas the data do not exist to describe the sex distribution of the different migrant streams, it is clear that the East Coast stream is predominantly male and travels with a crew leader, while the Texas and West Coast streams are predominantly families, often of three or four generations, and have women and children active in the field work.

There is conflicting data over the relative proportion of certain ethnic and racial groups in the total migrant labor force. One source states that the majority are Mexican-American and blacks,[5] while another states that, contrary to popular belief, the majority are white, and that Mexican-Americans comprise only about 25 percent of the total migrant population.[6] In considering these numbers, it must be kept in mind that it was not until the early 1970s that minority advocates were successful in getting the government to collect and document the presence of various ethnic groups, both in the workforce and in the population at large. In general, however, the authors' experience coincides with these estimates.

According to USDA data for 1979, 49 percent of migrant farmworking women were Hispanic, 45 percent were white, and 6 percent were "Black and Other"[7]—in other words, 55 percent were classified as belonging to minority groups. However, our numerous visits to fields and labor camps in many states raise doubts about the accuracy of these figures, for we never saw a white woman migrant farmworker.[8] If so, the USDA figures do not accurately portray the ethnic composition of the total migrant workforce.

Farmworker earnings in the United States are low, and those of immigrant farmworkers are lowest of all. In 1970 Economic Research Services, which analyses data for the USDA, reported that the average annual income of a farmworker was $5,501. A large percentage of this money must have been generated from nonfarm employment, however, since full-time farm laborers brought home annual earnings of less than $3,000—less than the agricultural minimum wage.

Within this highly exploited group of workers there are great disparities. In 1979 the average daily income of a male farmworker (including supplementary wages from nonfarm work) was a mere $27.01, and for a female it was even less—only $22.39.[9] Further, the annual average salary for a farmworking male (who engaged in both farm and nonfarm work) was $4,689, while that for a female (who also engaged in both types of work) was only $2,370—despite a differential of only 68 days' labor. The California Commission on the Status of Women attempted to quantify the inequities encountered by farmworking women. It found that women farmworkers have lower annual incomes because they are tracked into different jobs than men, and because they are paid less for the same jobs; that women have no chance for upward mobility—better jobs are presumed to require "male strength"; that an overwhelming majority of women (and men) want to leave farmwork unless the work conditions, pay, benefits, and housing improve; and that women farmworkers in particular would like affordable and nearby child care centers.[10]

One reason that the women are paid less is that the women are required to do piecework while the men are paid by the hour. Since the women can pick less, they are paid less, while the hourly wage for men gives the employer control.[11] Another is that a great number of women are employed only during the peak of the harvesting season, while men are hired for the few jobs in the off season. As one farmworking woman noted, "For women the work runs out sooner than for men."[12]

Since the majority of female farmworkers are members of minority groups, racial and language barriers are further obstacles to attaining adequate pay, as is the generally low level of educational attainment. In 1979 the median amount of completed education of a Hispanic farmworker was 5.4 years, while for the "Black and Other" category it was 7.7 years, and for the white category it was 12.3 years.[13] Migrant workers thus have less ability to compete for other jobs in the labor market, and are therefore more easily exploited as farmworkers. And the nature of the migrant's life only perpetuates illiteracy, since parents have to move their children from school to school as they follow the harvest.

In addition, children are expected to work in the fields at a very early age: the average farmworker family cannot survive unless all its able members work. Even children in school often rise at 5 A.M., work side by side with their parents, and then put in a full day in the classroom.[14] Violations of child labor laws—which prohibit children under twelve from working—are clearly flagrant. In the past the Department of Labor gave permits to growers of short-season crops to use ten- and eleven-year-old children as laborers, but the National Association of Farmworker Organizations fought a successful, though lengthy, court battle to establish twelve years of age as the legal limit. Ironically, firmer enforcement of these laws only worsens the farmworker's already deplorable economic situation, so that Legal Services lawyers—who have an obligation to see that the laws are enforced—are forced to overlook children working in the onion fields, planting the buds as they quickly crawl through the rows. Farmers like to employ children for jobs such as these since their small size allows them to move quickly through the fields.

The children of farmworkers face hazards greater than other children. In the fields they are exposed to pesticides and other toxic substances—often as babies, when their mothers are forced to bring them to the fields for lack of day care. One woman described a typical incident:

When we work in the fields our whole family goes, my children, ranging from 6 years to 1 year. While we were working . . . a duster plane started spraying the field right next to us. The wind started blowing the pesticide toward us. That day when we got home I felt very dizzy and had a lot of blurred vision. . . . My children who were playing outside got a lot of burning sores all over their bodies.[15]

Migrant children are also prone to accidental drowning—working parents cannot adequately protect their children from falling into the irrigation ditches that cross the fields.[16]

The irrigation ditches are a hazard in another way. The water in the ditches (and in the spigots) is often the only source of water for the workers. Unlike every other workforce—including that in the construction industry, which is after all as mobile and temporary as that in agriculture—farmworkers are not provided with such basic sanitation facilities as drinking and wash water and portable toilets. In 1972, farmworker advocates petitioned the Occupational Safety and Health Administration (OSHA) to develop agricultural field sanitation standards. The result has been ten years of litigation as to whether farm laborers should or should not have drinking water in the fields! During recent hearings in Washington, D.C., a Texan farmworking woman gave the testimony regarding toilet facilities in the fields: "Whenever there is a ditch or woods nearby, we go there. When this does not exist, we just have to wait. Or otherwise a group of us get together and stand around the person and cover him or her up."[17] Prolonged retention of urine has been associated with a high rate of urinary tract infections (UTI) among farmworkers,[18] and such infections are common among farmworking women.

Inadequate human-waste disposal is a principle factor in the transmission of numerous infectious diseases, including dysentery, typhoid, hepatitis, and parasitic infections. The largest outbreak of typhoid fever in the United States in recent history occurred in a migrant labor camp in Dade County, Florida, and was traced to a contaminated water supply.[19] Parasitic infections—also a result of fecal contamination, often of the drinking water—among migrant adults and children are frequent and result in gastrointestinal problems.

The lack of toilet facilities is a serious hazard not only to the farmworker but also to the consumer. Workers who must evacuate in bushes or open fields may contaminate edible food.[20] This possibility is supported by data included in a report by the National Institute of Occupational Safety and Health that shows that parasitic infections in the general population parallel migrant-worker travel routes, and that in Florida the highest rates of these infections were in those areas with the greatest intensity of fruit and vegetable harvesting.[21]

Farmworkers who use irrigation water for drinking and washing face the additional hazard of ingesting chemicals: the irrigation system is often used for the application of pesticides. These have been linked with cancer, genetic mutations, birth defects, and neurological and behavioral problems,[22] and many have been banned by the government—but not before thousands of workers have drunk them daily.

The housing provided to migrant workers varies from farm to farm. It ranges from relatively comfortable structures to converted chicken coops with no indoor plumbing or electricity, no sewage system, and no fresh water supply. One worker described a not atypical camp:

> The living quarters are very bad here where we've been coming for 15 years. There is hardly a house that has a bathroom or hot water to bathe, which is very essential. After working the way we do we need a bath to feel better. Without a bathroom, we have to heat the water and take a bath in the toilet compartment, which is falling down and stinks. We have to line up and go one at a time. . . . This really makes me mad, but I can't say anything. Apa says we'll be leaving in a week so we can put up with it. But I don't think it's fair we should go through this every year. Though no one says anything for fear of losing their job. And then what?[23]

Occassionally a child dies in one of these camps and the public outcry leads to fleeting attempts at reform. An article in the *Washington Post*, for instance, reported the death of a nine-month-old migrant child in a labor camp in Maryland. The paper described the camp as follows:

Most migrants had been living in squalid conditions, often crowded into small rooms with few sanitary facilities. Visitors reported seeing clogged latrines, stagnant pools of water, dank mattresses, and gang showers, and there were reports of widespread disease.[24]

Yet conditions at this particular camp had frequently been criticized by migrant reform groups and had already been the subject of a commission report. A Washington law firm had even recommended to the Maryland Department of Health and Mental Hygiene that the camp be closed down unless dramatic improvements were made. Nothing has been done.

Although OSHA is charged with enforcing the Temporary Labor Camps Standard Act, the standard was written in a manner that makes worker protection difficult.[25] A major loophole is that the camp must be inhabited at the time of inspection: if a worker asks for a OSHA inspection, but leaves before the inspector arrives, and a new crew has not yet come, the inspector cannot give the grower a citation. This happens frequently since there are far too few inspectors.

These conditions are obviously oppressive to all farmworkers, but because women are considered responsible for domestic life, it is they who suffer most heavily. It is they who must struggle to feed, clothe, and care for their families under such primitive conditions.

Most of us do not consider the weather a hazard, but for the migrant farmworker it is—both at work in the field and at home in the camp. Scorching sun, wide temperature swings between day and night, harsh winds, and driving rains permeate the migrant farmworkers' lives as they move from state to state. At times it is so cold that farmworkers put on several pairs of socks, extra pants, and layers of jackets and scarves. At other times the heat is so extreme that workers suffer from heat cramps (from loss of salt), heat exhaustion (from loss of body water), and heat stroke (when the body can no longer maintain its temperature control). All are compounded by the lack of drinking water. What shelter there is in the field is more often used to protect the machinery than the workers. Those who try to seek the shade these shelters provide risk being fired. One worker in Texas noted that potatos that were picked during the heat of the day and fell to the ground literally baked.[26] Another noted:

> This summer has been one of the hottest. It gets so bad that there are days when the workers just can't stand it and they leave the field early. People complain then that migrants don't want to work but I'd like to put them all in the fields for just a

half a day in 90-degree heat and see how they like it. I mean even mules get put in the shade in the heat of the day. Are migrants less than animals?[27]

Since the "general environment" is the farmworker's workplace, employers have argued that it cannot be controlled by engineering methods and other typical industrial safeguards. But this only allows them to evade their responsibility to provide a safe and healthy workplace.

The general public, however, views the agricultural workplace as a low-risk environment. In fact, they often think it is a "healthy" place—plenty of fresh air, sunshine, and lots of exercise. But the reality is that agriculture is just as chemical-laden and machine-intensive as any other area of industry. Machinery and other types of equipment are used at every point of the agricultural cycle. Tractors, spray rigs, irrigation poles, movable bins, conveyor belts, hauling trucks, ladders, hoes, scissors, knives, and saws are all used routinely by farmworkers. Those who call agriculture un-skilled labor speak out of ignorance. Anyone who picks grapefruit must be highly skilled to maintain his or her balance on a flimsy ladder while filling a huge sack. Any abrupt movement brings the worker tumbling down. The rapidity of these workers is a source of amazement to those who can barely stay on the ladder and avoid the sharp citrus thorns.

Aside from machinery accidents, pesticide exposure is the most highly publicized health and safety problem for agricultural work-ers. The term "pesticide" refers to any chemical that is used to eliminate a targeted pest. For example, insecticides, herbicides, and fungicides are chemicals that kill insects, weeds, and funguses respectively. But these chemicals are not target-specific—they poison the workers in the fields as easily as the plants they are aimed at. Yet since only a limited amount of information is avail-able on the long-term health risks of pesticides, the farmworker is in effect a human guinea pig.

The most common categorization of pesticides is by chemical class. This breaks them down into organochlorines. In the past organochlorines (such as DDT, chlordane, and heptachlor) were the most commonly used, but because they persist in the environ-ment and accumulate in human tissues they have gradually been phased-out. Their replacement, the organophosphates, were origi-nally developed as nerve gases during World War II. Although these breakdown more easily in the environment, and thus pose less of a long-term threat, in the short term they are more likely to cause severe poisoning. Organophosphates and carbamates have been shown to have profound effects on the body's immunological system, and their use may account for the high incidence of respiratory diseases among farmworkers.

The responsibility for issuing pesticide standards for agriculture falls to the Environmental Protection Administration (EPA), rather than OSHA, which can only issue standards that affect their formulation and manufacturing. The Federal Insecticide, Fungicide, and Rodenticide Act (FIFRA) is administrated by EPA and is the only legislation that provides farmworkers with some protection from pesticide exposure. FIFRA states that no worker should be in the field when a pesticide is being used unless that worker has been trained as a pesticide applicator and is provided with protective equipment. Further, no worker may re-enter the field until the pesticide dust has settled or the liquid has dried. Specific re-entry intervals—the amount of time that must elapse before a worker is allowed to re-enter the field—have been established for some chemicals and may range from 24 to 48 hours. Yet FIFRA is seldom enforced, as numerous eyewitness accounts make clear:

> The planes are always spraying pesticide, sometimes directly over us and sometimes around us. I work during the cabbage, cotton, and onion seasons. We have never been told to leave the fields while the spraying is going on. This has happened to me many times.[28]

> The planes are usually dusting where we are working, especially during cabbage harvest. I get a severe rash and a nagging cough every time I work where pesticide has been sprayed. They tell us to get out of the field while the spraying is being done. But we go back to work right after the plane leaves. The pesticide is still wet and gets all over our clothes.[29]

There are three ways in which chemicals can enter the body: through inhalation, ingestion, or absorption through the skin. Field workers are subject to all three: they inhale the drift, and come into contact with residues on crop leaves (foliar residue), which are then transferred from the hands and arms to the mouth, nose, and eyes, and can also be inhaled directly. Exposure to foliar residues often results in dermatitis, skin allergies, and eye problems. Gloves afford some protection, but it is sometimes difficult to harvest efficiently while wearing them: most farmworkers feel they cannot harvest grapes and raisins, for instance, while gloved.[30] The following testimony presented by farmworking men at an EPA hearing in south Texas shows some of the ways which pesticide poisoning can happen:

> We were working in the fields north of Mercedes when a duster plane was spraying the field next to us. That was last year in

April of 1979. Ever since then I have had a permanent sinus [problem] in which blood comes out of my nose, severe headaches, and rash.

It was in the early morning hours about 9:00 A.M. when an airplane came right over us and started spraying pesticide. Some of the workers were eating their breakfast just outside the field. Pesticide fell over their food, yet they didn't notice it. An hour or two later, I felt a severe chest pain and other people did too. The ones that were eating at the time the plane came by got very ill and were taken to the hospital. They were treated and released and were told it was just the hot weather and cold drinking water. I still get headaches and severe chest pain.[31]

To what extent are agricultural workers actually harmed by pesticides? The estimate cited by an HEW official during Senate hearings on migratory labor was that there were approximately 800 deaths and 80,000 injuries from an improper use of pesticides every year.[32] This figure was criticized for being too high, since it was said to be an extrapolation from data for one county in Florida. On the other hand, a 1976 California report attributed 1,452 occupational diseases to pesticides in California alone.[33] This was said to be an underestimate of the number of poisonings. In a study of 400 farmworkers in rural Florida, 48.5 percent stated that "at least once in their careers they had been sprayed directly with pesticides while they were harvesting crops, and 52 percent of the respondents became noticeably ill after the spraying incident."[34] A preliminary analysis of data collected in south Texas by the National Association of Farmworkers' Organizations revealed that 53 percent of the 260 workers interviewed had been in the fields during the application of pesticides; only 21 percent of these had been asked to leave the field and 61 percent complained of routinely being sprayed by pesticide drift.[35] The warning label, which is the only means of communicating protective information to the field worker, is in fact seldom available. And even if it were, it is unlikely that it could be understood, since it is written in highly technical language—and only in English.

One of the major potential risks from pesticides is to reproductive potential. The response of government agencies when dealing with the reproductive risk faced by men contrasts strongly with its response to the risk faced by women. For instance, DBCP is a pesticide that has been shown to cause sterility in men, a fact that was established in 1976 when men working in its manufacture were affected. However, it was not until 1979 that the EPA suspended the use of this chemical and put a temporary ban on its use in the agricultural fields of all states but Hawaii. In contrast, when only animal data showed that the pesticide TOK caused birth defects, the EPA issued a statement as follows:

An active ingredient of this product causes birth defects in laboratory animals. Women of childbearing age should not be involved with mixing/loading or application of this product. Exposure to this product during pregnancy must be avoided.[36]

Nevertheless, in contrast to DBCP, TOK has not been banned—so that the EPA caution has become a handy excuse for a grower to refuse to hire women. Thus while it may seem that women are being more quickly protected, in fact it is a form of protection that only serves to further segregate them into the lower rungs of the agricultural workforce.

Consumers too are affected by pesticides. We eat pesticide-coated fruits and vegetables, whether they are grown in the United States or imported from the third world—where fields are often sprayed with chemicals that are banned in the United States but sold overseas. This maneuver not only subjects farmworkers in the developing world to the most dangerous chemicals, but exposes the very U.S. consumer whom the ban was supposed to protect! And it is not as if there was no alternative: integrated pest management for instance—pest control strategies that use minimal amounts of pesticide along with such farming techniques as mixed crop planting and biological controls—offer an alternative to the heavy reliance on dangerous chemicals.

Like workers in other industries, farmworkers have organized in order to better their working conditions. Although the National Labor Relations Act excludes farmworkers from those who have the right to bargain collectively, some states—including California and Arizona, have passed legislation that provides these rights. And the unions, led by the United Farm Workers, have taken advantage of their contracts to win prohibitions against the use of certain pesticides while their members are in the fields. Unions have also made sure that, where state sanitation standards exist, they are properly enforced.

Women have been instrumental in the effort to organize unions among farmworkers. As one organizer put it, "women provide a lot of leadership, for example, in keeping the strikes nonviolent. When you have women, you also have children, and children bring out a different type of feeling."[37]

Dolores Huerta, vice-president of the United Farmworkers' Union is a leader in establishing union health centers, and a prime catalyst in obtaining health and safety protections for all farmworkers in California.

Union-busting tactics in agriculture have included the malicious spraying of workers with pesticides. One worker testified:

> Last year just before the onion strike, we were clipping onions just northwest of Raymondville [Texas]. . . . A duster plane suddenly appeared and started spraying while we were working. No one ever instructed us to leave.[38]

Similarly, in August 1978, during a strike among tomato workers in Ohio, members of the Farm Labor Organizing Committee were deliberately sprayed by a grower. The EPA's response was to issue—in April 1980—a warning to the farmer that they had reason to believe that he had violated the instructions on the pesticide label![39]

But while organizing farmworkers in the effort to pressure the courts, Congress, and the growers to provide the wages and standards of living and health they deserve would seem an urgent neccesity, farmworkers have not proven easy to organize. Differences in race, ethnicity, and language are used by the growers to divide the workers from each other. In Florida, for instance, Haitians, Jamaicans, and black Americans are given different housing and eating areas. They are segregated so that they cannot get to know each other, and made to compete against each other so they will not get together to fight a common—larger—cause. Farmworking women are particularly isolated—from the men by the extra burden of work they have to bear, and from the women in surrounding communities by their constant moving from place to place. The plight of farmworking women and men is not a romantic social cause. It is very real. And the struggle goes on . . .

Notes

1. Susan L. Pollack, *The Hired Farm Working Force of 1979*, USDA/ERS, *Agricultural Economic Report #473* (Washington, D.C., August 1981), p. 4.
2. Ibid., p. 24.
3. Rural America, Inc., *Where Have All the Farmworkers Gone?*, September 1977, p. 13.
4. Kathryn A. Bissell, *The Migrant Farmworker* (Washington, D.C.: Institute for Multi-Disciplinary Graduate Research, Catholic University, 1976), p. 1–1.
5. Comptroller General of the United States, Report to the Congress, *Impact of Federal Programs to Improve the Living Conditions of Migrant and Other Seasonal Farmworkers*, February 6, 1973.

6. Bissell, The Migrant Farmworker, p. 1–1.
7. Pollack, The Hired Farmworking Force of 1979, p. 24.
8. Labor camps visited included those in the states of Florida, Texas, California, North Carolina, South Carolina, Michigan, Wisconsin, Illinois, and Oregon.
9. Pollack, The Hired Farmworking Force of 1979, Appendix Table VII, p. 34.
10. California Commission on the Status of Women, Campesinos: Women in the California Agricultural Labor Force (Sacramento, CA, June 1978).
11. Rural New York Farmworker Opportunities, Inc., Farmworking Women's Equity Project (June 1976): 26.
12. Ibid.
13. Pollack, The Hired Farmworking Force of 1979, p. 8.
14. Paula De Perna, "Despite Child Labor Laws 8-Year-Olds Cut Asparagus," New York Times, 6 July 1981.
15. Affidavit by a farmworking woman in Willacy County, Texas, April 10, 1980, notarized by Andrea H. Hurtado.
16. Drowning is the second most common cause of death among migrant children. The first is car accidents. See Education Commission of the States, Interstate Migrant Education Task Force—Migrant Health, Report No. 131 (Denver, CO, November 1979), p. 17.
17. M. Semler and C. Feinberg, "Seems OSHA's Washing Its Hands of Farm Worker's Basic Sanitation," New York Times, 15 September 1981.
18. Personal communication with Mario Manecci, Office of Migrant Health, Bureau of Community Health Services, U.S. Department of Health and Human Services, September 1980.
19. U.S. House of Representatives, Subcommittee on Agricultural Labor, Hearings on Typhoid Outbreaks in Dade County, Florida, 93rd Congress, 1974.
20. J. Ortiz, "The Prevalence of Intestinal Parasites in Puerto Rican Farm Workers in Western Massachusetts," American Journal of Public Health (1980): 70, 2203–05.
21. National Institute of Occupational Safety and Health, A Report to the Occupational Safety and Health Administration on Field Sanitation, March 1981.
22. "The Pesticide Dilemma," National Geographic 57, no. 2 (February 1980).
23. The Harvester 4, no. 2 (March-April 1982): 13.
24. A. Muscatine and A. Guillermoprieto, "Baby from Controversial Maryland Migrant Labor Camp Dies," Washington Post, 22 July 1982.
25. Occupational Safety and Health Standards, 29 CFR 1910.142, Temporary Labor Camps.
26. Personal communication from Lupe Rivera and Maria Mazorra.
27. Karlyn Baker, "The Nightmare," Washington Post, 22 September 1980.
28. Ibid., 16 April 1980.

29. Ibid., 17 April 1980.
30. W. J. Popendorf and R. C. Spear, "Preliminary Survey of Factors Affecting the Exposure of Harvesters to Pesticide Residues," *American Industrial Hygiene Association Journal* 35 (June 1974): 379.
31. Affidavit, April 9 and 15, 1980.
32. N. Ashford, *Crisis in the Workplace: Occupational Disease and Injury* (Cambridge: MIT Press, 1976), p. 529.
33. "Farmworker Health and Safety Is a Right—Not an Issue," *National Farmworker* 2, no. 9 (November-December 1979): 1.
34. Florida Rural Legal Services, Inc., "*Danger* in the Field: The Myth of Pesticide Safety," May 1980, p. 34.
35. National Association of Farmworker Organizations, in conjunction with the Farmworker Consultation, "A National Perspective on Farm Labor Issues," September 29, 1980.
36. EPA Reg. No. 707-92-AA, EPA Est. No. 477-MD-1, TOK WP-50, Rohm & Haps.
37. *The Harvester* 4, no. 2 (March-April 1982).
38. Affidavit, April 19, 1980.
39. M. Mazorra, "Farmworkers under the Spray Gun," *Not Man Apart* (Magazine of the Friends of the Earth), September 1980.

5
Sexual Harassment and Women's Health
Peggy Crull

Carmita Wood worked as an administrator in a large university. Her department head let it be known that he didn't think a woman should be doing her job. He stared at her breasts, made suggestive remarks, and brushed against her. She began dressing in pants to discourage him and taking a circuitous route to avoid passing him in the hall. When these methods failed to stop his advances she complained to her supervisor, who responded that a "mature woman" should be able to handle him. She asked for and was denied a transfer. The situation was making her so tense that she began suffering neck pains that eventually put her in traction. Finally, after an especially embarrassing incident in which her harasser grabbed her at a department Christmas party, she quit her job. She was denied unemployment benefits and, at her appeal, where hearing officers made jokes about how her harasser had been a "pain in the neck," she was turned down again because they didn't believe her story.

At the same time Diane Williams was involved in a protracted court battle against the United States Department of Justice, where she had formerly been employed. She had been fired from that job after her supervisor became irritated when she did not accept his invitations for dates or respond to the love notes he left on her desk. Williams' was one of the first sexual harassment cases to reach the courts.[1]

The cases of Wood and Williams, and of other women who have had the courage, foresight, and perseverance to insist on public recognition of their dilemma, brought the phenomenon of sexual harassment on the job to public attention and sparked the formation of advocacy groups such as Working Women's Institute and the Alliance Against Sexual Coercion in the mid 1970s.[2] Stories from women who had previously been silent led to the recognition of yet another form of sexual abuse of women. Like street harassment, rape, battery, and incest, sexual harassment is an outrage because it is an invasion of a woman's personal integrity and safety. In the case of sexual harassment, the mechanism of coercion is a woman's need to make a living; going to work makes her a target for sexual degradation.

Rising consciousness has resulted in an explosion of information which points out that beyond the inherent injustice of sexual invasion, sexual harassment has a damaging impact on women's work. Statistics on jobs, raises, and training that were lost because women refused to be sexually available at work suggests that sexual harassment has served as a major, though hidden, barrier to women's economic security and advancement.[3] Sociologists and economists have begun to measure the economic losses to women in terms of salary, sick days, opportunities for promotion, and benefits in an attempt to establish the degree to which women's depressed and segregated status in the workforce is aggravated by sexual harassment.[4]

Recognition of the implications of sexual harassment for women's mental and physical health came much later than recognition of its direct economic effects. My own consciousness of sexual harassment as a health issue dates from reading the following letter in the files of Working Women's Institute:

> Dear Ms. Meyer and Ms. Sauvigne:
> I saw you on television last week and even though I think you were great, you left something out. I have gone to the doctor twice in the last month to get something for my stomach. When my harasser (I call him Romeo) is around and putting his hands on me, my stomach gets totally churned up. It has gotten to the point where I can't eat and now my doctor thinks I'm getting an ulcer, so I'm on a strict diet. Unfortunately, I need this job and Romeo, who is one of the most popular businessmen in this little town (you know, Jaycees and all) is not about to leave me alone because he can't help himself. He would gladly go to bed with every woman who works here if they would let him. Anyway, I wish there was some way to get him to pay my doctor bills! Seriously, maybe you could give some advice to women about how to keep this from getting to them and making them sick.

This paralleled Carmita Wood's descriptions of physical discomfort and alerted me to those themes in many of the letters we received. It inspired a series of investigations at Working Women's Institute of the possible stress effects and other ramifications for health that might grow out of sexual harassment on the job.[5] This chapter describes the results of those investigations, as well as several other studies that have looked at the connection between sexual harassment and health. It speculates on the mechanisms through which sexual harassment acts as a hidden occupational health hazard and suggests methods for eliminating the problem.

The Context of the Problem

In order to be comprehensible, the stress effects of work-related sexual harassment must be viewed as part of a larger system of causes and effects. Sexual harassment grows out of the economic and psychological inequality between the sexes that is built into the workforce as well as the whole culture and is reinforced by the class system that pervades every institution of our society. Men can force sexual attention on women at the workplace because of the greater economic power they hold. On the whole, they have higher status jobs, higher salaries, more formal training, and more seniority than women.[6] They are more likely to be in unions or to be more closely connected with informal "old boy" networks. This superior status protects men from any repercussions that could arise when a woman complains about being targeted for sexual attention. Indeed, sexual harassment may be a demonstration of that status and power, and not primarily motivated by sexual feelings.[7] It may also be a route through which men bolster class and status differences among themselves.[8]

Gender-based differences in internalized feelings about power are also at play in sexual harassment. Men are taught that it is their prerogative to make sexual comments to and about women. Indeed, their success at this often proves their masculinity.[9] Further, sexual comments can serve to trivialize women when their potential equality becomes threatening. On the other hand, women believe that they are supposed to acquiesce to uninvited sexual attention, even when it is derogatory, because it is an affirmation of their femininity. Their socialization even encourages them to blame themselves when male sexual behavior gets out of line.[10] In sum, sexual harassment is a manifestation of the powerlessness wrought by women's economic situation and reinforced by their psychological training.[11]

Once we see the relationship between sexual harassment and power, preliminary research which suggests that sexual harassment is widespread wherever women and men come into contact at work comes as no surprise. Using a variety of definitions of sexual harassment, various polls have produced rough estimates of the extent of the problem. One of the earliest surveys, conducted by *Redbook* in 1976, found that 88 percent of 9,000 female readers who mailed back its questionnaire reported some form of unwanted sexual attention in their work lives.[12] A 1980 survey of government workers in Illinois showed that 59 percent of the women had been harassed on their jobs. In a study of 23,000 federal government employees, 42 percent of the women told of sexual harassment within the last two years of their federal service.[13] Two considerably smaller surveys have produced very tentative information about the incidence of sexual harassment in blue-collar jobs. A telephone interview study of 139 unskilled female auto workers revealed that 36 percent of the interviewees had experienced sexual harassment.[14] Fifty-three percent of the women in a small survey of coal miners had been propositioned by a boss, and one-third of those propositions had been accompanied by a threat. Seventy-six percent had been propositioned by co-workers and 17 percent had been physically attacked.[15]

While these figures indicate that sexual harassment is widespread in several industries, they are too sketchy to provide us with any information about variations according to industry and occupation.[16] At Working Women's Institute we have attempted to develop some hypotheses about possible variations based on records of women who contact us for help.[17] Our clients come from a wide range of industries and occupations. Their distribution among them is very similar to the distribution of women in the workforce as a whole. For example, 39 percent of the women we hear from are clerical workers, a field in which 34 percent of all women in the workforce are employed.[18] We therefore speculate that sexual harassment occurs across the board. We have begun to suspect, however, that there are some differences in the *forms* of harassment encountered by women in different occupations. These differences in form cannot be understood without a broader description of the experience of sexual harassment on the job.

A Profile of the Sexual Harassment Experience

The sexual harassment which prompts women to mail back survey questionnaires, or call a women's group for advice, or even go to court is not the light sexual banter or "harmless" chase around the desk frequently depicted in popular humor. More often than not it is an inescapable series of acts which invade the woman's personal and/or physical privacy and escalate to the point of interfering with her work or even her safety. In the words of one client:

> We had to travel together a lot because he was training me to be a buyer in his division. I always tried to ignore his constant complaints about how bored he was with his wife in bed and

his veiled suggestions that we could save money by getting a room together. One night after he had a few too many drinks at dinner, he kept calling my room all night telling me how frustrated he was. I was afraid to tell him off since I was up for a promotion in a month.

A client in a nontraditional job reported:

The other surveyors seemed fascinated by what I wore, even though I tried always to dress in baggy clothes. Every few days I would find a note in my tool box with some comment about my body like "You have the best tits out here." I had no idea who put them there, but they all seemed to stand around and wait for me to open the box on the days they appeared. When I complained to the head surveyor everyone started ignoring me and refusing to work with me when I needed a partner.

The typical pattern of sexual harassment consists of two elements, sexual actions and work harassment. The sexual actions may consist of comments, jokes, propositions, touches, kisses, grabs. Although the most frequently reported type of sexual behavior is verbal, about half of the women who contact the institute for help have been subjected to physical advances. In almost 20 percent of the cases physical force has been used:

One day he followed me into the storage closet and grabbed me and started to unbutton my uniform. He twisted my arm so hard that I could hardly move it the next day. I was afraid he was going to try to rape me, but someone walked by and I ran out.

Sometimes the sexual actions, whether verbal or physical, are more subtle than the ones described in these quotes. They may take the form of grafitti and "girly" pictures on the wall of the mailroom, the ribald jokes about women that pass as sales kick-offs, or the disguised requirement that receptionists in outer offices wear sexy blouses and skirts. They emanate from the customer who can't seem to talk to the waitress without putting his arm around her, or the older male faculty member who takes an interest in every newly hired female faculty member until it becomes obvious that she is not sexually interested in him, or the patient who constantly reminds the nurse that she is supposed to put up with a few "feels" as part of her nursing duties.

The second element of the pattern, work harassment, is retaliation for noncooperation. If the woman is uncooperative with the sexual attentions or complains to someone about them, her harasser (or harassers) seeks vengeance through her work. She finds that the minute details of her work are scrutinized, that she is forced to work overtime, that her boss is ridiculing her work in front of other workers, that her foreman is ignoring safety precautions on her equipment, that she is not being trained properly. Here are two further examples from our sample:

> They started complaining about my typing even though it had been fine the week before. George hinted that things would go easier if I hadn't refused his two dinner invitations and that Bill was just going along with it because they were friends. Then George started insisting I get to work earlier, even though there wasn't anything to do at that hour. His liberal attitudes sure died when he didn't get his way.

> Things started disappearing from my work station. Then someone threw acid all over my slides. I could never be sure, but I think the other technicians wanted me to have trouble getting my job done because the graffitti and porn magazines they left on my desk had not ruffled me.

About 66 percent of the women in the Working Women's Institute sample have reported that their sexual harassment experience included some type of retaliatory behavior. In many cases it occurs after a series of unreciprocated sexual overtures. In other cases it seems simply to be part of a whole spectrum of behaviors, sexual and nonsexual, designed to let the woman know that she is not welcome at her job. This second form frequently occurs in work situations where women were not found previously.

The type of sexual harassment that was first legally recognized concerned women who were propositioned by a superior at work and then fired or denied some job benefit because they refused. This type appears benign at first because it seems motivated by sexual attraction—until work harassment reveals it as an exploitation of power. It is likely to occur in more traditional job settings, such as clerical work, where there are definite power differences between the woman and the men with whom she works. In a second type of sexual harassment there is an atmosphere of sexual comments, jokes, or leers directed at women. It may contain elements of flattery ("you have the best legs on this site") but there is usually a hostile edge to the message ("legs like that should be in bed, not in overalls"). In a pattern similar to the harassment of racial and ethnic minorities, it usually starts as soon as the woman comes on the job, is mixed with other actions that are clearly hostile and discriminatory, and is intended to force her to leave.[19] Those in Working Women's Institute's sample who report this type of harassment are likely to be in nontraditional jobs for women, such as the trades or in work situations where there are few women. The harassers often have much the same job status as the women.

Despite its hostile tone, many women initially minimize this harassment, thinking it is just part of the ritual hazing of new workers that occurs in all-male work situations.[20]

The most devastating feature of either type of sexual harassment is that it frequently results in the loss of a job, promotion, raise, training, or other benefits for the woman. In many cases dismissal from the job is explicitly linked with the woman's refusal to date or sleep with her boss. An example is the case of a bookkeeper, Doreen Romano, who received a letter on company stationery from her boss saying he could no longer stand to work with her if she didn't go to bed with him.[21] Other cases are more subtle. The woman is told there are "budget cuts" and is laid off after she complains about the persistent come-ons of a powerful manager in her company. Or a woman who has been the target of verbal slurs yells back at one of her harassers and is then let go for not being able to get along with her co-workers. More than one-third of the women in our sample had been fired or laid off as a result of refusing sexual attentions.

Another 25 percent of our contacts were forced to resign from their jobs because the pressure of the sexual or related work harassment became too great. Many women quit, realizing that there was no way to avoid the ultimate confrontation with their powerful boss and that they would not be supported by personnel departments. Some who faced harassment in a nontraditional job left totally discouraged, convinced that women were not welcome, that they would never feel comfortable or confident with their co-workers, and that their unions were reluctant to deal with sexual harassment. A significant number of women left out of fear for their physical safety after being attacked or put in situations that could have resulted in a serious accident.

Figures from survey data on such loss of jobs and promotions vary widely. Nearly half of the 9,000 *Redbook* respondents said they or someone they knew had left or been fired from a job due to sexual harassment.[22] In the federal government study about 16 percent of the women reported that they had lost a promotion or job or had quit a government position because of sexual harassment.[23] In the Illinois study about 9 percent of the women had been fired or denied a promotion because of sexual harassment, while 7 percent had quit.[24] The issue of job loss was not addressed in the auto-work and coal-mining studies, but respondents in both indicated that sexual harassment had resulted in unfair handling of their promotions.[25]

The ramifications of sexual harassment go beyond job loss. In order to get a new job, the woman usually needs to get a letter of reference from the very employer she is fleeing. Frequently, unemployment officials don't believe the woman really was sexually harassed or, even worse, they blame her. Trying to file a complaint with an enforcement agency often involves struggling through a bureaucratic maze and always takes a long time. Union representatives sometimes are unsympathetic or have no idea how to handle a sexual harassment grievance. Family members themselves frequently don't comprehend the seriousness of the situation or understand why the woman couldn't easily resolve it.

The Impact of Sexual Harassment on Health

In addition to its serious economic consequences, sexual harassment has far-reaching health consequences. Because stress, physical illness, and problems with self-confidence and job performance are recurring themes in our counseling at the Institute, we began a systematic exploration of the ways in which sexual harassment drains a woman's health. The remainder of this chapter will describe and interpret our findings and compare them to those of other researchers who have asked the same questions.

We began by analyzing the contents of the letters we received and derived three distinct categories of stress effects: (1) effects on work performance, (2) effects on general psychological well-being, and (3) effects on physical health; under each category there were a number of more specific effects. Using these, we summarized the types of health complaints and proportions of our client population making them.

Even though women express pride at being able to do their jobs despite harassment, 46 percent of the 518 cases said it interfered with their work performance.[26] The two most common effects on work performance were that the women were distracted from their tasks and dreaded coming to work. Having to worry about what the harasser is going to do next or to fend him off takes energy away from the task at hand and interferes with the development of new skills. A substantial number of women reported that they sought to avoid face-to-face contact with the harasser by taking circuitous routes or calling in sick:

> I would not go into the computer center and work alone with him. Sometimes this wasted my time since I needed to work early in the morning when no one else but him was there.

The ramifications for job performance go far beyond the immediate situation. The lack of respect, and the retaliation through sabotage and criticism, make her doubt her abilities and in some cases question her own career choice:

> I loved acting, but suddenly I wondered if any of his compliments were real or just based on his interest in my body. After I rejected him he picked at every detail. I began having trouble with him in rehearsals. You know, you have to be able to trust the director and yourself. By the end of that summer I decided I didn't have what it takes to act.

In an attempt to minimize her contact with a potential harasser, a woman often switches from male-dominated occupations to traditionally female occupations or goes into business for herself. Both choices tend to result in lower incomes. Others leave the workforce for an extended period of time.

In many situations, sexual harassment serves to exacerbate safety hazards that already exist in a job. On an assembly line, construction site, or police beat it is imperative to be alert and well rehearsed. If the women and men working together in these settings are distracted by interpersonal confrontations, they will fail to maintain those conditions. In recent years women in coal mining have protested that the men they worked with jeopardized their safety by attempting to grab them in the mines rather than following the usual routines. Intentional neglect of safety precautions is often part of the hostility that goes along with an atmosphere of "sexual teasing." One of our client's foreman refused to give her the proper fitting mask for welding and she was burned as a result.

The negative effects of sexual harassment are not limited to the work setting. They invade every aspect of the woman's life and often are manifested as general psychological stress symptoms. At least one negative effect was reported by over 94 percent of the women in our sample. The reaction most often mentioned was excessive tension:

> I was nervous all day at work to the point where I dropped a whole tray of food when I saw that the obnoxious customer had brought a bunch of his buddies with him. I knew that each of them would try to get a feel. It got to the point where I couldn't relax at home because I was fuming about the customers. I asked my husband to give me some of his valium, but he said I should quit.

Anger and fear were other frequently reported responses, as were depression, embarrassment, sleeplessness, and guilt. Anger may spur the woman to fight back, but it was not uncommon for it to reach debilitating proportions, causing the woman to feel outrage at anyone who did not immediately understand and sympathize with their plight, including union officials, lawyers, doctors, and prospective employers. Fear and anger often interfered with relations with lovers, friends, and family, creating sexual difficulties, impatience with children, and general estrangement. In order to suppress their agitation, some women turned to drink or took tranquilizers at work and home. Finally, depression was a common outcome of the entire situation. (This accords with the theory that depression stems from supressing feelings of anger.)

About 36 percent of the women involved in our study pointed out physical ailments they thought had been brought about by sexual harassment. The most prevalent ones were nausea, tiredness (a frequent sign of depression), and headaches:

> I would vomit every day before going to work and I was so tired that even the smallest job seemed like too much effort. I really knew something was wrong when I had an accident driving to work for the night shift.

Another symptom high on the list was drastic weight change: the woman was either too nervous to eat, or overate out of anxiety. Some women complained of lowered resistance, saying that they caught every infection that was going around and had trouble shaking it.

The psychological and physical symptoms described by our sample are not limited to mild or temporary problems. About 25 percent of the sample had sought medical or psychological help. Many suffered from stress and illness that they had not connected with sexual harassment until some outside circumstance alerted them. For example, one secondary school teacher told us of her year-long experience with headaches. When they started getting so severe that she couldn't work, she went to her doctor. As a result of his questions about her job, she suddenly realized that the headaches were associated with her bouts with a principal who propositioned her whenever they attended meetings outside the school.

Ours was the first of several efforts to investigate the possible parameters of harassment's health hazards.[27] Two more recent studies present further analyses. Although their data and that of Working Women's Institute are not easily compared due to differences in methodology, they appear to confirm and extend our findings.

The 1980 federal study discussed earlier asked six questions designed to assess the influence of sexual harassment on emotional and physical conditions, feelings about work, and ability to work.[28] A large proportion of respondents indicated that their feelings about work and their emotional or physical condition had been damaged by their experience. A smaller proportion noted that their attendance at work or their ability to work had suffered. (See Table 1.) The federal researchers calculated the cost of sexual harassment

Table 1
Impact of Sexual Harassment on Merit Systems Respondents
Percentage of Respondents Who Indicated These Aspects
of Their Lives "Became Worse"

Aspect	Percentage of victims of actual or attempted assault	Percentage of victims of pressure for dates or sexual favors, letters, and phone calls
Feelings about work	62	41
Emotional or physical condition	82	37
Ability to work with others on the job	32	18
Time and attendance at work	48	14
The quantity of work	28	13
The quality of work	21	12

Source: U.S. Merit Systems Protection Board, Office of Merit Systems Review and Studies, "Sexual Harassment in the Federal Workplace: Is It a Problem?" (March 1981): 81.

in terms of job turnover, absenteeism, and the use of health benefits and concluded that it cost tax payers $189 million over a two-year period.[29]

The Merit Systems Protection Board, which authored the report, and the congressional committee that commissioned it, were puzzled: Why had so few people reported damage to the quantity or quality of their work when so many felt emotional and physical ramifications of harassment?[30] We have found a similar phenomenon in our case material and a possible explanation for that discrepancy. Although 46 percent of our sample reported reduced work performance, and 95 percent described some emotional distress, a vocal subgroup maintained that they were impervious. The frequent reply to our question, "Did this situation affect how you did your job?" was a fierce "No." Many insisted that they had worked harder to show that they would not be defeated by harassment. At the same time, they admitted discrete ways in which their job performance had been altered by the presence of the harassment. In fact, therefore, it is probably the very determination to overcome the harassment by maintaining a good work record that causes the stress symptoms. Women may not be aware of how thoroughly harassment has interfered with their work. After talking to our counselors, many began to remember ways in which the experience had impaired their work performance. It is not surprising that this awareness was not stimulated by Merit System's questionnaire, since it was not a face-to-face interview.

The other research that touches on the (primarily psychological) health effects of sexual harassment is an interview study of 139 Detroit auto workers.[31] The investigators concluded that sexual harassment affects feelings about work and general self-worth. They found correlations between frequent sexual harassment and poor relationships between the woman and her co-workers and supervisors, as well as the inability to develop job skills. Finally, the more the woman had encountered sexual harassment, the lower was her self-esteem and general life satisfaction. As in the previous research, general well-being (self-esteem and life satisfaction) is disrupted more than work performance.

The Significance of the Findings on Stress

The findings presented here leave at least two important questions unanswered: (1) are the stress symptoms elicited in these studies really caused by sexual harassment? and (2) does it result in serious or permanent damage to health?

There is almost no empirical evidence on the question of causality. Because this is a new area of research, most of the studies cited here—including ours—used the "fishnet" approach, rather than being systematic and tightly controlled. But in order to establish a causal link between sexual harassment and stress symptoms, it will be necessary to compare populations of harassed and nonharassed women to know more about the stress symptoms experienced by *all* workers, and to use standardized measures, in addition to self reporting.

Short of empirical proof, however, logic and available theory support the likelihood of such a causal connection. The economic powerlessness of women noted earlier places her in a double bind when faced with unwanted sexual behaviors at work. On the one hand, she does not want the intrusion. On the other hand, she fears that if she complains she will risk losing some job opportunity, yet that if she tries to ignore the situation it will only escalate. (Working Women's Institute's research shows that most complaints have negative results or fall on deaf ears, but that the harassment tends to get worse if ignored.)[32] Her only choice is to remain in a constant state of vigilance, one in which her body is always prepared to meet some physical or emotional demand. Research has shown that when this state, called the stress response, is chronic, it leads to health problems.[33] In addition, the necessity of suppressing anger toward the harasser and denying fear leads to the confusion, depression, and abnormal tension that typically result when feelings are not expressed.

The double bind is complicated by cultural assumptions about women's roles. Because of the idea that women are responsible for controlling male sexual behavior, many women who become the target of sexual harassment may feel guilty. Many in our study blamed themselves for being "too friendly" or not having "caught on" sooner. Indeed, the New Right has recently echoed this victim-blaming attitude by suggesting that women who dress properly are not harassed.[34] The belief that women should put their families before their jobs adds to the guilt. Finally, the self-blaming reactions we have observed make sense in the light of what we know about women's self-esteem, which research has shown tends to be fragile, especially when women are attempting traditionally male jobs.[35] All of these cultural attitudes make it more likely that women will internalize their problems and suffer the resultant health consequences rather than speak out against the sexual harassment.

The question of the severity and permanence of the health problems stemming from sexual harassment requires further research. Women who have undergone the experience believe that the damage to their health has been far-reaching. For example, some felt that the trauma had exacerbated abuse of drugs or alcohol. Even though some of the complaints listed in our case material may seem mild, they can be precursors to more serious illness, such as high blood pressure, ulcers, or heart disease. Sexual harassment may also have profound effects on mental health. The interpersonal difficulties we have described sometimes end in separation, divorce, and alienation from friends and family. Job loss and self-doubt can hamper a job search and send a woman into chronic unemployment and depression. In many instances harassment triggers memories of earlier experiences of incest, child abuse, and rape, leaving the woman psychologically disoriented. We know that stress caused by other sexual traumas can lead to mental and physical illness that is difficult to reverse. For example, the psychological repercussions of rape can last for years.[36] It remains to be seen whether this will hold true for sexual harassment.

Research that verifies the seriousness and permanence of the stress effects of sexual harassment will be an important mechanism for helping women to get immediate relief for this problem. For example, it is the recognition of these effects that has laid the groundwork for women to win unemployment and worker's compensation in sexual harassment cases. As law and policy in this area become more refined, there will be a need for more comprehensive and detailed data to support broad protections.

Toward Solutions to Sexual Harassment

In order to eliminate the stress caused by sexual harassment, basic work conditions must be changed. Ultimately this means that the unequal economic and social power now held by men in the workplace must be evenly distributed between both sexes. Short of this revolutionary change, and as a step toward it, both individual and group protections can be, and are being, established. Over the last nine years progress has been made at every level, from personal awareness to institutional structures. The four major vehicles for this change have been service, education, organizing, and legislation.

One of the earliest and most tangible results of the awareness of sexual harassment that emerged in the mid-1970s was the growth of a myriad of service and advocacy groups. Groups such as Working Women's Institute in New York, the Alliance Against Sexual Coercion in Cambridge, and the Coalition Against Sexual Harassment in Minneapolis counsel women on coping strategies, offer them legal information, refer them to lawyers and therapists, and conduct support groups.[37] Services such as this are now offered by YWCAs, women's crisis centers, and college counseling services. Other groups, such as the Women's Alliance for Job Equity in Philadelphia, have concentrated their efforts on advocacy and publicity as a way to raise community and institutional consciousness about specific sexual harassment cases.

Although it is critical to assist individuals in overcoming personal difficulties brought on by sexual harassment, those who have instituted service programs recognize that they must make a parallel effort to bring about more permanent protective and preventive measures. Because of the complexity and subtlety of sexual harassment, it has been necessary to conduct a massive educational campaign to convince the public and public officials to consider such measures. Public resistance has taken several forms. At first there was a general disbelief in the gravity of the problem. There was also a fear that institutional controls would interfere with natural attractions and interactions between the sexes. Even unions and working women's groups were reluctant to take up the issue, saying that bread-and-butter issues such as equal pay and daycare had priority.[38] But many of the established women's and workers' rights groups, professional associations and unions, along with the sexual harassment service/advocacy groups undertook educational programs based on careful research among their constituencies. Such diverse groups as the Coal Employment Project, the American Federation of State, County, and Municipal Employees (AFSCME), and the Modern Language Association have published handbooks explaining the issue and possible protections.[39] Organizations like

United Tradeswomen in New York City, the Coalition of Labor Union Women, Office Workers of New Haven, and the American Federation of Government Employees (AFGE) have made sexual harassment a topic of their workshops, task forces, and training sessions. Others, like Working Women's Institute, the Alliance Against Sexual Coercion, the Michigan Task Force on Sexual Harassment, the Women's Legal Defense Fund in Washington, and the NOW Legal Defense and Education Fund have aimed their educational efforts not only at individual women but at officials in government, unions, academic institutions, and corporations. They have used the media, testimony at national, state, and local legislative hearings, technical assistance, and distribution of printed educational materials.

Important organizing efforts have taken place both within established unions and outside of them. At the urging of their female members, some unions have sought to provide permanent protections in several ways. The United Auto Workers (UAW), AFCSME, and AFGE have issued policy statements condemning sexual harassment of employees by supervisors, and in some cases by co-workers. The UAW was one of the first unions to include a sexual harassment clause in a contract and presently has such clauses in its contracts with Chrysler and Ford. District 65 (Distributive Workers of America) also has a sexual harassment clause in its contract at Boston University. These official actions have been supported and pushed forward as the result of rank-and-file initiatives. In a number of instances union members have rallied to the support of women in their ranks who are being harassed. For example, members of Local 201 of the International Union of Electrical Workers walked off their jobs when a secretary at their plant was harassed by two managers.[40] A similar situation in a lumber mill in Washington led to discussions among members about whether or not sexual harassment of even a single woman is a breach of their contract. In California, a sexual harassment incident in which a lawyer grabbed the breast of a receptionist spurred a group of legal service workers to organize the California Rural Legal Assistance Workers. To date the policies and contract clauses have treated sexual harassment as an issue of sex discrimination and urged that grievances be carried out under that rubric. However, because of the growing recognition that sexual harassment creates stress and impairs health, unions are beginning to look at the possibility of including it in contract provisions covering worker health and safety.

Unions and other groups concerned with women's and workers' rights are still struggling with some of the specific problems involved with enforcing provisions against sexual harassment.

The problems which have sometimes caused them to shy away from the issue altogether are worth mentioning here. The first is that sexual harassment charges are sometimes selectively enforced. Management can use them as a pretext for getting rid of workers whom they consider troublemakers or undesirable because of their race, class, or political beliefs. Conversely, if the employee is highly valued management will look for a way to ignore or cover up the charges. Second, union members may harass each other. Like other problems of sex and race discrimination, this forces the union to look within its own ranks as well as outside for the sources of worker oppression, and thus risk criticism from anti-union forces. Most union constitutions have no mechanism to handle a grievance of one member against another; officials prefer to deal with such situations through internal education.

Because of the vigilance of worker's and women's groups and the courage of individual women in bringing their cases to court, the laws and legislation on sexual harassment have developed in an encouraging fashion. By and large, the rulings in the federal courts have been in favor of the claimants and have moved toward establishing that sexual harassment in its various forms is a violation of Title VII of the 1964 Civil Rights Act. Such findings have been made both in situations where women have been fired or denied some job benefit as well as in those in which they felt forced to quit. One of the most important advances in the federal arena was made in 1980 when the Equal Employment Opportunity Commission issued guidelines clearly spelling out the ways in which sexual harassment is a violation of the nation's antidiscrimination laws. In addition to providing a model for the courts and for state and local fair employment practices agencies, these guidelines put employers on notice that it was their responsibility to prevent the occurence of sexual harassment among their employees.

Because of this, many employers have developed and distributed policy statements against sexual harassment in their workplaces. Again, however, such policies are frequently a mixed blessing for women workers. While they may serve to alert potential harassers to the illegality of their acts and to provide women with official channels for complaint, they may also be used as a smokescreen by companies to make it appear that they have good intentions. For example, in the case of Miller v. the Bank of America, the company unsuccessfully argued that it could not be held responsible for the individual acts of a harasser since there was an official policy against such behavior.

Other laws besides Title VII, especially at the state level, have been used to rectify the damage done by sexual harassment. One important area has been in unemployment law, where many states have guaranteed that women can receive unemployment if they are fired or have to quit because of sexual harassment. Avenues of action such as criminal statutes, worker's compensation, and torts (civil lawsuits for acts such as assault, battery, and infliction of emotional distress) have been successfully pursued in recent years. While many legal approaches can be used to help individual women obtain their rights in these circumstances, sex discrimination laws have the most value as a permanent vehicle for change. They make the point that a powerless group has been singled out for unequal treatment whereas other laws tend to treat sexual harassment as a random violation of individual comfort and job security.

None of the tactics discussed here is sufficient to prevent or eliminate sexual harassment permanently. Although each of them must be vigorously pursued in order to protect individual women, they are not a resolution to the problem of sexual harassment or the stress it produces. They must be combined with efforts to eliminate the basic cause of the problem—the inequality between women and men in the workforce and in society. Without power differences in the form of sex segregation of the labor force, unequal pay, and limited opportunities for advancement of women, the possibility of sexual harassment would be drastically reduced. It is not until women have obtained political power both inside and outside the workplace that they will be able to create a work environment free of such harassment.

Notes

This paper is the result of research based on the ongoing activities of Working Women's Institute. I want to thank the staff, students, and consultants of the institute for their contributions. I am especially grateful to the hundreds of counseling clients who have cooperated in providing information and feedback during the research process. All quotes and anecdotes from institute information, referral and counseling clients have been adapted to protect the confidentiality of the women.

1. Carmita Wood was one of the founders of Working Women's Institute. Information on her case and that of Diane Williams is available in legal documents which are catalogued in the Working Women's Institute's legal brief bank. Information about the brief bank is available from the *Women's Rights Law Reporter*, Rutgers Law School, 15 Washington Street, Newark, N.Y. 07102.

2. The phenomenon of sexual harassment at work is not new; it was

simply unnamed until the mid-1970s. For a historical treatment of the phenomenon see Mary Bularzik, "Sexual Harassment at the Workplace: Historical Notes," *Radical America* (July-August 1978): 24-43.

3. Claire Safran, "What Men Do to Women at Work," *Redbook* (November 1976); Lin Farley, *Sexual Shakedown: The Sexual Harassment of Women on the Job* (New York: McGraw-Hill, 1978).

4. Peggy Crull, "The Impact of Sexual Harassment on the Job: A Profile of the Experiences of 92 Women," in *Sexuality in Organizations: Romantic and Coercive Behaviors at Work*, ed. Dail Neugarten and Jay Shafritz (Oak Park, ILL: Moore Publishing Co., 1980), pp. 67-71 (also available from Working Women's Institute); U.S. Merit Systems Protection Board, Office of Merit Systems Review and Studies, *Sexual Harassment in the Federal Workplace: Is It a Problem?* (March 1981); Barbara Hayler, Testimony Before the House Judiciary II Committee, State of Illinois (March 4, 1980): 1-5.

5. Crull, "The Impact of Sexual Harassment on the Job"; Peggy Crull, "The Stress Effects of Sexual Harassment on the Job: Implications for Counseling," *American Journal of Othropsychiatry* 52, no. 3 (July 1982): 539-44; Peggy Crull and Marilyn Cohen, "Expanding the Definition of Sexual Harassment on the Job," *Occupational Health Nursing* (forthcoming, March 1984).

6. Martha Hooven and Nancy McDonald, "The Role of Capitalism: Understanding Sexual Harassment," *Aegis* (November/December 1978): 31-33; U.S. Department of Labor, Office of the Secretary, Women's Bureau, "20 Facts on Women Workers" (1980).

7. Peggy Crull, "Sexual Harassment and Male Control of Women's Work," *Women: A Journal of Liberation* 8, no. 2: 3-7; Farley, *Sexual Shakedown*, pp. 28-51; Catherine MacKinnon, *Sexual Harassment of Working Women* (New Haven: Yale University Press, 1979), pp. 1-18, 143-221.

8. Some research indicates that men are attempting to compete with other men in the status hierarchy through the sexual conquest or intimidation of female co-workers. See Alliance Against Sexual Coercion, "Three Male Views on Harassment," *Aegis* (Winter/Spring 1980): 52-59.

9. Susan Griffin, "Rape: The All-American Crime," in *Women: A Feminist Perspective*, ed. Jo Freeman (Palo Alto: Mayfield Press, 1975), pp. 24-39.

10. Linda Phelps, "Female Sexual Alienation," in ibid., pp. 16-23; Lucy Gilbert and Paula Webster, *Bound by Love: The Sweet Trap of Daughterhood* (Boston: Beacon Press, 1982). See also Claudia Dreifus, "Pre-Adolescent Sexuality," *Women: A Journal of Liberation* 3, no. 1 (1982): 2–6.

11. It is not clear that the theory about women's psychological powerlessness with respect to sexual behavior applies to any but white middle-class women. While certain of the dynamics described here probably take place in *all* male/female interactions, different cultural and economic would be expected to result in different patterns of sexual

power and powerlessness among men and women. Only a few published works deal with this possibility vis-à-vis sexual harassment. See Judy Ellis, "Sexual Harassment and Race: A Legal Analysis of Discrimination," *Journal of Legislation* 8, no. 1 (1981): 30-45; Yla Eason, "When the Boss Wants Sex," *Essence* (March 1981): 82ff.; James Gruber and Lars Bjorn, "Blue Collar Blues: The Sexual Harassment of Women Autoworkers," *Work and Occupations* 9, no. 3 (August 1982): 271-98. The institute is presently involved in a research project in which women are asked to explain how their race and ethnic group played a part in their harassment experience.

12. Safran, "What Men Do to Women at Work."

13. Merit Systems Protection Board, *Sexual Harassment in the Federal Workplace*, pp. 3-6; Hayler, Testimony Before the House Judiciary II Committee, p. 2.

14. Gruber and Bjorn, "Blue Collar Blues," pp. 282-83.

15. Connie White, Barbara Angle, and Marat Moore, "Sexual Harassment in the Coal Industry: A Survey of Women Miners," unpub. paper, Coal Employment Project, Oak Ridge, Tennessee, 1981, pp. 3-6.

16. There are a few other studies that touch on the incidence of sexual harassment. Aside from those described in this paper, see Barbara Gutek and Charles Nakamura, "Sexuality and the Workplace," unpublished paper, University of California at Los Angeles, 1979; National Commission on Working Women, *National Survey of Working Women: Perceptions, Problems, and Prospects* (June 1979); Katie Leishman and Kathy Minton, "Sex and Power at Work: Results of Our Questionnaire," *Working Mother* 3, no. 5 (September 1980): 15ff.; Eliza Collins and Timothy Blodgett, "Sexual Harassment . . . Some See It . . . Some Won't," *Harvard Business Review* 59, no. 2 (March-April 1981): 77-95.

17. Working Women's Institute keeps track of demographic and other data on the women who are clients of its information, referral, and counseling service. Such information as occupation, type of harassment, presence of stress symptoms, and how women found out about our service is regularly coded, recorded, and summarized for research and evaluation purposes. The data base for the figures in this paper is case records of our client population from 1979 and 1980 and questionnaires filled out and returned by a group of women who wrote us letters asking for help with a harassment situation. For a further explanation of our methodology, see Crull, "The Impact of Sexual Harassment," p. 67; Peggy Crull, "The Stress Effects of Sexual Harassment on the Job," unpublished paper, Working Women's Institute (1981), pp. 1-3.

18. For our comparison we used "Employment and Unemployment During 1978: An Analysis," U.S. Department of Labor, Bureau of Labor Statistics, 1979. Our sample tended to have more people in the Professional/Technical and Managerial/Administrative categories than the national sample of the Department of Labor because of the composition of the New York-Metropolitan workforce.

19. Ellis, "Sexual Harassment and Race," p. 32.
20. Suzanne Carothers and Peggy Crull, "Contrasting Sexual Harassment in Female- and Male-Dominated Occupations," in *My Troubles Are Going to Have Trouble with Me: Everyday Trials and Triumphs of Women Workers*, ed. Karen Sacks and Dorothy Remy (New Brunswick: Rutgers University Press, in press).
21. Vivian Cadden, "Doreen Romano, Plaintiff, Versus Irving Lehat, Defendant . . .," *Working Mother Magazine* 3, no. 3 (May 1980): 31ff.
22. Safran, "What Men Do to Women at Work."
23. Merit Systems Protections Board, "Sexual Harassment in the Federal Workplace," pp. 79-80.
24. Hayler, "Testimony Before the House Judiciary II Committee," p. 4.
25. Gruber and Bjorn, "Blue Collar Blues," pp. 288-90; White, Angle, and Moore, "Sexual Harassment in the Coal Industry," p. 6.
26. This and the subsequent percentages reported here were derived in the following manner: First, we examined the letters we receive to find the recurring categories of symptoms reported. Then we sent a questionnaire to everyone who had written to us, asking specifically what physical, psychological, and work effects their sexual harassment had produced. We received 92 replies out of about 325 questionnaires. We then used the same type of content analysis used on the letters on counseling records of an additional 426 women we had talked to in person. In the counseling sessions clients were not directly asked whether their mental or physical health or work was affected. Therefore, the percentage represents the proportion of women who responded positively to specific questions in the mail survey and who *spontaneously* mentioned symptoms in counseling.
27. Two earlier studies touched on women's feelings in response to sexual harassment. They are Safran, "What Men Do to Women at Work," and Sandra Carey, "Sexual Politics in Business," unpublished paper, University of Texas at San Antonio, 1977. The Working Women Education Fund also touches on stress stemming from sexual harassment in its report, "*Warning: Health Hazards for Office Workers—An Overview of Problems and Solutions in Occupational Health in the Office* (Cleveland, OH: 1981), pp. 1–9.
28. Merit Systems Protection Board, "Sexual Harassment in the Federal Workplace," pp. 75-84.
29. Ibid., pp. 75-79.
30. Ibid., p. 84.
31. Gruber and Bjorn, "Blue Collar Blues," pp. 288-95.
32. Working Women's Institute, "Sexual Harassment on the Job: Results of Preliminary Survey," *Working Women's Institute Research Series Report No. 1* (Fall 1975): 1-2.
33. Working Women Education Fund, *Warning: Health Hazards for Office Workers*, pp. 5-8; Jeanne Stellman, *Women's Work, Women's Health: Myths and Realities* (New York: Pantheon, 1977), chapter 2.
34. Walter Berns, "Terms of Endearment," *Harpers*, October 1980, pp. 14ff.

35. Eleanor Maccoby and Carole Jacklin, *The Psychology of Sex Differences* (Stanford: Stanford University Press, 1974). This research, like much research on sex differences, applies mainly to white middle-class women.
36. Ann Burgess and Lynda Holmstrom, "Rape Trauma Syndrome," *America Journal of Psychiatry* 131, no. 9 (September 1974): 981-86.
37. See, for example, Alliance Against Sexual Coercion, *Fighting Sexual Harassment: An Advocacy Handbook* (Cambridge, 1979).
38. See, for example, "On-the-Job 'Favors': Equal Rightists Say Sexual Harassment Issue is Overplayed," *Dayton (Ohio) Daily News*, 9 January 1978.
39. Coal Employment Project, "Sexual Harassment in the Mines: Legal Rights, Legal Remedies"; American Federation of State, County, and Municipal Employees, *On the Job Sexual Harassment: What the Union Can Do*; and Modern Language Association of America, *Sexual and Gender Harassment in the Academy: A Guide for Faculty, Students, and Administrators* (New York, 1981).
40. Marcia Hams, "Electrical Workers Wildcat over Sexual Assault on Union Member," *Labor Notes*, 25 June 1981, p. 7.

6
Minority Women, Work, and Health
Leith Mullings

The health of minority women is conditioned by their status as workers, as members of a minority group, and as women. This chapter will discuss the way in which the inequality structured into U.S. society has resulted in a special oppression of minority women, subjecting their health to the hazards of ethnic and gender discrimination in the workplace, of poverty, and of the stress entailed in the "double day." While I will be primarily concerned with Afro-American women, other minorities share many of the same conditions. Thus the general outlines of this analysis may be applied to other minority women, keeping in mind the differences generated by their different histories of incorporation into the U.S. economy.[1] That very little information on the problem of occupational health and minority women exists is itself an indication of the problem. This chapter therefore constitutes an introductory and exploratory discussion that will hopefully stimulate further research.

Afro-American men and women experience greater morbidity (illness) and mortality (death) from certain cancers, and from hypertension, diabetes, and other occupational and chronic diseases.[2] For example, if we look at diseases of the heart, the first leading cause of death, statistics for 1977 show an overall age-adjusted heart disease rate of 322 per 100,000 for Afro-American men, compared with a rate of 294 per 100,000 for Euro-American men; for Afro-American women, we find an age-adjusted rate of 204 per 100,000, compared with 137 for Euro-American women. For cancer, the second leading cause of death, Afro-American men had an age-adjusted death rate from cancer of 222 per 100,000 in 1977 compared with a rate of 133 per 100,000 for Euro-American men; Afro-American women had a rate of 130 deaths per 100,000 compared with a rate of 108 per 100,000 for Euro-American women.[3]

The picture for occupational injuries and illness is equally grim. As Morris Davis has stated:

We enter the 1980's with the following statistics. Fifteen percent of the black work force (one to one and one-half million) are unable to work due to permanent or partial job-related disabilities. Black workers have a 37 percent greater chance than whites of suffering an occupational injury or illness. Black workers are one and one-half times more likely than whites to be severely disabled from job injuries and illness and face a 20 percent greater chance than whites of dying from job-related injuries and illnesses.[4]

For minority women there are special problems. The probability that an Afro-American woman, for instance, will die of childbearing complications is five times that of Euro-American women.[5] Hypertension, a disease in part related to stress, kills Afro-American women between the ages of twenty-five and forty-four seventeen times more frequently than Euro-American women.[6] Not surprisingly, in the 1975 Health Interview Survey Afro-American women reported the lowest level of emotional well-being across sex and race, with 63 percent of Afro-American women reporting moderate to severe levels of distress.[7]

Following the lead of the dominant social science interpretations of societal inequality, theories seeking to explain the incidence of illness among minorities and low-income groups have tended to focus on alleged biological or cultural differences, rather than on an analysis of the position that population occupies in society.[8] The astoundingly higher rates of cancer in the Afro-American community, for instance, have been attributed to biological and genetic differences on the one hand, and to lifestyle characteristics, such as smoking, diet, and cultural and personal practices on the other. Genetic explanations are attractive despite the fact that high rates of cancer, for instance, were uncommon before 1935;[9] or that the incidence of cancer mortality among Afro-Americans exceeds that of Africans, with rates among Afro-American men being three times those of men in Ibaden, Nigeria, for example. For Afro-American women, the rate is twice that of the African women in the same study.[10] The precipitous rise of genetic screening of employees by industry is one indication of the policy ramifications of such genetic explanations. In 1982 fifty-nine major industrial companies had informed the Congressional Office of Technology Assessment that they intended to begin genetic screening of employees in the next five years; according to the agency seventeen had begun carrying out such tests in the past five years, and more than five were in the process of doing so.[11]

Similarly, the growing emphasis on lifestyle explanations for cancer tend to exaggerate their role and minimize that of occupational carcinogens and involuntary exposures.[12] Further, such explanations frequently ignore analysis of the interrelationship of structural constraints and lifestyle/personal practices: the type of work one does or how much money one makes will have an impact on what one eats, how much one exercises, how often one sees the doctor, how much one smokes, and so on.

Both the biological and cultural/personal explanations tend to shift attention from the environment to the individual; the emphasis is on removing the allegedly susceptible worker from a dangerous environment or changing her lifestyle rather than on cleaning up the workplace or removing structural barriers to equal opportunity. Yet there is much evidence to demonstrate that patterns of morbidity and mortality are directly conditioned by the structure of the society. For example, we find a marked decline in mortality from tuberculosis in the United States during the first three decades of the twentieth century, although chemotherapy did not become widely available until the 1950s—suggesting that changing social conditions were the major factor. It has been clear since the Industrial Revolution that social relations mediate the incidence and prevalence of a disease by shaping the conditions for its emergence and by determining the distribution of risk. With industrialization, the radically transformed relations of production created an environment for the rise of diseases related to the new conditions of work. Most important were the new relations of production—the creation of a class of workers who are by virtue of their position in the social division of labor, most susceptible to certain diseases.

In the United States workers have been differentially incorporated into the labor market along racial/ethnic lines. While Euro-Americans constituted a free, although exploited, labor force, captured Africans were enslaved. As time went on Afro-Americans (as well as Mexican-Americans, Puerto Ricans, and Asian-Americans) were restricted to the most dangerous jobs, receiving the lowest wages for their labor. They have frequently been denied legal and civil rights, and have been excluded from social services such as health and education, and from organizations such as trade unions through which their status might be improved.[13] Further, their more exploited status in the labor market has been explained and rationalized by the larger society on the basis of their biological or cultural inferiority.[14]

To understand the differential patterns of certain types of disease among minorities, we must first examine the health ramifications of their social conditions. The rest of this chapter will focus on these social conditions, arguing that the issue of occupational health among Afro-American women can only be understood within the context of an analysis of their status as workers, as minorities, and as women.

Work, Compensation, and Health

Afro-American women have always participated in the labor force as workers. During slavery they were often forced to do the same work as men, in the fields and in the factories.[15] Despite the defeat of slavery, Afro-American men have rarely received wages sufficient to support their families, and the women have always had to work in order for their families to survive.

In 1890 the labor force participation of Euro-American women was 16.3 percent, compared to 39.7 percent for nonwhite women.[16] Since at that time it was the ideal that a woman leave the labor force after marriage, more telling is the difference in participation of married women: for married Euro-American women the labor force participation rate was 2.5 percent, compared to 22.5 percent for married nonwhite women.[17] By 1980 the gap between groups had narrowed considerably, however, with official statistics reporting 54 percent of Afro-American, 52 percent of Euro-American, and 47 percent of Spanish-origin women in the workforce.[18]

Despite historically high rates of labor force participation, work options for Afro-American women have always been conditioned by gender and ethnicity: bound by the confines of a sex-segregated market, minority women are still further restricted by their ethnic status. Prior to World War I Afro-American women were generally barred from higher paid jobs in factory employment, and later from the white collar positions in offices and stores that were open to Euro-American women; they were confined to domestic and laundry work.

As militant collective action forced the removal of some employment barriers, Afro-American women gradually moved into jobs that were previously segregated. Yet discrimination continues to limit minority women to the lowest paid and most dangerous jobs in an already lower paid sex-segregated market. The broad categories used by official statistics (i.e., clerical, professional and technical, operatives) often mask the real stratification within these categories and the fact that minorities are not evenly distributed from top to bottom in the wage hierarchy. This has implications for economic status which in turn has ramifications for health, as well as for the health hazards encountered on the job.

Restriction to the lowest paying, dead-end jobs means that minority women have a greater chance than others of being poor.

For example, in 1977 33 percent of Afro-American women who worked year round were below the poverty line.[19] In 1983, the average full-time year-round female worker earned 59 percent of the average man's earnings; Afro-American women earned only 54 percent, and Hispanic women only 49 percent, of the average man.[20] In 1981, 15.6 percent of Afro-American women over the age of sixteen were unemployed, as compared to 6.9 percent of Euro-American women.[21]

When we examine family income we see even greater discrepancies. Because of the discrimination against both men and women, Afro-Americans as a group have incomes considerably lower than do whites, with this inequality growing in many regions of the country. In 1980 the median income for Afro-American families was $12,674, as compared to $21,904 for white families.[22] Since Afro-American men working full-time year-round earn substantially less ($13,874) than Euro-American men ($19,719),[23] Afro-American women continue to have a heavier responsibility in providing subsistence for their families. The disproportionate unemployment rates effect family income. The October 1982 unemployment rate of 20 percent—one out of every five Afro-Americans was unemployed—does not even take account of those who involuntarily work part-time, discouraged workers, and labor force dropouts.[24] The fact that Afro-American men, too, are forced to work at the most dangerous jobs, subjecting them to higher rates of job-related death and disability, further effects family income. Morris Davis has pointed to the relationship of elevated cancer rates found among Afro-American workers to the jobs to which they are confined in rubber, steel, chromate, and other industries.[25]

The high rates of unemployment, morbidity, and mortality combine with other factors to modify family structure, which affects income. It is not surprising that the complex factors that have promoted a rise—for all races—of families maintained by women has had a disproportionate impact on Afro-Americans, where the rate is 45 percent.[26] The fact that approximately one-half of these families were below the poverty line in 1979[27] has led some investigators to assert that "family instability" is a major cause of poverty among Afro-Americans.

When we look closely at the facts, however, we find that although working-class households certainly fare better with two incomes, the following question remains unanswered: If single parent families are the problem, why is poverty far less prevalent among households headed by Euro-American females and by unmarried white or black men? If, for instance, we look at all households headed by women who worked full time in 1976, we find that the incidence of poverty was four times greater for minorities than for whites.[28] Further, in 1979, while 50 percent of households headed by black women had incomes above the poverty line, this was true for almost 80 percent of those headed by white women or nonmarried black men, and for 90 percent of those headed by nonmarried white men.[29] Since the majority of households with single parents are not in poverty, it would seem that the problem lies not with the fact that Afro-American women are supporting families, but with the limited options they have in the job market.

Numerous studies have demonstrated that in placing constraints on the ability of people to purchase adequate housing, food, and medical care, poverty itself increases health risks. Poverty and discrimination often force minorities to live in more polluted environments. Thus the inability to procure safe housing, food, and so on may increase the risk of being exposed to occupational pollutants even where people are not directly exposed as workers. For example, a study of mothers in the Mississippi Delta who had not been directly exposed to DDT during most of the study period found residue levels highest among rural Afro-American mothers and newborns; the study suggests that the differences were not related to metabolism, but degree of exposure determined by quality of housing, availability of running water, and sources of food and water.[30]

In a fee-for-service health system such as that in the United States, employment and income bear directly on the ability to purchase adequate medical care. With the soaring cost of health care, third party payment becomes the only means by which most people can afford to use the system. Because most people acquire insurance coverage through the workplace, discrimination in employment has serious ramifications for access to adequate medical care. A 1982 study by the U.S. Commission on Human Rights found that because minorities and women have greater rates of unemployment, have lower paying jobs, and are more likely to be employed in part-time, seasonal, or "poor risk" jobs such as private household service or agriculture, they are severely disadvantaged in obtaining health insurance. While unemployment lowers the rate of health insurance coverage for everyone, unemployed minority women lack health insurance to a greater degree than unemployed Euro-American women. Further, minority children are less likely than others to be covered by medical insurance.[31]

In addition to the health vulnerabilities that result from inadequate compensation for work, minority women also face direct dangers to their health in the jobs at which they work. We will turn now to brief examination of some of the industries in which minority women are concentrated.

The largest proportion of Afro-American women workers—34.4 percent—are employed in cleaning, food, health, and personal and protective services.[32] If we look at the health industry, for example, we find that minorities constitute a disproportionately large number of health service workers. The health industry is rigorously stratified by race and gender. The top echelon of physicians, administrators, and scientists remain overwhelmingly male and Euro-American; in 1970, 9 percent of the predominantly female "paraprofessionals" (nurses, therapists, and technicians) were Afro-American, while 30 percent of the auxiliary, ancillary, and service personnel (who were 84.1 percent female) were Afro-American.[33] In 1980, 21 percent of *all* health service workers were Afro-American women.[34] The 1970 median income of the auxiliary, ancillary, and service personnel in the health industry was $4,000, as compared to $6,000 for paraprofessionals and $40,000 for professionals.[35]

Studies have shown that hospital workers have a generally high level of occupational diseases (see chapter by Coleman and Dickinson).[36] In some illnesses, such as hepatitis infection (which is three to six times higher among medical personnel than the general population), disadvantaged socioeconomic status interacts with job category to influence the incidence of disease.[37] A recent study of mortality among nonprofessional hospital workers in New York City, where minority workers make up the bulk of the lower echelons of health service workers, suggests that nonprofessional workers may be at elevated risk for certain types of cancers. The study found particularly high rates of liver cancer among Afro-American men and breast cancer among Afro-American women. While it was difficult to ascribe specific cancers to specific chemicals, the investigators noted that hospital workers are constantly exposed to ionizing radiation, anesthetic gases, benezene, ethlylene oxide, formaldahyde, and alkylating agents—substances that have been linked to cancer. The study also raised the question of whether the excess of liver cancer among health service workers is associated with exposure to Hepatitis B virus, through cleaning, handling of patients' laundry, and so on.[38]

A NIOSH report based on Health Interview Surveys (HIS) of 498,580 people between 1969 and 1974 found elevated morbidity rates for a range of diseases, particularly among persons in private household service as compared to workers in other job categories.[39] These findings no doubt partially reflect the age of these workers. More important, however, are the hazards of housework (see chapter by Rosenberg), aggravated by the stress of performing it for someone else, in conditions where the wages are low, and there is often no limit to the working day, no medical coverage, and no such benefits as sick pay and vacations.

As a result of the expansion of the service and clerical sectors, along with the struggle against discrimination, Afro-American women have moved out of private household work, an occupational niche to which they had long been confined. While in 1967 24.5 percent of all Afro-American women workers were in private household service, by 1980 only 7.5 percent placed themselves in this occupational category, and these were primarily older women.[40] However, this is not a dying occupation. As unemployment rises among all minority women, more and more, of all ages, will be forced to turn to "day work." And for many immigrants from the Caribbean, for instance, private household work is in any case one of the few occupational options—and an important way to regularize their status in this country. A year after the 1965 liberalization of the immigration laws more live-in maids had been approved for entry than any other category.[41] Many others come in without documents, and, as I shall show below, undocumented status further threatens the health of the worker.

Thirty percent of Afro-American women workers are clerical workers.[42] The hazards of clerical work include muscular and circulatory disorders, fatigue, and exposure to dangerous chemicals such as benzene, toluene, and other organic solvents (see chapter by Fleishman). Clerical workers also seem to be particularly vulnerable to stress-related diseases. A major study examining the relationship of employment status and employment-related behaviors to the incidence of coronary heart disease found that women clerical workers with children experienced coronary heart disease at a rate twice as great as those of other comparable nonclerical workers or housewives. Increased risk of coronary heart disease among clerical workers appears to be related to features of the work environment, including the lack of control and autonomy, nonsupportive relationships, and limited physical mobility.[43]

These conditions may have a particular impact on minority women, who are concentrated at the lowest levels of the office hierarchy. Afro-American women, for example, tend to be underrepresented among the higher paid legal and medical secretaries,[44] and among secretaries and receptionists, but over-represented among file clerks, mail handlers, key-punch operators, and telephone clerks[45]—jobs that are often subject to speed-up, isolation, and lack of job mobility. A recent, and as yet unpublished, study of the psychological health effects (including anxiety, depression, and isolation) of the new office technology concluded that clerical workers at the lower end of the office hierarchy were subject to health risks similar to those of assembly line workers and "exhibit psychological strains due to low utilization of skills and abilities, low participation in decision making, lack of social support at work, and job insecurity."[46] Given the high rates of hypertension among Afro-American women, these relationships warrant further study.

Among operatives, minority women workers hold jobs that put them at particular risk. In 1980, 40.4 percent of all clothing ironers and pressers and 23.3 percent of all laundry and dry cleaning operators were Afro-American women.[47] A study conducted by the National Cancer Institute compared the death rates of laundry and dry cleaning workers to those of the general population, using records kept by a St. Louis trade union local from 1957 to 1977. Analysis of the distribution of deaths found a predominance of women—particularly nonwhite women—and excess rates of cancers among the workers, particularly of the lungs, cervix, uterus, and skin. Most significant, the death rate for Afro-American males and females was *double* that for Euro-American males and females. The study suggests that elevated cancer risks result from multiple exposures to various dry cleaning fluids, including tetrachloroethylene, carbon tetrachloride, and trichloroethylene.[48]

Minority women also work in health-threatening jobs in the textile and apparel industries. In 1980, 57 percent of the 240,000 textile workers were women,[49] while 20.7 percent of all operatives and 13.8 percent of all sewers and stitchers were Afro-American women.[50] In New York City, where much of the garment industry is located, the bulk of workers are minority women. Puerto Rican women, for example, constitute almost 25 percent of those employed in apparel.[51] The ILGWU estimates that in 1983 there were approximately 20,000 unionized workers in New York City's Chinatown garment factories, the vast majority of whom are Asian women.[52] Although accurate statistics are difficult to obtain, it has been estimated that undocumented workers, most of whom are people of color, constitute over 30 percent of New York City's apparel industry.[53]

The apparel industry increasingly relies on sweatshop labor and piecework. According to federal government and ILGWU statistics, there are at least 500 sweatshops in New York City alone.[54] Conditions in these shops are unsafe and unhealthy, reminiscent of sweatshops at the turn of the century—crowded, poorly lit, badly ventilated, and vulnerable to accidents and fires. The tenuous legal position of these workers often discourages them from filing complaints.[55] The *New York Times* described these shops as:

> situated in dank cellars and broiling lofts, in barricaded storefronts and back-alley garages, in dingy attics and rundown apartments. They exploit minorities and illegal aliens, paying

wages below the Federal minimum of $2.90 an hour, often operating from sunrise to sunset but not paying for overtime and sending out cut fabric for illegal sewing at home. They prey on fears of workers who worry about losing their jobs or being deported as illegal aliens.[56]

In addition to the miserable work conditions, the compensation is minimal. In 1974 the average hourly wage in apparel was $2.99—the lowest in any industry, comparing unfavorably to manufacturing as a whole, where the average hourly wage was $4.40.[57] For undocumented workers the wages are even lower. A report to the New York State Assembly estimated the undocumented workers' average rate of pay in 1981 to be less than $2.00 an hour ($15.00 a day) outside Chinatown and even lower in Chinatown itself.[58] In order to care for their children at home, some workers do piecework, which brings in even less; for sewing together an entire dress a woman may earn between $.75 and $1.00.[59]

In the textile industry, byssinosis (brown lung) and other respiratory ailments (such as chronic bronchitis, asthma, and breathlessness) from the cotton dust constitute a major health hazard. Minority workers tend to be concentrated in high dust areas, such as the opening, picking, and carding operations, and have disproportionate rates of respiratory disease.[60] For both the textile and apparel industries, workers are constantly exposed to the various chemicals—dyes, formaldahyde, arsenic—used to treat fabrics.

Of the estimated 5 million migrant and seasonal farmworkers, 75 percent are Chicano and 20 percent Afro-American.[61] There are many hazards in farmwork (see chapter by Jasso and Mazorra), but the use of organophosphates in pesticides is a major one and it is often minorities who are assigned to mix, formulate, and spray them; and it is minorities who have the highest rates of organochlorine pesticide residues and in some areas, the highest rates of pesticide-induced liver and renal dysfunction.[62] Women (and children), who do the weeding, are often directly sprayed with pesticide.

In addition to the direct health hazards of the workplace, minority women also face special risks as members of households of minority men who themselves hold dangerous jobs. Studies of families of asbestos, lead, and beryllium workers have found that contamination of the home environment through such mechanisms as soiled work clothes may be associated with elevated disease levels in the families of the workers.[63]

One of the means by which the subordinate position of minorities has been maintained is the denial of legal and civil rights. This may take the form of special legislation directed against them, such as the laws codifying legal segregation, or of formal or informal exclusion from the protection offered by existing laws. With reference to occupational health and safety, Afro-Americans and other minorities often work in small shops (ten or fewer employees) that are not covered by federal accident and illness recordkeeping requirements. Even where shops are covered by federal regulations, threats to lay off or terminate workers who are already disproportionately unemployed and subject to job discrimination, or whose undocumented status makes them vulnerable to deportation, act to limit complaints about hazardous conditions and reports of violations.

The Double Day and the Triple Day

Given their history of forced participation in the labor market, Afro-American women have generally escaped the psychological damage of confinement to their own homes, but instead have been subjected to the stress of the double-day syndrome. For most Afro-American women this means that, in addition to a full day of work outside the home, they also have the responsibility of running the household,[64] made much more difficult by a limited budget. Afro-American and other working-class groups have developed creative means for collectively addressing the situation, including extended family networks, fictive kin, and ritual kin—ways of getting a wide range of people to share the resources and responsibilities.[65] But this becomes yet another task for women, who tend to be the nodes of these networks and to bear the major responsibility for organizing and maintaining them.

All these responsibilities become even more difficult in a situation where social services are being reduced by the government. The high rate of unemployment and inflation, the dismantling of OSHA, and the increasing wage differential between minorities and other workers disproportionately affect minorities and result in rising morbidity among minority children, deterioration of the education system, teenage unemployment, and increasing poverty among the elderly. It often falls to women to deal with the serious problems caused by these policies in the face of cuts in health care, child care, education, social services, and food stamps.

Under these circumstances, childbearing brings additional problems and hazards. Compared to Euro-American women, a greater proportion of minority women work during their childbearing years, when the presence of children makes working more difficult but more necessary.[66] In 1976, 62 percent of minority women with children 6 to 17 years of age were workers, as were 53 percent of those with children under 6; the comparable figures for Euro-

American women were 55 percent and 38 percent.[67] Thus minority women are disproportionately affected by cutbacks in child care. The fact that minority women frequently work at low-wage jobs in small, nonunion shops decreases the likelihood that they will receive adequate benefits for prenatal and postnatal care, or maternity leave. The conditions of work and the household responsibility influence the health of the fetus as well as the mother. A recent study analyzed data collected on 7,722 pregnancies of Afro-American and Euro-American women in the following categories: (1) those who did not work outside the home, (2) those whose employment required sitting (students, clerical workers), and (3) those who had stand-up employment (retail sales workers, private household workers, service workers, and "laborers"). Of the women in the second and third categories taken together, 81 percent of the Euro-American women had sit-down jobs, compared to only 32 percent of the Afro-American women. The study found lower birth weights among children of mothers who held employment outside the home than among those of mothers who remained at home during the last trimester of pregnancy and concluded that the "growth retardation was most severe when mothers had stand-up jobs, continued working until near term, were hypertensive, or had children at home to care for when they returned from work."[68] For most of these variables, Afro-American and other minority women are more likely to be at risk.

The heavy responsibilities of work and household, as well as limited access to adequate nutrition, housing, child care, and medical services, certainly have a bearing on the fact that minority women die in childbirth at five times the rate of Euro-American women and that the infant mortality rate among Afro-Americans is nearly double that of Euro-Americans.[69]

In attempting to juggle the burdens of work, household, and reproduction, sterilization may be an extreme and irreversible solution to a limited range of alternatives. The 1977 case of the four women who charged that they were sterilized because they were given the choice of sterilization or being transferred to lower paying jobs has dramatized the widespread policy among industries to exclude vulnerable women from jobs where they may be exposed to reproductive hazards rather than clean up the workplace.[70] The possibilities of losing a job and of being unable to support another child weigh heavily on minority women, who have fewer options to begin with. Outright sterilization abuse, in addition to limited alternatives, has produced a situation where minority women continue to be sterilized in disproportionate numbers. Accurate statistics are hard to come by, but those that exist give some indication of the situation. According to a study by Princeton University's Office of Population Control, 20 percent of all married Afro-American women have been sterilized; other sources suggest that approximately 20 percent of Chicana women and over 35 percent of all Puerto Rican women of childbearing age have been surgically sterilized.[71]

Afro-American women and men, and other minority women and men, have always been involved in efforts to resist the conditions foisted upon them—slavery, segregation, and discrimination. In this sense, many minority women may be said to have a triple day. Such struggles are carried out on a variety of levels, from individual actions, such as the everyday resistance to harrassment, to collective mass struggles, such as the civil rights movement of the 1960s. Actions may be directed toward the dominant structure or the victimized group; they may be aimed at changing the social organization of work, the legal restriction and denial of civil rights, or the ideologies of racism that rationalize such conditions.[72] Rosa Parks is an example of the militant role played by a working-class Afro-American woman. A private household worker who had toiled all day, she refused to give up her seat on a bus to a white man. This action sparked the Montgomery bus boycott and an important phase of the massive civil rights movement of the 1960s.

Space does not permit a full discussion of the history of these struggles, but I want to briefly discuss those directed toward reorganizing the social organization of work. After mass struggles brought about advances in breaking down discriminatory barriers in industry and the trade unions, Afro-Americans became the ethnic group in the workforce with the highest proportion of unionized members—33 percent.[73] Afro-American women have generally seen unionization as a necessary instrument for improving their conditions of work, and have, often under dangerous and difficult circumstances, played an active part in the struggle to organize trade unions and in subsequent trade union actions.

Today, minority women are active in the leadership of such trade unions as District 1199 of the National Union of Health Care Employees, the United Food and Commercial Workers International Union, and the National Education Association, the largest union in the country. Recognizing that some unions have adopted the policies and practices of the corporations in accepting unequal treatment of women and minorities, Afro-American women are active participants in national organizations such as the Coalition of Labor Union Women and the Coalition of Black Trade Unionists that press for equality in the trade union movement and in society at large.

This chapter has described the way in which the triple oppression of class, race, and gender affect the health of minority women. Given these circumstances, it is appropriate to question those explanations and policies that focus primarily on alleged biological, cultural, and lifestyle differences—and ignore structural constraints—in explaining ethnic and class differences in rates of morbidity and mortality. Such explanations, which shift the responsibility to the victimized populations, are accepted as part of a long history of rationalizing slavery, gender, and race discrimination on the basis of biological and cultural inferiority. Refined in academic circles and disseminated by the mass media, these notions attempt to vindicate the corporate structure that profits from these conditions, to blame the victim, and therefore to undermine any movements for social change. Yet, being triply oppressed, minority women are also a triple threat. With their consciousness shaped by their experiences as workers, as members of a minority group, and as women, they are at the core of resistance.

Notes

1. Leith Mullings, "Ethnicity and Stratification in the Urban United States," *Annals of the New York Academy of Sciences* 318 (1978):10–22.
2. For example, see M. Radov and N. Santangelo, "Health Status of Minorities and Low-Income Groups," Department of Health, Education, and Welfare, Publication No. 79-627 (1979); *Health, United States*, 1975 edition, Department of Health, Education, and Welfare; D. Levin, et al., "Demographic Characteristics of Cancer of the Pancreas: Mortality, Incidence, and Survival," *Cancer* 47, no. 6 (1981); C. Mettlen and G. Murphy, eds., *Cancer Among Black Populations*, Proceedings of the International Conference on Cancer Among Black Populations, Roswell Park Memorial Institute, Buffalo, New York, May 1980.
3. Kyriakos S. Markides, "Mortality Among Minority Populations: A Review of Recent Patterns and Trends," *Public Health Reports* 98, no. 3 (1983):253–55.
4. Morris Davis, "The Impact of Workplace Health and Safety on Black Workers: Assessment and Prognosis," *Labor Law Journal* 31, no. 12 (December 1980):724.
5. June J. Christmas, "Black Women and Health in the 80's," keynote address to the First National Conference on Black Women's Health Issues, Atlanta, Georgia, June 24, 1983, p. 3.
6. William West "Drug Action in Management of Hypertension," *Urban Health* 4, no. 3 (June 1975):36.

7. Christmas, "Black Women and Health," pp. 4–5.
8. There is, however, a body of literature in epidemiology that describes class as a variable that overrides race and culture in most diseases.
9. Andrew Rowland, "Black Workers and Cancer," *Labor Occupational Health Program Monitor* (January-February 1980), p. 14.
10. John L. Young, et al., "Incidence of Cancer in United States Blacks," *Cancer Research* 35 (November 1975):3536.
11. *Women's Occupational Health Resource Center News* 4, no. 4 (September 1982): 2.
12. Samuel Epstein and Joel Swartz, "Fallacies of Lifestyle Cancer Theories," *Nature* 289 (January 1981):127–30.
13. Stanley Lieberson, *A Piece of the Pie* (Berkeley and Los Angeles: University of California Press, 1980); Mullings, "Ethnicity and Stratification"; Victor Perlo, *Economics of Racism* (New York: International Publishers, 1975).
14. Leith Mullings, "Rationalizing Inequality," *Journal of Academic Skills* 3, no. 1 (Spring 1982):6–17.
15. Angela Davis, *Women, Race, and Class* (New York: Random House, 1981), chapter 1.
16. Claudia Goldin, "Female Labor Force Participation: The Origin of Black and White Differences," *Journal of Economic History* 37 (1977):87.
17. Ibid.
18. Margaret Wilkerson, "Working Women in the United States," in *Black Working Women* (Berkeley: Center for the Study, Education and Advancement of Women, University of California, 1982), p. 5.
19. Philip Foner, *Women and the American Labor Movement*, vol. 2 (New York: The Free Press, 1980), p. 555.
20. *WREE Review: Journal of Women for Racial and Economic Equality* 8, no. 1 (January-February 1983).
21. Barbara A. P. Jones, "The Economic Status of Black Women," in *The State of Black America 1983*, ed. James D. Williams (New York: National Urban League, 1983), p. 153.
22. David Swinton, "The Economic Status of the Black Population," in ibid., p. 50.
23. U.S. Department of Labor, Women's Bureau, *Equal Employment Opportunity for Women: U.S. Policies*, 1982, p. 11.
24. Swinton, "The Economic Status of the Black Population," p. 45.
25. M. Davis, "The Impact of Workplace Health."
26. The meaning of the term "female headed household" continues to be in dispute. Studies such as that by Carol Stack (*All Our Kin* [New York: Harper & Row, 1976]) have demonstrated that although the residential unit may not include men for a variety of reasons, men continue to contribute to the households of their sisters, mothers, and the mothers of their children.
27. Jones, "The Economic Status of Black Women," p. 119.
28. Wilkerson, "Working Women in the United States," p. 5.
29. Jones, "The Economic Status of Black Women," p. 119.
30. A. J. D'Ercole, R. Arthur, J. Cain, and B. Barrentine, "Insecticide Expo-

sure of Mothers and Newborns in a Rural Agricultural Area," *Pediatrics* 57, no. 6 (1976):869–74.

31. U.S. Commission on Civil Rights, *Health Insurance: Coverage and Employment Opportunities for Minorities and Women*, Clearinghouse Publication 72 (September 1982).

32. Jones, "The Economic Status of Black Women," p. 152.

33. Vicente Navarro, *Medicine Under Capitalism* (New York: Prodist, 1976), p. 138.

34. Jones, "The Economic Status of Black Women," p. 152.

35. Navarro, *Medicine Under Capitalism*, p. 138.

36. *Women's Occupational Health Resource Center News* 4, no. 4 (September 1982):6; Martha Tabor, "Health Care, Job Stress," *Occupational Health and Safety* (December 1982); pp. 20–35.

37. C. J. Maynard Pattison, K. Berquist, and H. Webster, "Epidemiology of Hepatitis B in Hospital Personnel," *American Journal of Epidemiology* 101, no. 1 (1975):59–64.

38. Teresa Schnorr and J. Stellman, unpublished study cited in *Women's Occupational Health Resource Center* 4, no. 4 (September 1982):1.

39. Rose Kaminski and Rober Spirtas, "Industrial Characteristics of Persons Report Morbidity During the Health Interview Surveys Conducted in 1969–1974: An Exploratory Review," National Institute for Occupational Health and Safety, August 1980.

40. Jones, "The Economic Status of Black Women," p. 131.

41. Frank H. Cassell, "Immigration and the Department of Labor," *Annals of the American Academy of Political and Social Science* 3 (September 1966), p. 113.

42. Jones, "The Economic Status of Black Women," p. 152.

43. Suzanne Haynes and Manning Feinleib, "Women, Work, and Coronary Heart Disease: Prospective Findings from the Framingham Heart Study," *American Journal of Public Health* 70, no. 2 (February 1980): 133–41.

44. Julianne Malveaux, "Shifts in the Occupational and Employment Status of Black Women," in *Black Working Women* (Berkeley: Center for the Study, Education, and Advancement of Women, University of California, 1982), p. 137.

45. Diane Westcott, "Blacks in the 1970's: Did They Scale the Job Ladder?" *Monthly Labor Review* (June 1982), p. 32.

46. Gloria Gordon et al., "Psychological Effects of Office Workers' Job Conditions," paper presented at the annual convention of the American Psychological Association, Washington, D.C., August 24, 1982.

47. Westcott, "Blacks in the 1970's," p. 32.

48. A. Blair et al., "Causes of Death Among Laundry and Dry Cleaning Workers," *American Journal of Public Health* 69, no. 5 (May 1979): 508–11. A more recent study of laundry and dry cleaning women workers in Wisconsin found that some of the elevated risks found among these workers declined when compared to women workers in other low-wage occupations, pointing to the interaction of other socioeconomic variables. However, the small percentage of nonwhite fe-

males were "omitted for the sake of homogeneity." See Ronald Katz and D. Jowett, "Female Laundry and Dry Cleaning Workers in Wisconsin: A Mortality Analysis," *American Journal of Public Health* 71, no. 3 (March 1981):305–307.

49. *Women's Occupational Health Resource Center Fact Sheet* (March 1980), p. 1.
50. Westcott, "Blacks in the 1980's," p. 32.
51. Lois Gray, "The Jobs Puerto Ricans Hold in New York City," *Monthly Labor Review* 98, no. 10 (October 1975):12–16.
52. Abeles, Schwartz, Haeckel and Silverblatt, Inc., *The Chinatown Garment Industry Study*, report submitted to Local 23-25, International Ladies' Garment Workers' Union, June 1983.
53. Helen Safa, "The Differential Incorporation of Hispanic Women Migrants into the United States Labor Force," in *Female Migrants to the United States*, ed. D. M. Mortimer and R. S. Bryce-Laporte (Washington, D.C.: Smithsonian Institution, 1979).
54. Foner, *Women and the American Labor Movement*, vol. 2, p. 554
55. Conference on Undocumented Workers in New York City, Center for the Study of Human Rights, Columbia University, New York, May 6–8, 1982.
56. Cited in Foner, *Women and the American Labor Movement*, vol. 2, p. 554.
57. Safa, "The Differential Incorporation of Hispanic Women."
58. Franz S. Leichter, report to the New York State Senate, "The Return of the Sweatshop," 26 February, 1981.
59. Foner, *Women and the American Labor Movement*, vol. 2, p. 554; Leichter, "The Return of the Sweatshop."
60. M. Davis, "The Impact of Workplace Health," p. 729.
61. *Women's Occupational Health Resource Center News* 3, no. 5 (September/October 1981):4.
62. F. W. Kutz, A. R. Yobs, and S. C. Strassman, "Racial Stratification of Organochlorine Insect Residues in Human Adipose Tissue," *Journal of Occupational Medicine* 19, no. 9 (1977):619–22; and M. Davis, "The Impact of Workplace Health," p. 729.
63. See H. A. Anderson, I. S. Selikoff, et al., "Asbestos-Related Disease from Household Exposure to Occupational Dusts," paper presented to the American Conference of Chest Physicians, New Orleans, October 2–4, 1974; Edward Baker, et al., "Lead Poisoning in Children of Lead Workers," *New England Journal of Medicine* 296, no. 5 (3 February, 1977):260–61; and M. Eisenbud et al., "Non-Occupational Berylliosis," *Journal of Industrial Hygiene Toxicology* 31 (1949): 282–94.
64. While it is generally true that women bear major responsibility for the household, the issue of the extent to which working-class minority men share this responsibility needs more study. There is evidence to indicate working-class and minority men participate in household tasks to a greater extent than previously believed.
65. See, for example, Carol Stack, *All Our Kin* (New York: Harper & Row, 1974).
66. If we look at the proportion of women working in specific age groups in 1973, the differences in the overall impact of work experience can be

better understood. In the 25-34-year old range—the principle child-bearing years—there is a sharp decline in the participation in the labor market for Euro-American women, but an increase for Afro-American women. It is in this age range that the excess of Afro-American women over Euro-American women reaches its peak, with 61.1 percent of Afro-American women working, as compared with 48.6 percent of Euro-American women. See Perlo, *Economics of Racism*, p. 23.

67. United States Department of Labor, Women's Bureau, *Minority Women Workers: A Statistical Overview*, 1977.
68. Richard Naeye and Ellen Peters, "Working During Pregnancy: Effects on the Fetus," *Pediatrics* 69, no. 6 (June 1982):724–27.
69. Christmas, *op. cit.*, p. 3.
70. *New York Times*, September 9, 1980; and see chapter by Judith Scott in this volume.
71. A. Davis, *Women, Race, and Class*, p. 219.
72. See Cheryl Jilkes, "The Community Work of Racial-Ethnic Women," lecture presented at the Summer Institute on Women of Color, Center for Research on Women, Memphis State University, Memphis, Tennessee, 1983.
73. M. Davis, "The Impact of Workplace Health," p. 723.

7
Protection for Women: Trade Unions and Labor Laws
Alice Kessler-Harris

Feminists and the trade union movement find themselves at odds today over the issue of protective labor legislation for women. Laws that restrict women's capacity to hold certain kinds of jobs in the name of health, argue many feminists, actually serve to discriminate against them. Trade union officials, women among them, tend to point, in contrast, to a century of struggle for legislation that protects women as one of their great achievements. Accusations fly back and forth. Feminists are accused of negating the interests of most working women; trade unionists of being exclusionary and self-serving.

Although similar periods of mistrust between the women's movement and labor movement have existed in the past, it was not always so. When the issue of protective labor legislation for women first emerged in the 1870s, trade unions and women's movement activists more often cooperated than disagreed. Their relationship was never easy, but they were able to agree on certain basic principles, and they shared certain social assumptions that provided the underpinnings for cooperation between the two groups.

Trade unionists in the late nineteenth and early twentieth centuries faced a divided woman's movement. The majority of female activists, who I shall call reformers, argued that women's social roles, primarily home bound, vested women with a virtue and morality lacking in men whose lives were spent in the competitive worlds of work and business. These women wanted to extend the advantages conferred by women's "separate sphere" to their communities and into political life. Since the higher values resided in the home, women who guarded these qualities would bring to the public sphere a clearer perception of justice, a more humane set of concerns, a needed balance to the crass materialism encouraged by the daily grind of most men's lives. Women, they argued, could and should exercise a benign moral influence on society. As conservative as this sounds to us now, it provided, in the late nineteenth and early twentieth centuries, the rationale for much of the argument for the extension of property rights to married women, for the temperance crusade, and for woman's suffrage. And it also provided the basis for ameliorating the worst exploitation of working women. For if a woman's special role in the end inhered in her qualities as wife and mother, then the state had a legitimate interest in protecting her capacity to function at home, and the health of women workers became open to regulation.

In contrast to those who held that the state ought to protect women's home roles, a small and fluid minority, who I shall call women's rights advocates, believed that women deserved all the "human rights" enjoyed by men. Women as diverse as Elizabeth Cady Stanton, Anna Howard Shaw, and Alice Paul held that woman was first an individual and citizen of the state and that the roles that derived from her biological attributes were secondary. Arguing from the eighteenth-century notion of natural rights, women's rights advocates proposed to tear down barriers to equality between men and women and therefore opposed restrictive laws that limited women's ability to operate in any sphere of public life.

The early labor movement, especially after 1886 when the craft-oriented American Federation of Labor (AFL) became the dominant trade union federation, agreed not so much with the majority position as with the assumptions behind it. Most skilled workers shared prevailing beliefs about women's home roles. Brooklyn's iron molders, for example, insisted that women should be excluded from foundries because "We feel that the girl or the woman . . . is the future mother of the American boys and girls."[1] Such workers stood to benefit from wives with the time to perform personal services like laundry and meal preparation, wives who could relieve them of any responsibility for the care of household and children. As one ironworker put it, "One well known fact I know is that some women—I have worked with women for nineteen years—that they could not boil water without burning it, and to become the wife of a man they should have a training at home and learn housework."[2] The legislation that followed from that notion served the trade union's interest in another way. By removing some women from the labor force it offered to limit competition for jobs. Again, testimony from the iron molders provides a clear illustration. After testifying that men "get about $3.60 a day and the women make no more than $9 a week" for about the same work, one iron molder went on, "I think the men should be left to make living wages to support girls and their families."[3] For the trade union movement, regulating female labor was one aspect of a broader struggle to establish itself as arbiter of work-related issues.

Three competing principles have thus informed the achievement of protective labor legislation in this country. On the first—a shared belief in the state's interest in protecting the health of female workers—the labor movement and most elements of the women's movement have frequently agreed. They have usually disagreed on the second and third principles. The labor movement has insisted on its hard-won authority to rationalize conditions of employment for all workers, without regard to the specific impact of its decisions on excluded groups. And, especially as conditions for all workers began to improve, women's rights activists have increasingly moved to the fore in defense of each woman's individual right to make a place for herself in the workforce, even at the cost of challenging trade union authority and social conceptions of women's roles.

Historical circumstances have determined how these principles have played themselves out in the past. As family life and the structure of occupations have altered over the past century, so too has our understanding of women's social roles changed and the position of those concerned with equitable and reasonable work conditions begun to accommodate to new realities. Understanding how and why that has happened will help us to grasp the current debate over protective labor legislation. It will tell us something about where we are in the drama that pits two potential allies—women and workers—against each other, and forces women who are workers to choose sides instead of creating allies.

In the first phases of legislation, from the early 1870s to 1908, reformers struggled to establish the principle that the state could legitimately intervene to protect women's health. Wage-earning women, reformers, and unionists agreed that this was a desirable goal. But in a society that proclaimed the principle of freedom of contract for all workers, legislators with the support of the courts had consistently refused to intervene in the employer-employee relationship. They took the position that each worker must be "free" to negotiate with his or her employer about conditions of work, even where such freedom deprived workers of the capacity to organize and placed them at an evident disadvantage. In the 1840s, for example, associations of male and female workers and early trade unions had petitioned the Massachusetts State Assembly to shorten the number of hours in a working day. A legislative committee turned down the request, arguing that "labor is intelligent enough to make its own bargains, and look out for its own interests without any interference from us."[4]

But the Civil War and the depression of 1873 encouraged employers all over the industrial Northeast to drive workers beyond the limits of their capacities. In a period of rapid urban and industrial expansion, women lacked the small town and community life that had provided minimal protection before the war. Between a quarter and a third of the working women in every large city boarded with strangers or lived alone. Many were widowed and supported children. Without family to fall back on in periods of ill health and unemployment, without savings, and with no social insurance systems at all, they were entirely dependent on employers for life-sustaining work. Such women had little power to resist demands for more and faster work and they could scarcely protest such common abuses as heavy fines for coming in late, or their employer's failure to pay for completed work on time. Since most wage-earning women lacked industrial skills, they competed for jobs in an undifferentiated market, garnered only the lowest wages, and could organize with great difficulty. By the 1870s the working conditions of wage-earning women had become a national scandal.[5]

As working and living conditions for women steadily deteriorated, their health became a subject of general concern. Often weak and malnourished, wage-earning women in mills and factories died at a rate about 30 percent above that of male workers. They were susceptible to consumption and other lung diseases, and the conditions under which they worked threatened to cripple many for life. Standing on their feet for nine or ten hours every day, working in close rooms, unheated in winter and unventilated in summer, created innumerable problems. As Azel Ames pointed out in his influential volume, *Sex in Industry*, women suffered "nervous debility," menstrual dysfunction, perpetual backaches, and faintness and dizziness. And in the eyes of some, poor working conditions contributed to a general weakness that encouraged immorality. Though wage-earning women might disagree as to the uses to which such arguments were put, they served a useful purpose in publicizing the awful conditions under which most women worked.

Any hope that the labor movement might protect women disappeared when the Knights of Labor collapsed after 1886. The Knights had had a vision of a society run by producers' cooperatives. They welcomed as members all who shared that vision, including women, and they organized workers by industry as well as by craft. Among the half million or so members they are thought to have had at their peak in 1886, perhaps 50,000, or 10 percent, were women. They included housewives and farmers as well as skilled industrial workers. But membership in the Knights evaporated after the organization became associated with anarchism in 1886, and skilled crafts workers, already discontented, pulled out to form the AFL. Concerned with maintaining strength and unity, the AFL admitted to membership only unions of skilled craftsmen that charged dues high enough to support the local and national union and the parent federation. Unlike the Knights, its goal was to improve the living conditions of those who could most easily fight for themselves. Unskilled and poorly paid women found themselves excluded.

Yet the poor conditions of women could not be ignored by trade unionists who believed that these threatened to undermine the wages and jobs of all workers. Lower wages would prevent men from supporting their wives at all, thus throwing ever more women into the workforce and weakening the family as well. Reluctantly, trade unions came to the conclusion that legislation might serve to improve the conditions of those women who continued to work while it simultaneously placed onerous restrictions on employers of women, reducing their incentive to hire them as cheap labor. In the opinion of some, legislation could also serve as an entering wedge to shorten hours for all workers.

Female reformers approached the issue from a different perspective. In the late nineteenth century such groups as the National Consumers' League, the Women's Educational and Industrial Union, and the Working Women's Protective Union tried a variety of experiments to raise the living and working standards of wage-earning women. They provided lawyers to collect unpaid wages, they set up model boarding houses with clean rooms and wholesome food, they offered vocational training in the hope of moving women into better jobs, they publicized poor working conditions in factories, and they organized consumer boycotts of department stores that failed to provide rest periods and seats for their salespeople. But these efforts proved totally inadequate in the face of rapidly deteriorating conditions and increasing numbers of women workers. Fearing that the capacity of wage-earning women to bear healthy children would be permanently impaired and that wage work would create a class of deformed women, reformers, like many trade unionists, turned to state intervention as the most practical answer.

Given the history of opposition to any such legislation, persuading state legislatures to regulate women's working conditions was no easy task. It was not enough to argue only that working conditions were onerous. Rather, reformers had to emphasize the ways in which working conditions affected the larger public good. The courts had already recognized that reasonable differences distinguished one group or "class" of workers from another. On the basis of differences they could clearly identify and label, they had declared that certain classes of workers required the protection of the state. The courts recognized that child workers, for example, were a separate class in whom the state had a unique interest and they sustained legislation that limited the working hours of children. Sporadically they also recognized the special interests and needs of the state in protecting the health of workers in some hazardous occupations, including mining and railroads. The Massachusetts State Supreme Court was the first to acknowledge, in 1876, that women too constituted a class—a group of workers whose health and morals were of particular concern to the state. Other states followed suit in the 1890s, paving the way for legislatures to consider laws that protected the community's interest in women's well-being.

By the early part of the 1900s state courts began to affirm what had come to be the consensus. Upholding the interests of the state in sustaining women's capacity to reproduce, they agreed with legislators that states did indeed have the right to protect women's health by shortening the number of hours during which women worked. "If such legislation savors of paternalism," argued the Pennsylvania Supreme Court in 1900, "it is in its least objectionable form in that it cares for those who from their own necessities, ambition or the cupidity of their employers, may be prompted or required to jeopardize their health in unreasonable and dangerous employment." The court went on to argue that "sex imposes limitations to excessive and long continued physical labor as certainly as does minority. . . . Adult females are a class as distinct as minors, separated by natural conditions from all other laborers, and are so constituted as to be unable to endure physical exertion and exposure to the extent and degree that is not harmful to adult males."[6] From that assumption followed a series of others. Successive courts in such states as Nebraska and Washington held that since women could not "endure the same hours of exhaustive labor as male workers," the state "must be accorded the right to guard and protect women" in order to "conserve the public health and welfare."

The special concern with women's health inhered in their capacity to bear children. "That which would deleteriously affect any great number of women who are the mothers of succeeding generations must necessarily affect the public welfare and the public morals."[7] In their famous Muller v. Oregon decision in 1908 the U.S. Supreme Court capped this line of argument by accepting as evidence, and implicitly affirming, the validity of statistical data on the effect of work on women's health. The data presented in what became known as the "Brandeis Brief" attempted to prove conclusively that permitting women to work long hours was "dangerous to the public health, safety, morals or welfare." The court, concurring, noted that "healthy mothers are essential to vigorous offspring," the physical well-being of women becomes an object of public interest and care in order to preserve the strength and vigor of the race.[8] So saying, the court upheld statutory limits on the number of hours women could work in a day or a week.

As the courts legitimized the state's interest in protecting women's health, the separate states set out to assert their new prerogative. Even before the Brandeis Brief, states had taken up such rudimentary matters as seating, lighting, and sanitation in the workplace. Often the impulse behind such laws came from working women themselves or from reform groups like the National Consumers' League, which publicized a well-known "white list" of department stores that treated their employees well. But factory laws that provided for minimum amounts of ventilation, for adequate numbers of toilets and washbowls, for mandatory seats, and even for some rest periods during the working day were not controversial. They were rarely challenged in court—and often evaded by employers.

While most wage-earning women supported these regulations as a means of easing their daily lives, they were less enthusiastic about the parallel authority that the states simultaneously assumed for restricting the kinds of work women could do. For if states could regulate how women could work, they could also, on the grounds of protecting women's health and morals, restrict where and when they could work. In an apparently random pattern, states excluded women from mines, iron mills, saloons, concert halls, and other places "where intoxicants are seen." They prohibited women from operating dangerous machinery, from cleaning machinery in motion, and from working in places with high levels of dust. And this was only the beginning. Women were soon barred from operating elevators, serving as messengers, lifting heavy weights, and working a certain number of weeks before and after giving birth. State after state passed laws regulating the numbers of hours women could work in a day, and the number of days in a week. Legislators decided how those hours could be distributed over the twenty-four hour period, whether they could be at night, and in what industries. No doubt many women benefited from these laws; yet in regulating women's relationship to paid work, they served to affirm women's special place both at home and in the workforce.

The trade union movement accepted and generally supported this onslaught. Convinced that only organization could effectively protect workers in the workplace, the AFL adamantly opposed any extension of regulatory legislation to male workers. Leaders believed that the 90 percent of wage earners who remained unorganized in 1910 would hesitate to affiliate with unions if they could look to the state to protect them. In principle, at least, this belief applied to women workers too. In August 1913 the *American Federationist*, monthly journal of the AFL, "viewed with apprehension present sentiment in favor of setting up public and political agencies for securing industrial benefits for wage-earning women. Those agencies would constitute a restriction upon freedom of action . . . we should be foisting upon [women] fetters from which they would have to free themselves in addition to the problems that now confront them."[9] And in 1915 the journal editoralized: "Women work in industry side by side with men. Their relations to industry and their relations to employers contain no elements different from those of men's relations. Industrial protection and industrial betterment with freedom involve no elements that differ from the problems of men. Economic organization is the hope of all."[10]

But in practice the trade union movement was so ambivalent about organizing unskilled and transient women workers, and so convinced that women worked in areas not susceptible to organization, that their resistance broke down in the face of legislation that protected women. Tempted by the possibility of freeing all workers from the competition of unorganized women, the labor movement vacillated. The same year that the *Federationist* expressed fear of government intervention on behalf of women, Samuel Gompers, president of the AFL, told a Congressional committee that the AFL "urged as strongly as we could" a bill limiting the hours of women and children in the District of Columbia to eight per day.[11] And when the protective labor laws seemed to be threatened in the 1920s by a constitutional amendment advocating "that all laws shall apply equally to men and women" throughout the United States, the AFL characterized the proposal as "vicious" and called it "an attempt to break down all protective laws that have been placed around women to protect the potential mothers of the race."[12]

Many wage-earning women and their allies sympathized with this position. Through the decade and a half from the 1908 Supreme Court decision in Oregon v. Muller to 1923, when the debate over the first Equal Rights Amendment reached fever pitch, women argued, as a tactical issue, the question of whether they should organize into unions or seek legislative protection. The National Women's Trade Union League perhaps best epitomizes the struggle. Formed in 1903 to organize wage-earning women, the WTUL worked closely with the AFL from its inception. Until 1913 it emphasized organization as its major priority. Then, discouraged by the meagre support it got from the AFL, it began to turn its attention to legislation until by 1915 almost all of its money and efforts were pointed in that direction. The move, argues Nancy Schrom Dye, historian of New York's WTUL, reflected a shift "away from an emphasis on women as workers to be integrated into the labor movement to one on women workers as women with special needs, disadvantages and weaknesses."[13] It was a feminist position, but one based on the needs that distinguished women from men.

As in the WTUL, women in other reform groups had been in the vanguard of efforts to seek legislative restrictions on some kinds of women's work. Medical studies, led by the pioneer research of Alice Hamilton, increasingly substantiated the greater impact of certain industrial poisons on women. Lead, long banned as an industrial poison in Europe, came under fire in the United States at the beginning of the century when studies indicated that women employed around it tended to miscarry or give birth to deformed children. Benzene and phosphorous, widely used in women-employing industries, poisoned exposed women at three times the rate of exposed men.[14] Simultaneously, a growing consciousness of the effects of dust and lint in producing tuberculosis and silicosis in women led the WTUL and the National Consumers' League to support regulations that barred women from workrooms with excessive levels of dust. About the same time, many states forbade women from lifting heavy weights, or from operating grinding machines that threw particles of dust into the air.

Such restrictions were less controversial than those on women's work at night. On this issue, wage-earning women often divided from the reformers. Many women preferred to work at night for family convenience or better pay, rejecting the dangers to their morals or to their health that reformers insisted accompanied such work. But since 1906, when most European countries had sub-scribed to the Berne Convention which eliminated night work for women, reformers in the United States had worked painstakingly to get the states to adopt similar regulations. By 1920 most indus-trial states prohibited or limited night hours for women in in-dustry, a move that finally received the Supreme Court's stamp of approval in 1924. The court then declared that night work "so seriously affected the health of women, so threatened and impaired their peculiar and natural functions, and so exposed them to the dangers and menaces incident to night life that the State felt impelled to take cognizance of the situation, ... and that in so doing it was clearly within its rights."[15]

Women fought bitterly to retain jobs from which protective legislation removed them. They understood, as did the skilled craftsmen who often supported campaigns for legislative restric-tion, that limiting access to jobs created a permanent disability in the labor force in that it deprived them of opportunities for ad-vancement. Restrictive legislation therefore affirmed the job segre-gation of a divided labor market.

Some of the bitterest struggles between skilled craftsmen and women occurred over restrictive laws. New York's iron molders, for example, successfully used the assumption that women should not lift heavy weights to push women out of foundry jobs that they had held for more than a generation. Claiming that women had at first been employed only to "make little bits of cores," members of the molders' union argued that within a few years women were "using these monstrous rammers and making cores of great size . . . and there are very few men there now."[16] In an effort to undermine job segmentation and take advantage of cheaper female labor, employers argued that it would be a shame to deprive women who could do that work of relatively well-paid jobs. Male workers responded vociferously: "The foundry is no place for a woman as the future mother of our citizens. . . . Most of us are unalterably opposed to women working in a foundry." Similar arguments were used by street-railway union members, who used a night work law to push women out of their jobs as conductors after World War I, and by metal polishers, who first urged women's exclusion because of flying dust, and then when ventilation systems removed all dust from the room, claimed that the job was simply not appropriate for them.

Faced with exclusion from hazardous and unsafe jobs, women asked why such jobs could not be made safe for all workers. Trade unions had resolved the issue of hazardous work for men by seeking workmen's compensation legislation. But compensation was awarded only after an *accident* that could be attributed directly to work-related causes. Other illnesses, some of them contracted and developed over the course of several years at one job, were not covered. The term "occupational disease" moved only haltingly into public parlance. "Some U.S. Senators," reported the AFL's committee on health and safety to its national convention in 1914, "have shown a strong disposition to ridicule the term 'occupational diseases' where it is discussed in labor safety bills."[17] Without compensation for diseases, and given the prevalence of regulation for women only, the Women's Bureau of the Department of Labor noted, women were subject to potential discrimination. In 1921, when the body of protective legislation for women was all but complete in the United States, the bureau warned: "It is very possible that under the guise of 'protection' women may be shut out from occupations which are really less harmful to . . . them than much of the tedious heavy work both in the home and in the factory which has long been considered their special province. Safe standards of work for women must come to be safe standards of work for men also if women are to have an equal chance in industry."[18]

Women who had rejected the notion of women's primary domestic role and who argued from a position of women's strength recognized the danger immediately. With suffrage won, these more radical feminists turned their attention to the problems of securing women's right to compete equally with men for jobs. Led by Alice Paul's Woman's Party and joined by a variety of business and professional women's organizations, proponents of the first Equal Rights Amendment, introduced into Congress in 1923, argued that women should accept no legal status that limited their freedom of contract or placed them on an unequal footing with men. To ensure this, they proposed to write such a guarantee into the constitution. Now the principle of individual rights came into political conflict with that of the state's right to intervene to protect women's health. For, as then Professor of Law Felix Frankfurter put it, an amendment that asserted equality with men could not simultaneously sustain special class status for women. And it therefore "opens the door to evils far more serious and affecting a vastly greater number of women than the disabilities they would shut out."[19] Legal experts agreed, guessing that an Equal Rights Amendment would vitiate most protective labor laws at a time when wage-earning women were just beginning to benefit from them.

Most female trade union leaders and sympathizers therefore opposed the amendment. Faced with losing improved conditions, they resoundingly rejected the ERA and rallied behind legislation. Mary Anderson, head of the Women's Bureau and for seven years a National Women's Trade Union League organizer, perhaps expressed the position best. Calling herself a practical feminist, she noted that without laws women had two choices. They could either "wait for their eight-hour day until they are themselves sufficiently organized to bargain for it with employers. Or they can go on working nine or ten or eleven hours a day."[20] Alice Hamilton summed up the argument succinctly. "What I would urge upon the opponents of special legislation for women in industry," she wrote in 1924, "is that they work for the fundamental reform of industry first, later for the special reform they are now pressing, the equal status of men and women in industry."[21]

In the end the ERA was defeated. Reluctantly or enthusiastically, most influential groups—and, we must assume, many individuals—chose to sacrifice the rights of some individuals to what they thought would be the immediate greater good of healthy womanhood. The position was effectively articulated by Alice Hamilton: "That there are some skilled women workers who suffer from legal regulations of their trades is undoubtedly true, but they are a small minority compared to those who need these laws. . . . Surely it would be better for these exceptional women to turn their efforts toward the framing of amendments exempting their own class from the operation of a law rather than to oppose all legal control of the hours of work of less capable and fortunate women."[22]

But what looked like a defeat for individual rights was transformed within a generation by the shifting needs of the workplace. The depression of the 1930s offered, ironically, the first breakthrough. While discrimination against married women reached new peaks and the segregation of women into certain labor market sectors tightened, women benefited from the increased need for unskilled and cheap labor.[23] For New Deal programs intended to benefit male breadwinners also offered some advantages to women. In extending the protection of the state to all workers, the New Deal laid to rest at last the need to separate men and women before the law. And it annointed the trade union official representative of workers' collective interests. Neither of these steps dramatically changed the lives of most women workers, but together they put wage-earning women into a different relationship to both the trade union and the state. Ultimately the policies of the New Deal made room for women to insist on individual rights in the workplace.

The social realities behind this shift emerged from the devastating unemployment of the depression. With 25 percent of the labor force jobless, the state stepped in to help rationalize both industry and labor. The National Industrial Recovery Act, passed in the spring of 1933, encouraged the creation of industrial codes that reduced the working day to forty hours for all covered workers, and down to thirty-five for some. The codes regulated shift-work, sometimes limiting the numbers of hours factories could operate, and eliminating overtime and night work. They provided minimum wages for all covered workers. To determine appropriate wage levels and to give workers a voice in creating codes, the legislation provided for elected representatives of workers in each industry. For the first time, trade unions had at least semi-official sanction for their organizing efforts, and workers exhibited a rising surge of interest in the labor movement. Stubbornly, the AFL remained committed to organization by crafts. And thousands of workers in the new mass-production industries found that they lacked support for industrial organization. Leaders in coal, steel, autos, and textiles were among those who formed a dissident committee for industrial organization within the AFL to pressure for industrial unionism. When the AFL expelled the dissidents, the Congress of Industrial Organization (CIO) was born. Committed to recruiting on an industry-wide basis, the CIO admitted everyone in a plant—male and female, black and white—allowing women for the first time to become a regular part of trade union turf.

These developments generalized categories that had earlier been specific to women. For although the National Recovery Administration as often as not discriminated against women workers with regard to wages, it enfolded all workers within its categories, generating rules and conditions for men that had earlier encompassed women only. When the NRA ended, its successors—the National Labor Relations Act in 1935 and the Fair Labor Standards Act in 1938—both affirmed the principle of state intervention on behalf of all workers. And if the CIO organized mainly in the mass-production industries where women were not heavily represented, it no longer left out the few who had found places in industry on office staffs or behind machines. And it offered at least verbal encouragement to organize office workers, teachers, and

CUT MILITARY SPENDING — 25¢ NICKEL APPLE — ...ALS OUR PAY
COALITION OF LABOR UNION WOMEN

GET THE DEPRESSION OFF OUR BACK — NICKEL APPLE
COALITION OF LABOR UNION WOMEN

25¢ — NICKEL APPLE — INFLATION STEALS OUR PAY
COALITION OF LABOR UNION WOMEN

1199

social workers. It therefore provided the possibility of large-scale organization among wage-earning women, a possibility realized at least temporarily during World War II.

Taken together, these changes permanently mitigated some of the circumstances that had placed women in a "special class." Depression conditions encouraged women to think in terms of taking advantage of these benefits, rather than having to assert individual needs. They also allowed a new element to creep into the discussion: occupational disease. With the welfare of the worker now foremost, trade unions and women's organizations began to urge the investigation and control of occupational disease at the workplace. No longer comfortable with "compensation" given after the fact and for accidents only, the labor movement became concerned with mechanisms for creating safer machinery and controlling disease. The Women's Bureau and other women's organizations, satisfied that they need no longer fight for minimum wages and shorter hours, turned to disease as well.

In 1935, forty-four of forty-eight states had some form of compensation for work-related accidents, but only twelve states compensated for industrial disease. The Metropolitan Life Insurance Co. identified 94 poisonous substances used in 900 different occupations in 1933—up from 52 in 1922. Among those that affected women particularly were radium, dyes, lead, mercury, carbon monoxide, benzol, and dust. Labor leaders agreed with the Women's Bureau that all of these substances should be banned from industrial use. Short of that, workers exposed to suspect chemicals should receive free health check-ups; diseases that resulted from them should be reported to local health authorities and the victims compensated.

The war years strengthened the tendency for women and trade unions to cooperate with each other, increasing the proportion of male and female unionized workers and placing the federal government firmly in the position of arbiter of work-related issues. The trade union movement emerged from the war stronger than it had ever been and committed to joining business and government as a guarantor of the new prosperity. As in earlier incarnations, both the AFL and the CIO perceived that the main task was to increase the economic well being and job security of their membership.

As long as women had remained a fairly small percentage of the workforce (not more than 25 percent before the war), and as long as they conceived of wage work as secondary to the family and home, they had challenged the trade unions only nominally. But in the postwar period family and demographic factors pushed women into the labor force in increasing numbers. Faced with the need to earn a living on a permanent basis, women began to complain of job discrimination, of exclusion from the benefits provided by employers, unions, and the state, and of the limits imposed on them by outmoded protective labor legislation. To bar a woman from working in a saloon in the new climate or to prevent her in an age of automation from lifting heavy objects that required pushing a button on a machine seemed ludicrous. When the 1964 Civil Rights Act forbade job discrimination on the basis of sex (as well as race, religion, and color), the floodgates burst open and women found themselves able to compete directly with men for jobs.

Trade union leaders, still attached to the notion of women's primary domestic role and commitment to job security for their (mostly male) members, resisted women's requests for access. But now wage-earning women were united. In the early phases of a self-conscious feminist movement, they rejected old social prescriptions and insisted on the new reality. Like the women's movement activists of the early twentieth century, they argued from a belief that women were more like men than unlike them. Neither gender nor marital status could limit their natural rights.

External pressures have helped women to make their point. A decline in production industries and an expansion in the white collar and service sectors where women are employed have convinced unions that if they are to survive they must organize this new constituency. Slowly in the 1970s and 1980s some trade unions have begun to acknowledge that demographic and economic factors make it unlikely that women's domestic roles will ever again be primary. These developments have led them to join in removing women from the category of a special class. But accommodation to women's presence in the workforce requires a commitment to consider appropriate protection for biological differences without discrimination. And it is in this direction that both the labor movement and the women's movement need to go. A woman's movement in need of allies, and a trade union movement eager to protect its gains, may yet lead each to incorporate the basic goals of the other.

Notes

1. W. T. Provert testifying before the New York State Factory Investigating Commission, in Minutes of Public Hearings, Second Report to the Legislature, vol. 3 (1913), p. 934.
2. Edward Parker in ibid., vol. 4 (1913), p. 1811.
3. Ibid., p. 1810.
4. Quoted in W. Eliot Brownlee and Mary M. Brownlee, *Women in the American Economy* (New Haven: Yale University Press, 1976), p. 168.
5. For more detailed discussion see Alice Kessler-Harris, *Out to Work: A*

History of Wage Earning Women in the United States (New York: Oxford, 1982), chapter 4. For background on divisions among women, see Aileen Kraditor, The Ideas of the Woman Suffrage Movement: 1890-1920 (New York: Norton, 1981), chapter 3.

6. Elizabeth Faulkner Baker, Protective Labor Legislation with Special Reference to Women in the State of New York, vol. 116 of Columbia University Studies in History, Economics, and Public Law (1925; rept. ed., New York: AMS Press, 1976), p. 61.

7. Ibid., p. 62.

8. Louis D. Brandeis and Josephine Goldmark, Brief for the State of Oregon (New York: National Consumers' League, 1908), p. 10.

9. "Women's Work, Rights, and Progress," American Federationist 20 (August 1913): 626.

10. "Coming into Her Own," American Federationist 22 (July 1915): 519.

11. "Testimony Before House Committee," American Federationist 20 (December 1913): 998.

12. American Federation of Labor, Proceedings of the 44th Annual Convention, El Paso, Texas (1924), p. 73.

13. Nancy Schrom Dye, As Equals and as Sisters: Feminism, Unionism, and the Women's Trade Union League of New York (Columbia, MO: University of Missouri Press, 1980), p. 140.

14. Alice Hamilton, "Protection for Working Women," International Suffrage News (May 1924): 119.

15. "Federal Supreme Court Upholds State Law, Forbidding Late Night Work for Women," New York Times, 11 March 1924, p. 11.

16. Provert testimony, pp. 934-35.

17. American Federation of Labor, Proceedings of the 34th Annual Convention, Philadelphia, Pennsylvania (1914), p. 78. See also the proceedings of the 1915 convention in San Francisco, p. 96.

18. U.S. Department of Labor, Women's Bureau, The Employment of Women in Hazardous Industries, Bulletin No. 6 (Washington, D.C.: U.S. Government Printing Office, 1921), p. 8.

19. Felix Frankfurter to Ethel Smith, 8 September 1921, in file: Legislation, Equal Rights, Box 22, National Women's Trade Union League Collection, Library of Congress.

20. Mary Anderson, "Should There Be Labor Laws for Women? Yes," Good Housekeeping (September 1925): 53.

21. Hamilton, "Protection for Working Women," p. 119.

22. Ibid.

23. See Ruth Milkman, "Women's Work and Economic Crisis: Some Lessons of the Great Depression," Review of Radical Political Economics 8 (Spring 1976): 73-97; and Alice Kessler-Harris, Out to Work, chapter 9.

Part 2

Damned If You Do, Damned If You Don't: Work and Reproduction

Introduction

On the one hand, for the sake of sacred motherhood and the "protection of the unborn," fertile women are barred from certain jobs. On the other hand, they are pressured to consider surgical sterilization. In another setting, medical coverage excludes abortion. And, finally, benefits and leaves for maternity are nonexistent or limited. What's a working woman supposed to do?

These corporate directives and restrictions not only contradict one another; each is illogical on its own, and some are illegal. As Judy Scott explains in chapter 9, the exclusion of fertile women from the workplace on grounds of "fetotoxic exposure" violates the fundamental premise outlined by the OSHA General Duty Clause, the right to a safe and healthful workplace. After these exclusionary policies became public in 1978, Eula Bingham, then director of OSHA, specifically explained that reproductive health was included under general health. This understanding of the General Duty Clause was made concrete in the subsequent lead standard, which considered the effects of lead on male and female reproductive function in deciding upon permissible exposure levels on the job.

Moreover, policies that focus solely on women flagrantly ignore the known facts of reproductive physiology. Men do indeed play a role in reproduction. As Maureen Hatch explains in chapter 8, male endocrine function and sperm production can be compromised by toxic exposures. The sparse data available on this topic do not indicate male invulnerability; on the contrary, the data simply reflect the presuppositions of the questions asked—in this case, only harm to the fetus during pregnancy is a parameter of concern while other routes to reproductive malfunction are seldom considered. When they are, however, the inescapable conclusion is that the only way to safeguard worker reproductive health and the well-being of the next generation is to lower allowable levels of hazardous substances for *everyone* in the work environment.

But are the corporations truly concerned about motherhood? They fight to deny pregnant workers protection at work and job-related benefits like medical insurance, unemployment, or disability pay (see Wendy Chavkin, chapter 10). They certainly do not appear to be pro-*parenthood*, as men are usually allowed only one day paid leave at childbirth—compared to three days leave for a funeral or wedding. Rather than allow paternity leaves, in fact, many companies have chosen to eliminate maternity leaves.

Is the corporate world anti-reproduction altogether? Those companies that suggest sterilization for female workers, hire only those women who present proof of surgical sterilization or hysterectomy, and respond to the discovery that a pesticide causes male infertility by suggesting that workers wanting vasectomies volunteer to work with it may give that impression.[1] Yet some also want to restrict medical coverage so that it excludes abortion (see Judy Scott, chapter 9).

Faced with these glaring inconsistencies and lapses in logic, we have to look deeper for an underlying theme. The one that emerges is that there is a desire to *control* reproduction, but to deny that control to women—in whose bodies the major part of the drama takes place. The corporate push to maximize profits intersects neatly with ideological sexism, as it is to the companies' economic advantage to maintain women in an inferior position *and* to enhance control over workers.

The authors of these chapters maintain that women must confront this struggle over reproductive control head on. We must fight for full participation in public life, as well as for recognition and respect for our physical role in reproduction. We have to assert that physical needs related to reproduction are legitimate and should be met, not apologized for. Western philosophic tradition has considered "male" as the norm, thus defining women as "non-male" or "other," and citing this difference to justify their subordinate position. Unless women reject this framework and argue for a reformulation that recognizes two reproductive norms— female and male—we will continue to be on the defensive. We end up in the false position of trying to prove ourselves as "men plus" (or minus). True equality requires acknowledgment of these different physical experiences. It further requires distinguishing between the ongoing care of children and the physical work of pregnancy and childbirth. Child *care* responsibilities can be shared by both parents.

The labor movement has become embroiled in certain aspects of this struggle. Many unions have taken a firm stand against exclusionary policies based on fertility, including the Oil, Chemical, and Atomic Workers, the International Chemical Workers, the United Auto Workers, the Steelworkers, and the Rubberworkers (see Judy Scott's chapter). They argue that such policies violate OSHA, have left men exposed to hazardous substances, and violate Title VII of the Civil Rights Act by discriminating against women workers. Such policies interfere with unions' hard-won guarantees about seniority, advancement, and equal employment opportunities.[2]

In 1979 feminist groups, labor unions, civil libertarians, public interest groups, and occupational safety and health groups formed the Coalition for the Reproductive Rights of Workers (CRROW). Together, they developed legal, educational, and technical resources to debunk the corporate misfacts, lobbied and pressured OSHA and the EEOC to defend their mandates, and mobilized public concern and outrage at the notion that workers should be forced to forego healthy parenthood. Perhaps most important, feminist and union groups acknowledged that they need one another's support for some common goals.

The effectiveness of cooperation between organized labor and feminist groups had been demonstrated when together they pressured for the passage of the Pregnancy Discrimination Act, which forbids discrimination against pregnant workers. Unfortunately, this mutual support has not been smoothly maintained around the issue of abortion. Many unions, afraid of both general backlash and of prejudice from their male membership, have shied away from aggressively defending abortion rights. For example, in the course of CRROW's active years, there were at times fierce debates over whom to include in the coalition. The unions, wanting to muster all possible support against exclusionary policies based on fertility, could not understand why the feminists were refusing to work with anti-abortion groups. The unions conceived of the struggle on their own terms (i.e., interference with union prerogatives, seniority, and so on) and not as part of the battle for reproductive rights.

Similarly, when the American Federation of Government Employees refused to accept a congressional directive that their medical insurance exclude abortion, they did so on the grounds that this constituted interference with the negotiated contract, and not because of any explicit pro-abortion stance. On the other hand, feminists need to expand their horizons to understand that the unions' priorities are to win economic benefits for their members and to strengthen their organizations. Feminists make a mistake if they appeal to unions solely on ideological grounds, without taking the trouble to learn about labor's perspective. Rather, they need to make clear to unions that fighting for reproductive rights will further labor's long-range goals.

As long as women shoulder the major responsibility for children, they will remain constrained in their ability to participate fully as workers, much less have time for union activities. The *right* to abortion (no matter what choice an individual may make) is a prerequisite if women as a group are to gain control over their own lives. If unions want more active women members, they must help ensure that the conditions for their participation are realized.

Moreover, it is the New Right that made abortion the focus of its overall attack on women's rights, and is also committed to attacking organized labor and workers' rights. The New Right is using abortion as the redbaiting symbol of the 1980s. Many organizations and politicians are permitting themselves to be manipulated by this scare tactic and rushing to disavow support for abortion. Yet abortion is *legal,* and every poll confirms that the majority of Americans support it. Out of the desire to avoid controversy, those liberal sectors that seek to appease the Right on the abortion issue in the end divide and weaken the very forces that could together successfully challenge the conservative backlash. For example, unions may forfeit the support of women and the women's movement if they sidestep this critical issue. If progressive forces sacrifice abortion today, the door is opened for the loss of workers' rights and the rest of the Right's agenda tomorrow.

It is not surprising that feminists and labor leaders have different priorities. In the light of a century and a half of struggle between the two, new developments such as CCROW and the coalition for the PDA are very promising. They indicate that the two groups are being pushed to forge mutually acceptable goals, and that together they have the ability to move and involve working men as well as women.

Notes

1. David Burnham, "Pesticide Work Suggested for Those Seeking Sterility," *New York Times,* 27 September 1977. He cites R. K. Phillips of the National Peach Council: "If possible sterility is the main problem, couldn't workers who were old enough that they no longer wanted to have children accept such positions voluntarily? Or could workers be advised of the situation, and some might volunteer for such work posts as an alternative to planned surgery for a vasectomy or tubal ligation, or as a means of getting around religious bans on birth control when

they want no more children. . . . We do believe in safety in the
workplace, but there can be good as well as bad sides to a situation."
2. For more detailed discussion of these issues and the unions' attempts
to combat such policies see Rosalind Petchesky, "Workers, Reproductive Hazards, and the Politics of Protection," Carolyn Bell, "Implementing Safety and Health Regulations for Women in the Workplace,"
Michael Wright, "Reproductive Hazards and 'Protective' Discrimination," and Wendy Chavkin, "Occupational Hazards to Reproduction:
A Review Essay and Annotated Bibliography," *Feminist Studies* 5, no.
2 (Summer 1979).

For legal approaches to these same issues see Linda Howard,
"Hazardous Substances in the Workplace: Implications for the Employment Rights of Women," *University of Pennsylvania Law Review*
129, no. 4 (April 1981), and Wendy Williams, "Firing the Women to
Protect the Fetus: The Reconciliation of Fetal Protection with Employment Opportunity Goals under Title VII," *The Georgetown Law Journal* 69 (1981).

For some practical suggestions for both legal and collective bargaining approaches see Andrea Hricko, with Melanie Brunt, *Working for
Your Life: A Women's Guide to Job Health Hazards* (Berkeley, CA:
Labor Occupational Health Program and Public Citizen Health Research Group, 1976) and Women's Labor Project, *Bargaining for Equality* (San Francisco: WLP, 1980).

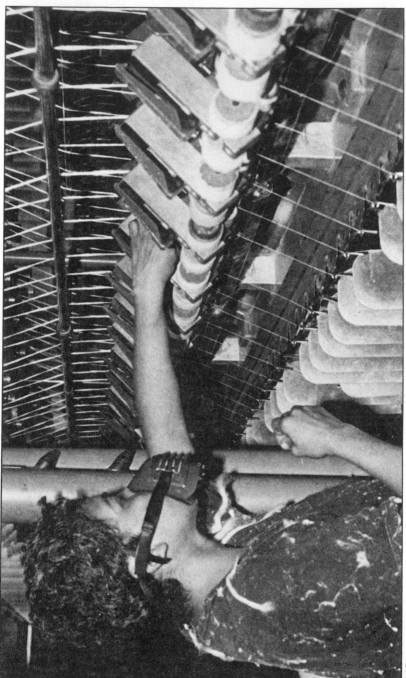

8
Mother, Father, Worker:
Men and Women and the
Reproductive Risks of Work
Maureen Hatch

This chapter will summarize what is currently known about the relation of hazardous occupational and environmental exposures to human reproduction. Bear in mind, however, that what we know is a function partly of the questions we ask, and partly of limitations in the methods available for exploring them.

Environmental effects on reproduction have usually been assessed by asking whether exposure to the mother during pregnancy increases the risk of birth defects in her offspring. Note the assumptions about the relevant route ("exposure to the mother"), timing ("during pregnancy"), and outcome ("birth defects"). But what about the father? Does paternal exposure also have adverse consequences? Can exposure that occurs *prior* to conception, rather than during gestation, also affect pregnancy outcome? And if exposure does not lead to the birth of a child with malformations, can we be sure that the substance in question is free of consequences, or might it lead to low birthweight, a miscarriage, or failure to conceive at all? A proper understanding of the relation between environmental exposure and reproductive health requires that we broaden the focus of research so as to examine a *range* of adverse reproductive outcomes and consider *both* parents as potential routes through which an exposure may exert its effects.

In this review I will therefore be particularly concerned with specifying which parent was studied, the timing of the exposure, and the endpoints that were evaluated. The intention is to help us see what biological models have been tested. Unfortunately, the literature is replete with conflicting findings and uninterpretable results, and there are large gaps in the available information. In part this is due to the nature of the research problem, in part to constraints in the research method, in part to the political context.

The Complexity of Evaluating
Reproductive Hazards

Once we agree that our concern is with a spectrum of reproductive problems, we need to consider the following outcomes in addition to birth defects: damage to the germ cells or sexual organs, reductions in libido or potency, sterility, and fetal loss; among liveborns, prematurity, functional deficit, and childhood cancer. This list is not exhaustive, but it should suffice to indicate the scope and types of reproductive effects that might follow exposure, and the range of processes involved.

Hazards to reproduction can involve any one of several causal pathways and consequences. The action may be on the mother, father, or fetus, so there are several targets to consider. There is seldom sufficient biological theory or prior experience to guide the investigator in selecting which of many potential lines of inquiry to pursue.

Occupational and environmental exposures are also problematic because a given exposure is rare in the general population as compared with agents like cigarettes or alcohol, and because it is difficult to test research hypotheses adequately when the sample of exposed individuals is small—small samples mean that there is little chance of detecting real associations (analyses using small samples have what statisticians call "low statistical power"). Moreover, occupational and environmental exposures are often poorly defined and measured, so that hazards are unlikely to be identified unless their effects are sizable or striking. If they entail a modest increase in a common condition, they are apt to elude us. For example, we know that prenatal exposure to the drug thalidomide causes limb deformities because this is a rare condition, but a moderate increase in an outcome as common as miscarriage or infertility may well be undetectable in the present state of knowledge.[1]

Our methods and the conditions of study are further impediments to an understanding of the environmental effects on reproduction. Investigations carried out among free-living populations are fraught with all the difficulties of uncontrolled research. Unlike laboratory scientists, epidemiologists must take things as they find them, and inevitable differences between exposed and unexposed individuals make it possible to propose alternative explanations for any observed effect. The validity of the research results will depend heavily on how well the investigator can identify and control these extraneous sources of variation.

As if these limitations were not enough, the social and legal

Table 1
Indices of Reproductive Dysfunction

1. *Fecundity*
Sexual dysfunction: libido, potency
Abnormal gonads, ducts, and external genitalia
Sperm abnormalities: number, mobility, shape
Menstrual irregularity: amenorrhea, anovulatory cycles
Delayed conception
Reduced age of menopause

2. *Fertility*
Infertility of male or female origin
Illness during pregnancy or parturition: toxemia, hemorrhage
Miscarriage (fetal loss up to 28 weeks gestation)
Stillbirth (fetal loss at or after 28 weeks gestation)
Fetal death during labor

3. *Sequelae in offspring*
Change in gestational age at delivery: prematurity, postmaturity
Reduced birthweight
Altered sex ratio
Multiple births
Birth defects: major, minor, mutations
Death in the first week
Infant death
Childhood morbidity
Childhood malignancies

Source: Adapted from "Report of Panel II: Guidelines for Reproductive Studies in Exposed Human Populations," in *Guidelines for Studies of Human Populations Exposed to Mutagenic and Reproductive Hazards*, ed. A. D. Bloom (New York: March of Dimes Birth Defects Foundation, 1982), pp. 37–110.

issues that surround environmental research create a highly charged atmosphere that is not conducive either to good science or to the impartial reception of research results.

With this as preface we can proceed to examine the evidence concerning the effects of ambient and workplace exposures on reproductive health. The next section will briefly discuss the various events that comprise reproductive function, and how these outcomes may interrelate. The following section will review some aspects of reproductive biology, distinguishing the male and female reproductive cycles in terms of those factors that could affect vulnerability to exposure. The final section will summarize our current knowledge of reproductive hazards.

The Range of Reproductive Effects

Table 1 sets out the numerous endpoints that are relevant to reproductive health, grouping them into three broad categories in order to provide a framework for discussing the evidence. The first category is labeled fecundity and refers to effects on reproductive potential: altered sexual capacity or behavior, changes in the hormonal functions of the testes or ovaries, anatomic anomalies in the reproductive tract, and damage to the sperm or egg. Such perturbations clearly arise prior to conception and may have the unrecognized effect of delaying it.

The second broad category relates to fertility. Here I include both the inability to conceive and the failure to produce live offspring when pregnancy does occur—miscarriage as well as sterility. The third category comprises all sequelae in liveborns, including those that only become evident later in life. DES (diethylstilbestrol, a drug prescribed for threatened miscarriage) is an example of an agent that exerted effects prenatally that were not recognized until the exposed offspring reached maturity.[2]

Factors Affecting Female Fecundity

The male and female differ considerably, perhaps even crucially, in the developmental processes involved in the production of germ cells or gametes. In the female, the entire store of germ cells is laid down in utero. They proliferate during gestation and by the time of birth have already partially completed the phase of the cell cycle in which the chromosome complement is halved, to prepare for fusion with the genetic material of the sperm. The oocytes, as they are known at this stage, lie suspended in mid-division until the time of ovulation, between 14 and 40 years later, when under hormonal stimulation of the menstrual cycle they resume cell division and develop into eggs, or ova.

Particularly because the supply of female germ cells is not renewable, considerable attention has been paid to the long latent period during which the resting oocytes may be subject to environmental insult. The association of increased maternal age with increased risk of Down syndrome, a condition arising from a chromosome imbalance in one of the germ cells, has suggested that the longer the germ cells are exposed to environmental insult, the greater the chance of error.[3]

We see similar age-associated effects in female mice.[4] This raises the question of whether we should regard aging as a strictly intrinsic process of progressive deterioration or as one that is dependent, at least in part, on the cumulative experiences of the woman. In other words, does the association of age with impaired or reduced fecundity simply reflect the increased period at risk of hazardous exposure?

Menopause is a case in point in that it occurs when the ovaries are depleted of oocytes. Since ovulation itself can account for at most a thousand among the million germ cells present at birth, clearly other factors are important in determining oocyte loss. But is it the internal process of cellular decay that is primarily responsible, or does exposure to environmental agents hasten the process by destroying eggs?

There are only two pieces of research that bear on this question. One is the association between cigarette smoking and the early onset of menopause,[5] which has been explained by either of two mechanisms: (1) is that cigarette smoking induces hormonal changes, or (2) that it leads to oocyte destruction, an effect observed in rodents exposed to a component of cigarette smoke.[6] The evidence is still too limited to permit any firm conclusions, but the association suggests that the exposure to smoke accelerates the aging process.

The other area of research concerns the effects of radiation, and relates more directly to the issue of whether exposure prior to conception influences pregnancy outcome; its results are conflicting. Studies in England and Canada support the view that exposure to radiation prior to conception is more common among mothers of children with Down syndrome. Other studies, however, including one of considerable scope at Johns Hopkins, suggest that this is not the case.[7] If a relationship does in fact exist, then the risk of bearing a child with Down syndrome as a result of maternal irradiation years before is very small compared to the risk conferred by age itself.

Thus while in theory any exposure may have an adverse effect on a woman's fecundity, there is little research that adequately demonstrates that exposure to hazardous agents in the environment before conception has an effect on a woman's offspring, mediated through the germ cells.

Factors Affecting Male Fecundity

One key difference between men and women is that we cannot readily observe the oocytes directly, but we can observe the sperm. In the male, the quality of the semen becomes an endpoint for evaluating the effects of exposure on reproductive function. The timing and location of germ cell production in males are quite distinct from in the female. At birth the stem cells transform into spermatogonia and are dormant until puberty. When sperm production does begin, it is not an all-or-nothing happening, as in the female, but is continuous and cyclical. A portion of the dividing spermatogonia continually buds off and undergoes the changes that produce mature sperm, a cycle which takes about eighty-four days. Thus at any one moment in the male testes there are sperm cells at every stage of development. The outcome of exposure is also different—in terms of the timing, nature, and duration of effect—depending on whether the exposure damaged the spermatogonia, the developing cells, or the mature sperm. The testicles, where the process of male germ cell production takes place, are less protected by the body than the ovaries and thus more accessible to exposure.

These differences between male and female reproductive biology indicate a potentially different susceptibility to environmental agents, and there is considerable evidence that characteristics of the sperm and/or semen are altered by such exposure. The finding, in 1977, that the pesticide DBCP (dibromochloropropane) substantially reduced sperm count in occupationally exposed men stimulated considerable interest in the relation of hazardous exposure to semen quality.[8] Since then, lead, irradiation, anti-neoplastic drugs, toluene diamine, and, with less certainty, cigarettes, marijuana, alcohol, DES, carbon disulfide, nonionizing radiation, and the pesticides kepone and carbaryl have all been shown to affect sperm concentration, sperm shape, or sperm mobility.[9]

The generalization that can be made from studies of laboratory animals and men is that exposure effects appear to be stronger at later stages of sperm development. Especially in humans, it may be that the spermatogonia—the stem cells that give rise to all future generations of sperm—are fairly invulnerable. This inference is based on evidence that the effects on the sperm are associated with current and recent exposure, but not exposure in the past (we see this with DBCP, for instance), and that once exposure is removed, recovery occurs—that is, healthy sperm regenerate.[10] Had the spermatogonia been affected, the damage would be expected to persist.

If this indication of a resistant spermatogonial cell population is borne out it should be reassuring, since in mice anomalies in offspring and transmission of germ cell defects seem to occur only when spermatogonia are affected.[11] In humans there is no evidence thus far that sperm alteration produces heritable damage. However, in man as well as in the mouse, effects on semen quality do appear to be associated with infertility and prenatal loss.

Effects of Paternal Exposure on Fertility

The association of semen quality with fertility is far from straightforward: while a complete absence of sperm produces sterility, conception is possible with quite a low sperm count; impairment of sperm motility seems to be a better predictor of infertility.[12] As for abnormal sperm shape, there is some evidence to suggest that abnormal forms are more common in husbands of women who have spontaneous abortions, especially recurrent ones.[13] But we do not yet know to what extent these abnormal forms indicate that the sperm have abnormal genetic or chromosome constitution—although it is difficult to imagine how else an association with fetal loss could arise.[14]

Systematic study is needed to clarify the relationship between alterations to sperm or semen and other reproductive outcomes. As it is, we are forced to piece together the evidence. Take DBCP as an example. The problem came to light as a result of frequent reports of infertility among men who worked with this pesticide. Subsequent semen analyses of men exposed in production plants or as field applicators identified the pesticide as a sperm suppressor;[15] however, the outcomes of pregnancies among exposed workers and their wives were not investigated. Conversely, a recent Israeli study evaluated the reproductive histories of DBCP users but did not do semen analysis. The study reports an excess of fetal loss following exposure to the fathers, but we do not know whether the men whose wives miscarried were the same ones who had abnormal semen analyses.[16] Such linked studies are needed if we are to fathom the mechanism at work. Similarly, paternal exposure to vinyl chloride and, more convincingly, to dental anesthetics has also been associated with an increased rate of spontaneous abortion in unexposed wives, but again the mechanism is unclear—although the effect must be directly on the male since it is unlikely with gases such as these that the husband has carried his exposure home on his skin or clothes to contaminate his wife.[17] Another case in point: a Bulgarian study of workers at a lead battery plant found a dose-response relationship between lead levels in the blood and abnormal sperm shape.[18] A sexual history was also taken from the men and the data suggested that exposure to lead impaired sexual function—but again the results of the semen analyses were not linked to the sexual histories, so that we do not know if the reported sexual dysfunction is correlated with damage to the sperm. On the other hand, a study at a lead-arsenic smelter in Sweden found that when both father and mother worked at the smelter, the risk of spontaneous abortion was increased over and above the excess associated with the woman's occupational exposure.[19] This implies that exposure to the father played a role in the spontaneous abortion rate.

Nevertheless, in all these cases we cannot be sure what the process is: Does the increased fetal loss arise because of fertilization with lead-damaged sperm, or is it that lead carried in the male ejaculate has entered the fetal milieu? Certainly lead has been found in seminal fluid, even in men without occupational exposure.[20] Distinguishing the underlying mechanism is not just a matter of academic interest, because if the effect is via the sperm, then our concern is with exposure prior to conception or at fertilization, whereas if the substance is transmitted during coitus, then paternal exposure throughout pregnancy is a potential threat. Thus it is important, for purposes of medical counsel and government regulation as well as for scientific understanding, to identify the route and mode of action that produce the observed effects.

Paternal Exposure and Sequelae in Offspring

When we turn to the last category of outcomes, sequelae in liveborns, the data on paternal exposure become even more sparse, in part because so little work has been done on this question. An initial finding that related radar and microwave exposure of fathers to Down syndrome in their children was reversed in a later study.[21] While we now know that in 20 to 30 percent of Down's cases the chromosomal error comes from the father, no risk factor has yet been clearly identified, although advanced paternal age does appear to be a contributing factor.[22]

A relationship between cancer in offspring and male workplace exposure has also been proposed. So far the evidence linking childhood cancer to paternal exposure to hydrocarbons is conflicting. There is one report relating childhood malignancy to paternal employment in the aircraft industry, however.[23] A careful case-control study found an excess of fathers in lead-related jobs (e.g., mechanics, solderers, metallurgists) among parents of children with Wilm's tumor, but again the association requires confirmation.[24]

Exploring Male Pathways

The endpoints that relate to paternal exposure—infertility, fetal loss, cancer, or chromosome anomalies in offspring—are all compatible with processes that occur around the time of conception—that is, with mutations or chromosome imbalance in the germ cell. Does this mean that exposure to the father *after* fertilization is without hazard, or do we simply not have the information to answer this question?

In fact, when we consider birth defects that are apt to result from action during the period of organ development in the growing fetus, the data on paternal exposure consist largely of anecdotal evidence or are the result of exploratory studies. For example, there are reports of neural tube defects in the offspring of men exposed to the herbicide Agent Orange in Vietnam, and also data on the relationship between cleft palate and painter-printer fathers from the Center for Disease Control's Birth Defects Monitoring Program.[25] But the lack of systematic research into the possibility that teratogenic effects, as they are known, can occur through the father reflects the common assumption that the mother is the sole route to the fetus once conception has occurred. This may indeed be the case, but it needs to be proved, not assumed. One way to put the theory to the test is to explore whether coitus during pregnancy is a mechanism whereby paternal exposure has postconceptional effects. Transmission of substances in the seminal fluid can and does occur through intercourse—an example is the hepatitis-B virus.[26] Infectious agents can attach themselves to motile sperm, which facilitates their passage through the mucous plug at the mouth of the cervix.[27] Moreover, experiments in animals have demonstrated an association between toxins in the ejaculate and adverse effects on offspring from matings with unexposed females.[28] The cervical plug may prove to be no more impervious than the placental barrier.

Reproductive Effects of
Maternal Occupational Exposure

The literature on maternal exposure is far more extensive than that on male exposure. It is therefore possible to be less speculative in this area and focus on reliable research findings. A number of studies, both here and abroad, have compared women who work during pregnancy with "nonworkers" (defined as housewives, students, women unemployed during pregnancy) on a range of reproductive indicators.[29] Nonworkers usually appear to be at lower risk. However, when workers are broken down into categories based on occupation, the risk associated with employment appears to be confined to particular jobs and their related exposure or characteristics; rates of outcome in some occupations are lower than in nonworkers.

A series of papers from Finland explores the effects of various maternal occupations on rates of spontaneous abortion and congenital defects. Women who work with industrial chemicals, particularly plastics like styrene, and with metals, in the electronics sector, have an increased risk of miscarriage, with similar trends observed among laundry and pharmaceutical workers.[30] Industrial and construction workers carry a greater risk of bearing children with central nervous system malformations.[31] A recent paper from Denmark found higher rates of spontaneous abortion among factory workers (presumed to be exposed to chemicals) than in supermarket workers (presumed to be unexposed).[32]

In Sweden, women in medical laboratories are reported to risk spontaneous abortion and perhaps birth defects if they work during pregnancy; exposure to solvents is presumed to be the hazard.[33] One recent Swedish study found an increase in congenital malformations and perinatal mortality among workers in chemical laboratories, but not in other laboratory workers. But another Swedish study, again in the pharmaceutical industry, found no difference in the rates of miscarriage between chemically exposed and unexposed lab workers, so that the evidence is not firm.[34] Nevertheless the suggestion persists that laboratory work during pregnancy may pose a threat to the fetus.

Medical occupations in general have come under scrutiny because of the risk of exposure to various chemical, physical, and infectious agents. One Swedish study found raised rates of perinatal mortality and malformations among women working in the medical field.[35] A recent New York City study, on the other hand, examined the relationship of miscarriage to a range of occupations and found no increased risk in female hospital workers as a group, or to those in specific medical occupations (e.g., nursing).[36] In Sweden again, delivery outcome was studied among physiotherapists to evaluate exposure to microwaves, shortwaves, and ultrasound during pregnancy. A marginally higher frequency of shortwave, and perhaps ultrasound, use was reported among women with dead or malformed infants, but the effect could also be explained by differences in recall; microwave exposure proved too uncommon to assess.[37]

Among other medical exposures, anesthetic gases appear to be associated with increased rates of spontaneous abortion in dental technicians, but the evidence for a similar effect among hospital nurses and anesthesiologists is less persuasive, with studies that do report positive findings marred by unequal response rates between the exposed and unexposed, or by unsuitable comparison groups.[38] Two recent studies of female hospital personnel that do seem more reliable—one with exposure data gathered prior to pregnancy outcome and the other utilizing records of exposure rather than self-reports—are both negative.[39] The dose and type of anesthetic agent are different in hospitals and dental settings, however, and this may explain the different results.

In relation to lead—a documented fetal hazard at the high doses to which populations were historically exposed—there is a surprising lack of data concerning its reproductive effects at current dose levels.[40] As regards maternal exposure, we have only a series of reports from a lead-arsenic smelter in Sweden, where spontaneous abortion, reduced birthweight, and malformations were noted in women exposed either as workers or as community residents.[41]

Epidemiologists in France have proposed an association between physical work stress during pregnancy and preterm delivery.[42] The specific components of occupational fatigue that were cited included the number of hours worked, the duration of employment during pregnancy, and the amount of physical effort required. A recent U.S. study provides some support for this hypothesis: active-duty air force women who were obliged to work until the day of delivery were found to experience a sixfold increase in preterm delivery compared with women at the same air force obstetric clinic who had the option of not working or of curtailing their work activities.[43] Similarly, the association between maternal employment in cleaning occupations and spontaneous abortion found in a New York City study may reflect the physical strains of the job, although it may also implicate exposure to household chemicals.[44]

When we move outside the workplace and into the broader environment there are several well-documented studies of fetal hazards. Skin-staining has been observed in the offspring of women exposed in pregnancy to PCB's through contaminated rice oil in Japan.[45] Again in Japan, mercury effluents from industries on Minamata Bay concentrated in the food chain and caused a cerebral-palsy-like syndrome in children born to women who had ingested contaminated fish.[46] In Turkey, the accidental contamination of grain stocks with hexachlorobenzene produced skin lesions in offspring exposed in utero, and almost all of them died within a year of birth.[47] At Love Canal in New York State, where toxic chemicals leached from a landfill, birthweight was lowered and the rate of miscarriage was raised.[48] From Seveso, Italy, following an industrial explosion that released dioxin into the environment, have come inconsistent reports of an increase in miscarriage and certain malformations in offspring.[49] Residents of areas sprayed with herbicides containing dioxin have also reported an increase in fetal loss.[50] The evidence does not allow us to determine definitively the extent to which these effects are real—but even if they were, in none of these instances can we sort out whether they reflect exposure to the mother, father, or both.

Conclusions

The relationship between occupational and environmental exposure and reproductive health is indeed complex and the data unclear, but we can nevertheless venture some answers to the questions set out at the beginning of this chapter.

(1) Does paternal exposure carry reproductive risk? Clearly yes. The sperm and semen are frequently altered by exposure to environmental agents, and a father's exposure seems to be related to an increase in spontaneous abortion. However, we still need to understand the specific links between changes in sperm characteristics, problems in conceiving, and unfavorable pregnancy outcome.

(2) Is preconceptional exposure also of concern? It probably is, but in the female at least the time of fertilization and after seems more susceptible to the effects of exposure than does the period prior to conception.

(3) Are there agents which do not cause malformations but that nonetheless carry risk for reproduction? There are, and this suggests that outcomes like sperm quality and spontaneous abortion may be sensitive indicators of potential hazard.

(4) Finally, based on the evidence to date from studies in humans, which occupational or environmental exposures can we say with certainty are reproductive toxins, and which appear suspicious enough to merit a priority in research? I would list as known toxins irradiation, DBCP, lead, PCBs, organic mercury, and hexachlorobenzene. I would class dental anesthetics and solvents/laboratory reagents as suspicious, along with the more general issue of physical work stress in late pregnancy.

This brings us to the political arena. At what point do we demand action? Do we wait for the accumulation of irrefutable evidence that a given substance causes a certain problem? Or do we decide that "suggestive" data are enough to warrant limiting exposure? Science can provide us with data, but the interpretations and decisions that follow are for all of us to make.

Notes

1. W. G. McBride, "Thalidomide and Congenital Anomalies," *Lancet* 2 (1961): 1358; W. Lenz and K. Knapp, "Foetal Malformations Due to Thalidomide," *German Medical Monthly* 7 (1962): 253-58.
2. A. L. Herbst, H. Ulfelder, and D. C. Poskanzer, "Adenocarcinoma of the Vagina: Association of Maternal Stilbestrol Therapy with Tumor Appearance in Young Women," *New England Journal of Medicine* 284 (1971): 878-81; A. B. Barnes, T. Colton, J. Gundersen, et al., "Fertility and Outcome of Pregnancy in Women Exposed in Utero to Diethylstilbestrol," *New England Journal of Medicine* 302 (1980): 609-13.
3. T. Hassold, P. Jacobs, J. Kline, Z. Stein, and D. Warburton, "Effect of Maternal Age on Autosomal Trisomies," *Annals of Human Genetics* 44 (1980): 29-35.
4. I. Maudlin and L. R. Fraser, "Maternal Age and the Incidence of Aneuploidy in First-Cleavage Mouse Embryos," *Journal of Reproduction and Fertility* 54 (1978): 423-26.
5. H. Jick, J. Porter, and A. S. Morrison, "Relation Between Smoking and Age at Natural Menopause," *Lancet* 1 (1976): 1354-55; D. W. Kaufman, D. Slone, L. Rosenberg, et al., "Cigarette Smoking and Age at Natural Menopause," *American Journal of Public Health* 70 (1980): 420-22.
6. D. R. Mattison and S. S. Thorgeirsson, "Smoking and Industrial Pollution, and Their Effects on Menopause and Ovarian Cancer," *Lancet* 1 (1978): 187-88.
7. For London, see E. Alberman, P. E. Polani, J. A. F. Roberts, et al., "Parental Exposure to X-Irradiation and Down's Syndrome," *Annals of Human Genetics* 36 (1972): 195-204; for Canada, see I. A. Uchida and E. J. Curtis, "A Possible Association Between Maternal Radiation and Mongolism," *Lancet* 2 (1961): 848-50. The Johns Hopkins study is B. H. Cohen, A. M. Lilienfeld, S. Kramer, and L. C. Hyman, "Parental Factors in Down's Syndrome—Results of the Second Baltimore Case-Control Study," in *Population Cytogenetics: Studies in Humans,* ed. E. B. Hook and I. H. Porter (New York: Academic Press, 1977), pp. 301-52.

174 / Maureen Hatch

8. D. Whorton, R. M. Krauss, S. Marshall, and T. H. Milby, "Infertility in Male Pesticide Workers," Lancet 2 (1977): 1259-61.
9. On lead, see I. Lancranjan, H. I. Popescu, O. Gavenescu, et al., "Reproductive Ability of Workmen Occupationally Exposed to Lead," Archives of Environmental Health 30 (1975): 396-401; on irradiation, see M. J. Rowley, D. R. Leach, G. A. Warner, and C. G. Heller, "Effect of Graded Doses of Ionizing Radiation on the Human Testis," Radiation Research 59 (1974): 665-78; on anti-neoplastic drugs, see S. M. Seiber and R. H. Adamson, "Toxicity of Antineoplastic Agents in Man: Chromosomal Aberrations, Antifertility Effects, Congenital Malformations and Carcinogenic Potential," Advances in Cancer Research 22 (1975): 57-93; on toluene diamine, see S. H. Ahrenholz and C. R. Meyer, Health Hazard Evaluation Determination, Report HE 79-113-728, Olin Chemical Company, Brandenburg, KY, U.S. DHHS, Centers for Disease Control, National Institute for Occupational Safety and Health (August 1980); on cigarettes, see H. J. Evens, J. Fletcher, M. Torrance, and T. B. Hargreave, "Sperm Abnormalities and Cigarette Smoking," Lancet 1 (1981): 627-29; on marijuana, see W. G. Hembree, G. G. Nahas, P. Zeidenberg, and H. F. S. Huang, "Changes in Human Spermatozoa Associated with High-Dose Marijuana Smoking," in Marijuana: Biological Effects, ed. G. G. Nahas and W. D. M. Paton (New York: Pergamon Press, 1979), pp. 429-39; on alcohol, see M. Semczuk, "Further Investigations on the Ultrastructure of Spermatozoa in Chronic Alcoholics," Z. Mikrosk. anat. Forsch. Leipzig 92 (1977): 494-508; on DES, see E. D. Whitehead and E. Leiter, "Genital Abnormalities and Abnormal Semen Analyses in Male Patients Exposed to Diethylstilbestrol in Utero," Journal of Urology 125 (1981): 47-49; on carbon disulfide, see I. Lancranjan, H. I. Popescu, and I. Klepsch, "Changes of the Gonadic Function in Chronic Carbon Disulfide Poisoning," Med. Lavaro 60 (1969): 566-71; on nonionizing radiation, see I. Lancranjan, M. Maicanescu, E. Rafaila, et al., "Gonadic Function in Workmen with Long-term Exposure to Microwaves," Health Physics 29 (1975): 381-83; on kepone, see W. J. Cohn, J. J. Boylan, R. V. Blanke, et al., "Treatment of Chlordecone (Kepone) Toxicity with Cholestryamine: Results of a Controlled Clinical Trial," New England Journal of Medicine 298 (1978): 243-48; on carbaryl, see A. J. Wyrobek, G. Watchmaker, L. Gordon, et al., "Sperm Shape Abnormalities in Carbaryl-Exposed Employees," Environmental Health Perspectives 40 (1981): 255-65.
10. R. I. Glass, R. N. Lyness, D. C. Mengele, et al., "Sperm Count Depression in Pesticide Applicators Exposed to Dibromochloropropane," American Journal of Epidemiology 109 (1979): 346-51; M. D. Whorton, and T. H. Milby, "Recovery of Testicular Function Among DBCP Workers," Journal of Occupational Medicine 22 (1980): 177-79.
11. For example, A. C. Chandley and R. M. Speed, "Testing for Nondisjunction in the Mouse," Environmental Health Perspectives 31 (1979): 123-29.

12. R. J. Sherins, D. Brightwell, and P. M. Sternthal, "Longitudinal Analysis of Semen of Fertile and Infertile Men," in *The Testis in Normal and Infertile Men*, ed. P. Troen and H. R. Nankin (New York: Raven Press, 1977), pp. 473-88; cited in A. J. Wyrobek, L. A. Gordon, J. G. Burkhart, et al., "An Evaluation of Human Sperm as Indicators of Chemically Induced Alterations of Spermatogenic Function," *Mutation Research* 115 (1983): 73-148.

13. M. Furuhjelm, B. Jonson, and C. G. Lagergren, "The Quality of Human Semen in Spontaneous Abortion," *International Journal of Fertility* 7 (1962): 17-21.

14. The relationship between abnormal sperm morphology and sperm chromosome constitution is a topic of current research. One approach involves the use of a technique for fusing human sperm with hamster eggs in order to examine the sperm chromosomes, which become visible only after fertilization. The strategy is to compare the proportion of abnormal karyotypes obtained from fertilizations with semen samples characterized by different proportions of abnormal sperm forms.

15. L. I. Lipschultz, C. E. Ross, D. Whorton, et al., "Dibromochloropropane and Its Effect on Testicular Function in Man," *Journal of Urology* 124 (1980): 464-68; R. I. Glass, R. N. Lyness, D. C. Mengele, et al., "Sperm Count Depression in Pesticide Applicators Exposed to Dibromochloropropane," *American Journal of Epidemiology* 109 (1979): 346-51; S. H. Sandifer, R. T. Wilkins, C. B. Loadholt, et al., "Spermatogenesis in Agricultural Workers Exposed to Dibromochloropropane (DBCP)," *Bulletin of Environmental Contamination and Toxicology* 23 (1979): 703-10.

16. M. Kharrazi, G. Potashnik, and J. R. Goldsmith, "Reproductive Effects of Dibromochloropropane," *Israel Journal of Medical Science* 16 (1980): 403-406.

17. P. F. Infante, J. K. Wagoner, A. J. McMichael, et al., "Genetic Risks of Vinyl Chloride," *Lancet* 1 (1976): 734-35; and E. N. Cohen, B. W. Brown, M. L. Wu, et al., "Occupational Disease in Dentistry and Chronic Exposure to Trace Anesthetic Gases," *Journal of the American Dental Association* 101 (1980): 21-31.

18. I. Lancranjan, H. I. Popescu, O. Gavenescu, et al., "Reproductive Ability of Workmen Occupationally Exposed to Lead," *Archives of Environmental Health* 30 (1975): 396-401.

19. S. Nordstrom, L. Beckman, and I. Nordenson, "Occupational and Environmental Risks in and Around a Smelter in Northern Sweden V. Spontaneous Abortion Among Female Employees and Decreased Birth Weight in Their Offspring," *Hereditas* 90 (1979): 291-96.

20. M. M. Plechaty, B. Noll, and F. W. Sunderman, "Lead Concentrations in Semen of Healthy Men Without Occupational Exposure to Lead," *Annals of Clinical Laboratory Sciences* 7 (1977): 515-18.

21. A. T. Sigler, A. M. Lilienfeld, B. H. Cohen, and J. E. Westlake, "Radiation Exposure in Parents of Children with Mongolism (Down's

Syndrome)," *Bulletin of Johns Hopkins Hospital* 117 (1965): 374-99; B. H. Cohen, A. M. Lilienfeld, S. Kramer, and L. C. Hyman, "Parental Factors in Down's Syndrome—Results of the Second Baltimore Case-Control Study," in *Population Cytogenetics: Studies in Humans*, ed. E. B. Hook and I. H. Porter (New York: Academic Press, 1977), pp. 301-52.

22. F. J. Mattei, M. G. Mattei, S. Ayme, and F. Giraud, "Origin of the Extra Chromosome in Trisomy 21," *Human Genetics* 46 (1979): 107-110; R. E. Magenis and J. Chamberlin, "Parental Origin of Nondisjunction," in *Trisomy 21—Down's Syndrome*, ed. F. F. de la Cruz and P. S. Gerald (Baltimore: University Park Press, 1981), pp. 77-93. On the contribution of advanced paternal age, see E. B. Hook, P. K. Cross, S. H. Lamson, et al., "Paternal Age and Down's Syndrome in British Columbia," *American Journal of Human Genetics* 33 (1981): 123-28; J. Stene, G. Fischer, and E. Stene, "Paternal Age Effect in Down's Syndrome," *Annals of Human Genetics* 40 (1977): 299-306; J. Stene, E. Stene, S. Stengel-Rutkowski, and J. D. Murken, "Paternal Age and Down's Syndrome," *Human Genetics* 59 (1981): 119-24.

23. The study that reports an association between paternal exposure to hydrocarbons and cancer in the offspring is J. Fabia and T. D. Thuy, "Occupation of Father at Time of Birth of Children Dying of Malignant Disease," *British Journal of Preventive and Social Medicine* 28 (1974): 98-100. Several later studies did not confirm the association, however; see T. Hakulinen, T. Salonen, and L. Teppo, "Cancer in the Offspring of Fathers in Hydrocarbon-Related Occupations," *British Journal of Preventive and Social Medicine* 30 (1976): 138-40; S. L. Kwa and L. J. Fine, "The Association Between Parental Occupation and Childhood Malignancy," *Journal of Occupational Medicine* 22 (1980): 792-94; M. Zack, S. Cannon, D. Lloyd, C. Heath, et al., "Cancer in Children of Parents Exposed to Hydrocarbon-Related Industries and Occupations," *American Journal of Epidemiology* 11 (1980): 329-35. For the report on the aircraft industry, see J. M. Peters, S. Preston-Martin, and M. C. Yu, "Brain Tumors in Children and Occupational Exposure of Parents," *Science* 213 (1981): 235-36.

24. A. F. Kantor, M. G. Curnen, J. W. Meigs, and J. T. Flannery, "Occupations of Fathers of Patients with Wilm's Tumor," *Journal of Epidemiology and Community Health* 33 (1979): 253-56.

25. J. D. Erickson, W. M. Cochran, and C. E. Anderson, "Parental Occupation and Birth Defects," *Contributions to Epidemiology and Biostatistics* 1 (1979): 107-17.

26. R. M. Scott, R. Suitbhan, W. H. Bancroft, et al., "Experimental Transmission of Hepatitis-B Virus by Semen and Saliva," *Journal of Infectious Diseases* 142 (1980): 67-71.

27. H. Gnarpe and J. Friberg, "T Mycoplasmas on Spermatozoa and Infertility," *Nature* 245 (1973): 97-98.

28. J. M. Joffe, J. M. Peterson, D. J. Smith, and L. F. Souka, "Sub-Lethal Effects on Offspring of Male Rats Treated with Methadone Before

Mating," *Research Communications in Chemical Pathology and Pharmacology* 13 (1976): 611-21; C. Lutwak-Mann, "Observations on Progeny of Thalidomide-Treated Male Rabbits," *British Medical Journal* 1 (1964): 1090-91.

29. For a recent review of this literature, see G. Chamberlain and J. Garcia, "Pregnant Women at Work," *Lancet* 1 (1983): 228-30.

30. On industrial chemicals, see K. Hemminki, E. Fransilla, and H. Vainio, "Spontaneous Abortions Among Female Chemical Workers," *International Archives of Occupational and Environmental Health* 45 (1980): 123-26; on the electronics sector, see K. Hemminki, M. L. Niemi, K. Koskinen, and H. Vainio, "Spontaneous Abortions Among Women Employed in the Metal Industry in Finland," *International Archives of Occupational and Environmental Health* 45 (1980): 53-60.

31. K. Hemminki, P. Mutanen, I. Saloniemi, and K. Luoma, "Congenital Malformations and Maternal Occupation in Finland: Multivariate Analysis," *Journal of Epidemiology and Community Health* 35 (1981): 5-10.

32. L. Z. Heidam, "Occupational Exposure to Chemicals Among Women and Their Implications for Reproduction," paper presented at the International Course in Occupational Hazards and Reproduction, Helsinki, Finland, August 1981.

33. O. Meirik, B. Kallen, U. Gauffin, and A. Ericson, "Major Malformations in Infants Born of Women Who Worked in Laboratories While Pregnant," *Lancet* 2 (1979): 91; M. Strandberg, K. Sandback, O. Axelson, and L. Sundell, "Spontaneous Abortions Among Women in a Hospital Laboratory," *Lancet* 1 (1978): 384-85.

34. For the first, see E. Hansson, S. Jansa, H. Wande, et al., "Pregnancy Outcome for Women Working in Laboratories in Some of the Pharmaceutical Industries in Sweden," *Scandinavian Journal of Work and Environmental Health* 6 (1980): 131-34; for the second, see B. Kolmodin-Hedman, L. Hedstrom, and B. Gronquist, "Fertility Outcome in Some Swedish Groups Occupationally Exposed to Chemicals," paper presented at the International Course in Occupational Hazards and Reproduction, Helsinki, Finland, August 1981.

35. B. Baltzar, A. Ericson, and B. Kallen, "Delivery Outcome in Women Employed in Medical Occupations in Sweden," *Journal of Occupational Medicine* 21 (1979): 543-48.

36. J. Kline, Z. Stein, M. Hatch, et al., "Surveillance of Parental Employment and Spontaneous Abortion," NIOSH Technical Report, 1982 (in press).

37. B. Kallen, G. Malmquist, and U. Moritz, "Delivery Outcome Among Physiotherapists in Sweden: Is Non-Ionizing Radiation A Fetal Hazard?" *Archives of Environmental Health* 37 (1982): 81-84.

38. For dental technicians, see G. N. Cohen, B. W. Brown, M. L. Wu, et al., "Occupational Disease in Dentistry and Chronic Exposure to Trace Anesthetic Gases," *Journal of the American Dental Association* 101 (1980): 21-31; for nurses and anesthesiologists, see Ad Hoc Committee

178 / *Maureen Hatch*

of the American Society of Anesthesiologists, "Occupational Disease Among Operating Room Personnel: A National Study," *Anesthesiology* 1 (1974): 321-40; R. P. Knill-Jones, L. V. Rodriguez, D. D. Moir, and A. A. Spence, "Anaesthetic Practice and Pregnancy: Controlled Survey of Women Anaesthetists in the United Kingdom," *Lancet* 1 (1972): 1326-28; P. O. D. Pharoah, E. Alberman, and P. Doyle, "Outcome of Pregnancy Among Women in Anaesthetic Practice," *Lancet* 1 (1977): 34-36.

39. For the first, see R. P. Knill-Jones, A. A. Spence, and C. Lawrie, "Occupation of Female Doctors and Outcome of Pregnancy," *Abstracts of Papers from the 9th Meeting of the International Epidemiological Association*, Edinburgh, August 1981; for the second, see A. Ericson and B. Kallen, "Survey of Infants Born in 1973 or 1975 to Swedish Women Working in Operating Rooms During Their Pregnancies," *Anaesthesia and Analgesia* 58 (1979): 302-305.

40. For a review of this literature, see K. Bridboard, "Occupational Lead Exposure and Women," *Preventive Medicine* 7 (1978): 311-21.

41. S. Nordstrom, L. Beckman, and I. Nordenson, "Occupational and Environmental Risks in and Around a Smelter in Northern Sweden: I. Variations in Birth Weight," *Hereditas* 88 (1978): 43-46; idem, "III. Frequencies of Spontaneous Abortion," *Hereditas* 88 (1978): 51-54; idem, "V. Spontaneous Abortion Among Female Employees and Decreased Birth Weight in Their Offspring," *Hereditas* 90 (1979): 291-96; idem, "VI. Congenital Malformations," *Hereditas* 90 (1979): 297-302.

42. N. Mamelle, "Travail et Grossesse," *Prévenir* 69 (1980): 724-27; M. Estryn, M. Kaminski, M. Franc, et al., "Grossesse et Conditions de Travail en Milieu Hospitalier," *Revue Française Gynecologie* 73 (1978): 625-31.

43. M. E. Fox, R. E. Harris, and A. L. Brekken, "The Active-Duty Military Pregnancy: A New High-Risk Category," *American Journal of Obstetrics and Gynecology* 129 (1977): 705-707.

44. J. Kline, Z. Stein, M. Hatch, et al., "Surveillance of Parental Employment and Spontaneous Abortion," NIOSH Technical Report, 1982 (in press).

45. M. Kuratsune, T. Yoshimura, J. Matsuzaka, and A. Yamaguchi, "Epidemiologic Study on Yusho: A Poisoning Caused by Ingestion of Rice-Oil Contaminated with Commercial Brand of Polychlorinated Biphenyls," *Environmental Health Perspectives* 1 (1972): 119.

46. For a review of the relevant literature, see B. J. Koos and L. D. Longo, "Mercury Toxicity in the Pregnant Woman, Fetus and Newborn Infant," *American Journal of Obstetrics and Gynecology* 126 (1976): 390-409.

47. C. Cam, "Une Nouvelle Dermatose Epidemique des Enfants," *Ann. Derm. Syph.* (Paris) 87 (1960): 393-97.

48. M. G. Nailor, F. Tarlton, and J. J. Cassidy, *Love Canal—Public Health Time Bomb: A Special Report to the Governor and the Legislature* (Albany: New York State Department of Health, 1981).

49. E. Homberger, G. Reggiani, J. Sambeth, and H. K. Wipf, "The Seveso Incident: Its Nature, Extent and Consequences," *Annals of Occupational Hygiene* 22 (1979): 327-67.
50. Environmental Protection Agency, *Six Years' Spontaneous Abortion Rates in Three Oregon Areas in Relation to Forest 2,4,5-T Spray Practices* (Washington, D.C.: U.S. Environmental Office, 1979).

9
Keeping Women in Their Place: Exclusionary Policies and Reproduction

Judith A. Scott

Some people might claim that Barbara C. had a choice in 1978 when she entered a West Virginia hospital for surgical sterilization. Her employer, American Cyanamid, had informed Barbara C. that if she wanted to keep her job in the pigments division at its Willow Island, West Virginia, plant she would have to be sterilized. She was made to believe that government support existed for the new policy and that neighboring chemical plants along the Ohio River valley would be implementing similar rules. So, with children to support, she submitted to the sterilization operation. Her decision was not a matter of choice, but one of economic necessity.

Barbara C. was not alone. Four of her co-workers at the American Cyanamid plant also underwent surgical sterilization in 1978 in order to keep their jobs when the company decided to implement a new policy barring fertile women from lead-exposed areas in seven of the factory's nine departments. Rather than face a layoff or a major cut in pay and transfer to the janitorial pool, these five women all took the drastic step of surgical sterilization. As one of them explained, "They don't have to hold a hammer to your head—all they have to do is tell you that it's the only way you can keep your job."[1] The bitter irony was that several months later the restricted departments were closed for other reasons. Barbara C. and her co-workers had relinquished their fundamental right to bear children for jobs that then disappeared.

The horrible choice that confronted these women is not unique to American Cyanamid. A number of companies, including General Motors, B. F. Goodrich, St. Joe's Minerals, Allied Chemical, and Olin, have implemented exclusionary policies that ban women from certain work locations unless they can prove they are sterile. Further, lead is not the only substance at issue: at least twelve other agents have sparked the practice, including vinyl chloride, cadmium, coal tar, acrylamide, toluene, and carbon disulfide. Sometimes the company has threatened to terminate or layoff women workers who fail to satisfy its new sterility requirement; in other cases the women have been reassigned to different departments, often with reduced pay. When the substance is present throughout the entire facility—as with lead in the GM battery plants—the company's hiring practice virtually forecloses the employment of women altogether. In addition, many of the jobs affected by the policy are the better paid, higher skilled production jobs that were previously off limits to women under the more blatant forms of sex discrimination.

The explanations the corporations give for these exclusionary policies may at first seem necessary, even laudable. The companies explain that a pregnant worker's occupational exposure to a toxic substance can cause damage to the fetus, particularly in the first three months (trimester) of pregnancy. They go on to argue that since the first trimester is an especially vulnerable period for the fetus, and since a woman may not know she is pregnant until well into this time period, *all* women of child-bearing capacity (ages 15-50) must be barred from the workplace exposure areas in order to protect the potential child. They call this exclusionary practice a "fetus protection policy."

Of course, everyone wants to avoid the horrible outcome of a deformed child. It is the means of obtaining this objective that has made this issue a public controversy. Those involved in the labor movement and/or committed to women's issues and civil rights see such corporate exclusionary policies as a serious setback to the advancement of employment opportunities for women and a wholly inadequate way to handle the grave occupational health issues at stake. The corporate mind-set that gives rise to these policies, according to its opponents, also threatens the employment rights of other vulnerable workers in our society (such as minorities) who may be susceptible to certain occupational diseases. Finally, it ignores the reproductive health hazards that these substances pose to male workers, as well as the other serious physical harm these agents can inflict. The basic policy dispute, then, centers on whether to clear out the worker or clean up the workplace.

The underlying assumption of the exclusionary approach is that *all* women capable of having babies will get pregnant, and that once pregnant all will carry the fetus to term. The policy ignores the fact that most women choose to control their reproductive lives, using birth control and abortion where necessary. In addition, by age 34 at least 89 percent of all women have borne all the children they expect to bear,[2] and still have over ten years of child-bearing capacity left. Moreover, working mothers, who numbered over 18.7 million in 1982, enter the workforce to earn a livelihood.[3]

They coordinate their child-rearing plans with their need to work. Some corporate decisionmakers, however, persist in maintaining the myth that blue collar workers are not intelligent actors who control their reproductive lives. The more sophisticated proponents of exclusionary policies respond by expressing concern over the few accidental pregnancies that may occur despite planning, and still maintain that it is necessary to exclude all nonsterile women in order to protect these fetuses from adverse health effects.

The companies do not simply champion the cause of the fetus, however: pecuniary interests are at stake. For one thing, they fear that a congenitally malformed child whose condition can be tracked back to the mother's occupational exposure to a toxic substance during pregnancy has a potential lawsuit against the employer[4]— one which, if successful, could prove very expensive. For another, in certain employment areas where female employees predominate, exclusionary policies have not been implemented (or even proposed), despite well-known reproductive hazards affecting the first trimester of pregnancy. Over 97 percent of nurses are female,[5] and exposure to the ionizing radiation of X-rays, to ethylene oxide (EtO), or to anaesthestic gases in operating rooms is known to cause reproductive damage (see chapters by Dickinson and Coleman, and by Hatch). Yet women have not been banned from these jobs. In elementary education, where more than 83 percent of all teachers are female,[6] and where German measles and other viral diseases present a significant risk to a fetus exposed during the first trimester, no one has seriously suggested that all nonsterile women be barred from teaching jobs in elementary schools. The significant wage differences between industrial jobs and those in education and nursing in part explains these different reactions: if all nonsterile women were banned from the low-wage fields of teaching or nursing, men could not be found to replace them at the same poor rates of compensation. On the other hand, women have only recently entered the industrial workforce in large numbers and are easily replaced, particularly in periods of high unemployment.

The issue extends beyond women workers, however. If we accept the exclusionary approach, we help establish the principle that a company can deal with a health and safety problem at the workplace by removing certain vulnerable workers, rather than cleaning up the workplace. If fertile women can be removed from the workplace, the development of pre-employment genetic screening could result in the exclusion of blacks and certain ethnic groups on similar grounds. In a disturbing series of articles in the New York Times in early 1980, reporter Richard Severo revealed that petrochemical companies, such as Dow Chemical and DuPont, have tested thousands of U.S. workers to determine if any of their genes make them vulnerable to certain chemicals in the workplace.[7] DuPont, for instance, has reportedly given routine pre-employment blood tests to all black applicants to determine whether or not they carried the trait for sickle-cell anemia—even though carrying this trait has not been demonstrated to put the carrier at greater risk than any other chemical worker.

The companies question the genetic acceptability of hiring Mediterranean and middle Eastern people, including Italians, Greeks, Yugoslavs, Spaniards, Portuguese, Arabs, Iranians, and Jews, as well as Chinese, Filipinos, and East Indians, among whom similar genetically-related blood disorders occur. The companies contend that people who have these disorders (or merely carry the trait) are at special risk when working with chemicals such as benzene, nitrosamines, nitrates, and lead.

It might be presumed from these policies that the white male population is "safe." But as the companies ban women and minorities from particular jobs, they leave behind a white male workforce that is still vulnerable to the adverse health effects that result from exposure to toxic substances. Several dramatic stories illustrate the tragedy of these policies. In 1977 in Lathrop, California, male workers at an Occidental Petroleum factory were found to be sterile after exposure to the pesticide dibromochloropropane (DBCP)—now banned in most instances by the Environmental Protection Agency. In 1975 workplace exposure to another pesticide, Kepone, was found to have sterilized the male workers at the Life Sciences Product Company production plant in Hopewell, Virginia.[8] And sterility is not the only reproduction-related damage inflicted by toxic substances: there is concern that some may have mutagenic effects, resulting in miscarriages suffered by the man's partner or in deformities to his children.[9]

While certain (company-financed) scientists advise that the scientific literature only supports a finding that substances such as lead are dangerous to female reproductive health, other members of the medical community feel the evidence must be read differently: "If scientific research reveals that a woman's reproductive health is at risk through occupational exposure to a particular substance, there is no scientific justification for concluding that a male co-worker is not similarly at risk, unless and until hard data proves otherwise," states Dr. Michael Silverstein, a medical doctor who specializes in occupational health issues at the United Auto Workers headquarters in Detroit. And indeed, the 1978 lead standard issued by the Occupational Safety and Health Administration (OSHA) recorded the adverse impact that lead exposure has on the reproductive health of men as well as women—including sterility, impotence, decreased ability to produce healthy sperm, and the possibility of fathering children with birth defects (see chapter by Maureen Hatch).[10] Moreover, a substance that poses a reproductive health risk usually threatens to cause other damage as well. For example, chronic exposure to lead may severely injure a person's blood-forming, nervous, and urinary systems, and can result in fatal kidney disease.[11] Other substances, such as cadmium and vinyl chloride, are carcinogens for which there is no known safe level of occupational exposure.[12]

The paucity of good scientific research into occupational health hazards is a national scandal, compounded in the reproductive health area by research projects that are restricted to female workers. The inevitable result is that employers too often seize upon sex-biased research to justify exclusionary policies and to divert attention from the overall deleterious impact of many workplace substances. The horrible burden that workers bear in these circumstances was poignantly described by a male employee from the BASF Wyanclotte plant in Rensselaer, New York, whose exposure to the plant's 1974-76 production of the weed killer oryzalin is suspected to have caused a serious rare heart abnormality in his son. Among the families of his sixty male co-workers, three other children conceived during this period were born with similar heart defects and another died at birth. After extensive surgery, only this man's son survived. He agonizes: "Do you have any idea what that [experience] does to a family? To a person that it has happened to? 'Dad, are we ignorant?' What do I tell my son when he grows up and he can't have any children? Through the amount of X-rays he has had he probably will be sterile. There has to be a better way. Believe me, there has to be."[13]

This grieving chemical worker is not alone in his conviction. Since the reproductive health issue surfaced, numerous trade unions have attempted to reverse the trend toward exclusionary policies and to force employers to clean up the workplace for everyone. Unfortunately, the traditional route of labor arbitration has not been the answer. In 1979, when the United Auto Workers challenged General Motors' exclusionary policy (banning fertile women from lead areas in its U.S. plants), the arbitrator was unable to make an independent analysis of the conflicting scientific assertions. The union's position was that instead of removing certain female workers, lead exposure should be substantially lowered due to its harmful effects on the reproductive health of both male and female workers. The arbitrator stated, however, that he was unable to determine the risk to potential fathers—thus leaving their fate to the caprice of the employer and the workplace. While conceding that there are alternatives to exclusionary policies that will protect women workers, the arbitrator upheld GM's approach, concluding that "it would be unrealistic to deal with women on an individual basis with respect to their childbearing intentions."[14]

The union also tried to attack GM's policy in an arbitration case over the corporation's use of the exclusionary approach in its Canadian facilities. While the arbitrator again refused to halt the policy, his decision nevertheless includes an astonishing recognition of the reproductive health hazards that male workers face in lead-exposed areas. He suggests "that male employees in their fertile years might well be able to refuse the type of work here in question without fear of discipline"[15]—a reflection that clearly runs counter to the exclusionary approach that the decision upholds. It also reveals the obvious bias in the GM policy: fertile men, but not fertile women, are given a choice as to whether they wish to risk their reproductive health for a particular job. Yet, if these jobs actually threaten the health of the larger worker population (*all* fertile males and females), the only acceptable solution is to reduce lead exposure to a safer level for *all* workers, or even to eliminate it entirely from the manufacturing process.

The unions that have grappled with American Cyanamid's exclusionary policies have tried other strategies besides labor arbitration, but have had mixed results. The sterilization tragedy at Willow Island, West Virginia, prompted the Oil, Chemical, and Atomic Workers (OCAW) to file a complaint with OSHA, and the company was subsequently cited for OSHA violations of the law's "general duty" clause and the lead standard and fined $10,000. This moderate penalty was then dismissed on procedural grounds upon review by the Occupational Safety and Health Review Commission. OCAW is now challenging this dismissal in court.[17]

The International Chemical Workers Union (ICWU), representing workers at approximately ten of American Cyanamid's facilities, encountered the exclusionary policy at the company's Pearl River, New York, location where pharmaceutical drugs are produced. Taking advantage of the fact that many ICWU members own American Cyanamid stock under a company stock ownership plan, the union joined with the Interfaith Center for Corporate Responsibility in 1980 to sponsor a stockholder resolution that called for a study of the company's reproductive health hazards, a full report to the shareholders, and the addition of a new member to the company's board of directors who would be especially concerned with this area. The stockholder initiative worried American Cyanamid, and in return for the withdrawal of the resolution, the company agreed to complete a reproductive health study and to appoint three of its current board members to a "public responsibility committee" to oversee corporate policies and practices concerning reproductive health and other related matters. The initial report identified six substances that posed a reproductive health risk, and named at least four thousand chemicals suspected of endangering reproductive health. These substances are now under study.

The United Steelworkers of America (USWA) has had the most success in confronting American Cyanamid. In October 1977 local management at the Warners plant in Linden, New Jersey, called its female production workers together to announce that women with child-bearing potential would no longer be assigned to approximately sixteen of the plant's twenty-one departments, and that those working in them had six months to transfer elsewhere. The company's rationale was that studies had shown that a number of the plant's chemical substances interfered with the normal development of the fetus, especially in the first trimester of pregnancy. A management memo to the workers concluded on this ominous note: "The company realizes that it is a very personal and private matter whether or not a woman cannot become pregnant because of surgical procedures. It must be pointed out, however, that this very personal matter will no longer be private if you are permitted, and choose, to remain in one of the [restricted] departments listed . . . above."

The USWA, which represents the 500 production workers at the Warners plant, would not tolerate this flat pronouncement because it failed to identify the specific chemicals in question and completely ignored the reproductive health of the men. During the months that followed the union insisted that the company document the scientific justification for each chemical it cited as a hazard and spell out its health effects on male workers and non-pregnant female workers. The union maintained that the health risks of all such chemicals had to be curtailed by engineering controls to reduce exposure levels, not by exclusionary policies. Further, the union demanded a comprehensive reproductive health policy for both sexes. In the face of the union's tough stance, American Cyanamid postponed implementation of the policy and then abandoned it altogether. Ten months after the October announcement, management informed its hourly female employees that since none of the suspected toxic chemicals were actually used at the plant, the exclusionary policy was unnecessary. Since then the union has been able to secure new engineering controls to cut down on chemical exposures—a benefit to workers of both sexes.

Nevertheless, even where the company gives up the exclusionary approach, there is no assurance that it will pursue the alternative course of cleaning up the workplace. A male or female worker who wishes to parent must thus often decide whether to risk remaining on the job. Some employers and unions have partially resolved this dilemma by providing that pregnant workers may temporarily transfer to a safer position for the duration of the pregnancy: the right to transfer off a job at no loss of pay was a novel component of the lead standard issued by OSHA in 1978. Under the direction of Dr. Eula Bingham, a highly respected specialist in the field of occupational health, OSHA rejected outright the notion of exclusionary practices to solve the reproductive health hazard question, stating: "Workers have the ability to plan and control when they will parent a child. They can be expected to act responsibly when informed of the reproductive hazards presented by lead, and of the special precautionary measure established by the standard."[18] Recognizing that lead exposure levels would not be low enough in many circumstances to protect future parents, the standard provides temporary medical removal protection for workers of either sex who desire to parent a child in the near future. This transfer option includes a guarantee of wage protection for up to eighteen months and thus enables a worker's blood lead levels to decrease before conception occurs.

Unions would like to see this concept broadened to cover other reproductive health hazards. One proposal calls for a system of "reproductive leave" to enable pregnant workers and male and female workers who are trying to conceive a child to voluntarily transfer off an exposed job with protection of pay, benefits, and seniority.[19] Such an interim solution to the reproductive health problem is not readily embraced by employers, as the recent controversy over video display terminals (VDTs) illustrates. When VDT operators, most of whom are women, began to complain of high rates of miscarriage and spontaneous abortion, employers did not rush to exclude fertile women from working with VDTs. Instead they reacted skeptically, relying on the scientific literature, which does not support a need for special concern. Employers also ignored the other potential health risks associated with VDTs (see section by Mary Sue Henifin).[20] Then in a test case in 1981, the Ontario Public Service Employees Union (OPSEU) forced the issue as to whether the worker or the employer should bear the cost of limited scientific research into the reproductive health hazards of VDTs. The union arbitrated the grievance of a pregnant data-processing technician employed by the Ontario Ministry of Education who had requested a transfer from her VDT job during her pregnancy because of her doctor's concern about possible risk to the developing fetus.[21] She was given a transfer to a clerical position, but with a cut in pay because her request was deemed "personal" rather than "health related." The grievance settlement board ordered the employer to compensate the grievant for lost wages, finding that her transfer was indeed for reasons of health. While expressly stating that it was making no determination as to whether work on a VDT was safe, the board upheld the pregnant worker's right to rely on her personal physician in matters of such significance. Noting the changing opinions about the harmfulness of such items as DDT, thalidomide, acid rain, PCBs, and asbestos, the board concluded that the nonscientific community is entitled to doubt scientists who, like the employer's expert witnesses, proclaim the safety of the workplace.

Several unions have also tackled the VDT issue at the bargaining table. In 1982 OPSEU won contractural protection which offers a model for resolving the reproductive health hazards problem until the workplace is totally clean. The agreement, which covers 58,000 public employees (50 percent of whom are female), confirms the right of a pregnant worker to transfer off a VDT job. The contract also addresses other health problems resulting from VDT use. The United Auto Workers obtained similar transfer rights with no loss of pay for pregnant VDT operators in the clerical units under the Canadian contracts at DeHavilland Aircraft and Northern Telecom. As yet, however, no contract provision goes as far as the 1978 OSHA lead standard in addressing the needs of the male or female worker who wishes to parent.

Frustrated and deeply concerned by employer resistance to cleaning up the workplace and by the growing number of exclusionary policies, the U.S. labor movement in 1979 joined with women's groups, civil rights organizations, and individuals from the scientific and legal community to form the Coalition for the Reproductive Rights of Workers (CRROW). The more than forty-four institutional members of CRROW have sponsored educational programs and have actively pressured governmental agencies such as the Equal Employment Opportunity Commission (EEOC), the Environmental Protection Agency (EPA), and OSHA to oppose exclusionary policies in carrying out their statutory responsibilities. For example, in 1980, the EEOC had a significant backlog of sex discrimination complaints based on exclusionary practices. CRROW was successful in convincing the EEOC to issue its proposed guidelines concerning reproductive health hazards—guidelines that were withdrawn as the Reagan administration took office, however.[22]

While the courtroom is a poor vehicle for regulating industry, it is an arena for challenging exclusionary policies that the Reagan administration cannot directly control. Several cases, based primarily on Title VII of the 1964 Civil Rights Act, have been brought against employers on behalf of the women like Barbara C. who have been victimized by exclusionary policies.[23] These lawsuits are aimed at preventing an employer from resorting to exclusionary policies in an alleged attempt to grapple with reproductive health hazards.[24] Targeting such companies as American Cyanamid for the Willow Island, West Virginia, tragedy, and Olin Corporation, the plaintiffs hope to win a ruling that this approach constitutes illegal employment discrimination and can no longer be used to divert attention from the employer's obligation to clean up the workplace for *all* workers.

Thus far only one higher court has directly addressed this issue, in a case appealing the approval of Olin Corporation's "fetal vulnerability policy."[25] Since 1978, Olin has banned fertile women from numerous job classifications at the company's Pisgah Forest, North Carolina, plant, where it produces cellophane, belts, and papers for the tobacco and printing industries. According to Olin's director of health affairs, the policy is necessary to protect the fetuses of pregnant employees from the damaging toxic effects of certain chemicals, principally lead. The trial court accepted this rationale as adequate justification for the exclusionary policy, but the higher court rejected it. While concluding that restrictions in female employment opportunities might be permissible in appropriate circumstances if reasonably required to protect the health of a fetus, the court spelled out several criteria that had to be satisfied before an exclusionary policy could be condoned:

(1) The employer must prove the policy is both effective and necessary to protect the unborn children of female workers from significant risks of harm. The employer must also show that the unborn children of *male* workers do not face significant risks of harm.

(2) The employer's proof must be based on independent, objective evidence, and supported by qualified experts in the relevant scientific fields.

(3) Even if the above factors are satisfied, the policy will still be illegal if its challengers can show that there are acceptable alternative practices that would accomplish the same purpose (protecting the fetus) while having a lesser differential impact on women and men workers.

The Olin policy was sent back to the lower trial court for evaluation in light of these strict standards. Based on the growing scientific evidence of the effects of toxic substances such as lead on male reproductive capacity and the availability of engineering controls to lower overall workplace exposure, it is doubtful that Olin will be able to justify its exclusion of fertile women workers under this closer judicial scrutiny.[26]

A related legal victory came in a 1982 appeals court ruling that upheld the right of a pregnant X-ray technician to take a temporary leave of absence in order to avoid the health risk of ionizing radiation on her fetus.[27] Her Texan employer, the Kleberg County Hospital, had forced her to resign out of a purported concern for both her fetus and the hospital's potential tort liability if a deformed child were born. The court held that the employer's termination of the pregnant worker (the first female X-ray technician ever employed by the hospital) amounted to illegal sex discrimination under Title VII because an available, less discriminatory alternative was available to achieve its purpose: simply put, the hospital could have granted the worker's request for a temporary leave of absence for medical reasons instead of forcing her resignation. This decision also lends support to the proposition that exclusionary policies cannot be justified when less discriminatory alternatives, such as the temporary medical removal protection in the 1978 OSHA lead standard, are available.

But the legal strategy has also suffered some setbacks. In a 1982 opinion an administrative law judge on the Illinois Human Rights Commission rejected a discrimination charge against B. F. Goodrich for its policy of excluding fertile women from jobs involving significant exposure to vinyl chloride.[28] The complaint had been filed by a forty-eight-year-old female chemical operator who was involuntarily transferred to another position in 1979 upon the company's adoption of the exclusionary policy. The decision was based on the artificial distinction between protecting the fetus and protecting the woman's and man's reproductive organs. The company was allowed to justify its policy without the rigorous analysis required in the Olin case.

It may be that the exclusionary approach will not be abandoned as long as employers continue to view all reproductive issues as strictly "female" problems that the workplace need not accomodate, or until they are forced to pay out large damage awards for deformities suffered by children whose fathers, rather than mothers, have been exposed to hazardous substances. The Teamsters are supporting the legal claims of male New York railroad workers against the Long Island Railroad on the basis that the children of these men were born with hip deformities and other birth defects as a result of their fathers' exposure to defoliant chemicals (2-4-5-D and 2-4-5-T) that they were ordered to spray in the rail yards and along the rights-of-way.[29] Male veterans exposed to Agent Orange in Vietnam and to nuclear radiation during military service are also pressing damage claims against the federal government for abnormalities suffered by their children.[30]

Except where constrained by law, employers persist in limiting the rights and benefits of women workers where reproduction is concerned. The 1978 Pregnancy Discrimination Act, for instance, although it made tremendous strides toward giving employment rights to pregnant workers, still exempts abortions from obligatory health care coverage, allowing employers also to exclude them except in the extreme situation where the mother's life is endangered if the pregnancy is carried to term. As a result, many employer health plans exclude elective abortions. And even under the best employer-financed health insurance plan, contraceptives are rarely, if ever, covered by prescription drug clauses. Elective sterilization procedures, such as tubal ligations, are also commonly excluded. In fact, a woman who agrees to comply with a company's exclusionary policy would probably have to pay for the sterilization herself!

The working woman's right to abortion is further threatened by the crusade for the so-called human life constitutional amendment, which would prohibit most abortions. Although attempts to adopt the amendment have so far floundered, the movement has dampened collective bargaining efforts to win full abortion insurance coverage: some unions hesitate to fight for this benefit, fearing adverse political reaction from anti-abortion groups among their members. Unions that have achieved gains in this area find they must fight the battle over and over again, just to protect these basic provisions. The American Federation of Government Employees (AFGE), for instance, which represents over 700,000 employees in the federal sector, won a health insurance plan that covers all therapeutic abortions but has been forced to wage an intensive struggle over the past several years to retain this benefit. AFGE has led a lobbying effort on Capitol Hill against a legislative proposal to bar the use of federal funds to finance abortions for federal employees or to subsidize any federal employee benefit plans, like that offered by AFGE, that cover abortions. Until recently, AFGE had been able to engineer the bill's defeat, although its existence prompted the Office of Personnel Management (OPM) in 1981 to refuse to sign the AFGE-negotiated health insurance contract because it covered abortions. Only a court order stopped OPM from carrying out this major offensive against abortion coverage.[31] Then, in November 1983, the anti-abortion forces prevailed: Congress passed the Smith amendment to the budget, prohibiting coverage for abortion in any federal employee benefit plans.[32]

Employer resistance to covering abortions in health insurance plans does not generally translate into support for the pregnant worker who chooses to bear her child, however. One of the starkest examples of this cruel dichotomy comes from Marengo, Illinois, where a tenured junior high school teacher, Jeanne E., was fired in January 1982 by the Board of Education for Hawthorn School District No. 17 because of her alleged "immorality." The charge was based on the fact that the teacher, who was an ex-nun, had become pregnant after being raped, had refused to have an abortion because of her religious beliefs, and had born a son whom she had chosen to rear herself. Six months after the child's birth she was dismissed. Fortunately, the Illinois Education Association fought her discharge and eventually won Jeanne E.'s reinstatement. The hearing officer's decision soundly rejected the board's accusation of immorality, finding that she was an "eminently moral person, a religious person, and staunch in her beliefs."[33] Contrary to the employer's claims, there was no proof that her situation damaged her teaching ability. The fact that some parents may disapprove of unwed mothers formed no standard for dismissing a tenured teacher.

Women like Jeanne E. and Barbara C. must sometimes question the priorities of a society that condones a worker's dismissal because of her refusal to have an abortion or to submit to sterilization. U.S. Congresswoman Barbara Mikulski, in addressing a CRROW conference, put it succinctly: "Too often in this society I find that the values we explicitly claim to honor we implicitly deny by our actions. We claim to honor motherhood and the family, yet we actually punish women for being mothers."[34]

It appears that in the U.S. workplace, women are punished for their reproductive capacity. Contradictory constraints hem women in on all sides: employment policies penalize them in the areas of fertility, sterilization, contraception, abortion, and pregnancy. The fight to improve women's rights and health on the job must therefore assert the right to control our reproductive lives as well as underscore men's role in reproduction. The growing attention being paid to this issue by unions, civil rights organizations, women's groups, and the media holds out the promise that soon workers will not be forced to choose between having children and having a job.

Notes

1. Joan E. Bertin, "Discrimination Against Women of Childbearing Capacity," address before the Hastings Center, New York, January 8, 1982.
2. "Current Population Reports," U.S. Bureau of the Census, Series P-20, No. 364, Table I, August 1981.
3. "Current Population Survey," Bureau of Labor Statistics, U.S. Department of Labor, March 1982.
4. In most states, workers' compensation statutes grant monetary awards for on-the-job injuries or occupational illnesses according to an established benefit schedule, with the worker having no independent right to sue for additional money damages unless there are unusual circumstances. While a worker may be barred from suing her company for a deformity suffered by her child while in utero, the child may not be covered by the same restriction. This theory is currently being tested in several cases, all involving children of male workers or Vietnam veterans who maintain that their exposure to Agent Orange caused birth defects. In addition, a growing number of lawsuits seek to advance the legal rights of the fetus, whether or not it is viable outside the womb. On this see Ruth Marcus, "Several Courts Weighing Legal Rights of Fetus," National Law Journal, 2 March 1981, p. 2. So far no court has been reported as awarding damages in either instance. If tort liability were established, employers could pursue insurance coverage for such claims, just as they currently secure insurance against injury claims by other nonemployees.
5. "The Registered Nurse Population: An Overview," National Sample Survey of Registered Nurses (November 1980), U.S. Department of Health and Human Services, Public Health Services Health Resources Administration, Bureau of Health Professions, Division of Health Professions Analysis, Report No. 82-5, June 1982.
6. Digest of Education Statistics 1982, National Center for Education Statistics, U.S. Department of Education, p. 52.
7. Richard Severo, "Genetic Tests by Industry Raise Questions on Rights of Workers," New York Times, 3 February 1980, p. A1; "Screening of Blacks by DuPont Sharpens Debate on Gene Tests," 4 February 1980, p. A1; "Dispute Arises over Dow Studies on Genetic Damage in Workers," 5 February 1980, p. A1. For a discussion of genetic counseling monitoring versus genetic screening see Sheldon W. Samuels, "The Management of Populations at High Risk in the Chemical Industry," Annals of the New York Academy of Sciences (1982).
8. For a more detailed discussion of the reproductive health hazards facing men, see Michael Castleman, "Why Johnny Can't Have Kids," Mother Jones, April 1982, p. 14.
9. Jane E. Brody, "Sperm Found Especially Vulnerable to Environment," New York Times, 10 March 1981, p. C1.
10. Lead Standard, adopted by OSHA, Attachment B to Preamble, 43 Fed. Reg. at 54,421 (November 21, 1978).
11. Lead Standard, adopted by OSHA, Appendix A to section 1910.1025, "Health Hazard Data," Para. B(2) (November 21, 1978).

12. The 1981 Cencer Policy, published by OSHA, 29 C.F.R. Section 1990.111.
13. Nick Crudo, member of ICWU Local 227, speaking at CRROW Conference on Reproductive Hazards in the Workplace, August 22, 1980, Transcript, p. 82.
14. UAW and General Motors (Norwood, Ohio) umpire decision Q-6, July 1978.
15. UAW and General Motors (Oshawa, Ontario), Arbitration Case No. CO-6, December 5, 1979.
16. District 9, IAM and Olin Corp., Olin Works, E. Alton, Illinois, FMCS Grievance No., 1-77-134, August 7, 1979.
17. Marshall v. American Cyanamid Co., OSHRC Docket No. 79-5762, April 27, 1981; on appeal to the U.S. Court of Appeals for the District of Columbia, Oil, Chemical and Atomic Workers v. American Cyanamid Company.
18. Lead Standard, adopted by OSHA, Attachment B to Preamble, 43 Fed. Reg. at 54,423 (November 21, 1978).
19. Michael J. Wright, "Reproductive Hazards and 'Protective Discrimination,'" Feminist Studies 5, no. 2 (Summer 1979).
20. Bob DeMatteo, The Hazards of VDT's (Toronto: Ontario Public Service Employees Union, 1981).
21. "In the Matter of an Arbitration Between the Ontario Public Service Employees Union (OPSEU) and the Crown in Right of Ontario (Ministry of Education)," Case No. 345/81, before the Grievance Settlement Board (January 21, 1982).
22. For an extensive discussion of the public comments offered by CRROW and affect industries on the 1980 EEOC proposed "Interpretive Guidelines on Employment Discrimination and Reproductive Hazards," which were subsequently withdrawn, see Ronald Bayer, "Women, Work, and Reproductive Hazards," Hastings Center Report, Institute of Society, Ethnic, and the Life Sciences, Hastings-on-Hudson, New York, October 1982. The proposed EEOC guidelines were published at 45 Federal Register 7514.
23. E.g. Barbara Cantwell Christman et al. v. American Cyanamid Company, United States District Court for the Northern District, West Virginia, Civil Action No. 80-0024-P.
24. At least two states, California and Connecticut, have enacted laws to expressly prohibit employers from conditioning employment, transfer, or promotion on the sterilization of the employee. However, these laws have not yet served as the basis for a court challenge to exclusionary policies practiced by employers within those states.
25. Wright et al. v. Olin Corp. et al., United States Court of Appeals for the Fourth Circuit, 697 F.2d 1172 (December 23, 1982).
26. The same month that the U.S. Court of Appeals ordered Olin Corp. to justify its exclusionary policy the corporation announced its agreement to pay $24 million in settlement of 1100 claims related to its manufacture of the pesticide DDT between 1954 and 1970 near Huntsville, Alabama. Environmentalists and community groups opposing

toxic waste dumping are clear allies of CRROW and the reproductive health crusade. See "Olin Is Settling DDT Litigation for $24 Million," *Wall Street Journal*, 28 December 1982, p. 6

27. Zumiga v. Kleberg County Hospital, F.2d (CA 5, 1982).
28. Steele v. The B. F. Goodrich Company, Illinois Human Rights Commission, No. 1980 CF 0617, November 17, 1982.
29. George Bailey et al. v. The Long Island Railroad, United States District Court for the Eastern District of New York, Civil Action No. 81-1162.
30. "Five Makers of Agent Orange Charge U.S. Misused Chemical in Vietnam: Companies Replying to Suit Say Federal Negligence Is Responsible for Any Harm to Veterans and Kin," *New York Times*, 7 November 1980, p. A14; Lombard v. United States, United States Court of Appeals for the District of Columbia, Civil Action No. 81-2261 (September 14, 1982).
31. American Federation of Government Employees v. Devine, United States District Court for the District of Columbia, No. 81-2239 (October 8, 1981).
32. "House and Senate Agree on Spending," *New York Times*, 12 November 1983, p. A1.
33. In the Matter of Board of Education of Hawthorn School District No. 17, Marengo, Illinois, and Dismissal of Jeanne Eckmann, decided by Hearing Officer Sidney Mogul, August 31, 1982.
34. Barbara Mikulski, speaking at CRROW Conference on Reproductive Hazards in the Workplace, August 22, 1980, Transcript, p. 14.

10
Walking a Tightrope:
Pregnancy, Parenting, and Work
Wendy Chavkin

Work Hazards and the Physical Changes of Pregnancy

Factory worker: I was so tired all the time I was pregnant. There were no women supervisors and the men couldn't come into the john after me. I had an old coat I left in the john. I would put it on the floor and lie down. It was gross but you do what you have to do. . . . If I asked for the right to do this, they'd tell me go jump in a lake.[1]

Machine operator: I felt nauseous because of the chemical smell around the plant. As soon as I came to work in the morning, I would head right to the bathroom. I'd get sick.

Lab technician: I used to have to use the bathroom all the time when I smelled something. Then I felt so weak. It takes a lot out of you.

Legal secretary: The supervisors didn't realize you need to get three meals and have snacks. They didn't understand that morning sickness isn't just in the morning.

Airlines clerk: The chairs in the office are very old and they teeter, they're not stable. The backs don't give good support, and there's no arm rest. And that's been my big problem. The bigger I get, the more prone to backaches. It's not very comfortable.

Machine operator: You don't get any pity at work for your back problems. I went to medical last week and asked to get off the machine for my eighth month. They wouldn't do it.

Exhaustion, nausea, backaches. These are some of the discomforts that can characterize a normal, healthy pregnancy. They are uncomfortable whether you are at home or at work, but rigid working conditions can certainly maximize the discomfort.

The first three months of pregnancy are a time of dramatic physical change for a woman.[2] The high levels of pregnancy-related hormones often cause her to feel nauseated. She may be extremely hungry, as this is a period when her body lays down stores for the work of gestation ahead. Increased blood flow to the kidneys, together with the pressure of the expanding uterus on the bladder, and hormonally induced changes all cause her to urinate frequently. As the pregnancy progresses, her increasing weight and size alter her posture and balance and put a strain on her back.

Inflexible work rules that don't allow snacking, easy access to the bathroom, changes in position, or rest breaks can aggravate these discomforts to the point of real hardship. Rigid work rules that prohibit snacking may not only aggravate nausea, but may also inhibit weight gain during pregnancy. Adequate maternal weight gain plays an important role in the infant's birthweight: infants that are born weighing much less than 5½ pounds have a harder time surviving.[3]

Some of the physical changes caused by pregnancy become a problem only in certain work situations:

Bank teller: I didn't have any problems, except my swelling ankles. I had a couple of instances where I was forced to stand at the [teller's] window as my ankles bulged out. You should have seen my ankles. They look like they're going to blow up. I said how big could they get?

Blood volume increases by about 50 percent during pregnancy.[4] As the uterus grows, it presses on the inferior vena cava, the major vein that returns blood to the heart. If a pregnant woman is required to stand for long hours everyday—or even to sit without changing position—much of this blood will become trapped in her feet, causing them to swell, or causing any varicose veins to expand. Moving the legs and having the opportunity to elevate them helps the blood return to the heart and alleviates the problem.

Waitress: I was afraid of slipping. Some of the dishes are heavy, with the ice and oysters. Each must weigh at least five pounds. I did cut down by carrying only two instead of three or four. The plates cause an imbalance so I walked slow.

One of the hormones elevated during pregnancy, relaxin, causes the ligaments of the back to soften and stretch. While this is functional in terms of allowing the pelvis to expand to accommodate the growing uterus, it also means that a pregnant woman's back is less well braced to handle heavy loads.

Clerical worker: Commuting was the worst part. Waddling off to the subway, standing around in the unbelievable heat, waiting to get a seat in a car which is air-conditioned, hoping to God you can get out of the car without being pushed or tripping. The subways have no air, I'd get so hot. My husband caught me the first time I passed out. The second time I was alone and woke up on the station floor. A doctor assisted. I didn't need medical attention; I needed a seat.

The increased overall metabolic activity and other pregnancy-related hormones (progesterone, human chorionic gonadatropin) cause a pregnant woman's temperature to rise about 1° higher than normal. Work conditions that are too hot—an uncomfortable strain for anyone—can be intolerable.

Many maternal physiologic functions operate at peak efficiency during pregnancy. It is a time of maximal production, storage, and turnover of maternal body constituents. It is a time when the woman's body ensures that it gets full access to oxygen and nutrients. Ironically, in an environment full of toxins this physiologic efficiency probably magnifies a woman's exposure to them:

Factory worker: The guys worked with all kinds of paint and got to wear big masks on their faces. We'd be like 10 feet from the guys with the masks and they said we didn't need them [masks]. I was scared that inhaling that stuff, I would hurt the baby. And the sawdust used to get into my lungs. My nose was all caked with black stuff. I don't know if it was the sawdust or the paint, but when you blew your nose all black stuff would come out of it.[5]

Inhalation is the major route by which substances in gas or aerosol form gain access to the bloodstream. Respiratory function undergoes marked changes during pregnancy.[6] The pregnant woman transfers 65 percent more of an inhaled gas across the lung's air sacs into the blood by breathing more deeply—not more frequently. She also empties her lungs more thoroughly when she exhales. Leftover air in the lungs serves to dilute the incoming gas; the amount of air left over in the lungs after exhalation decreases by about 20 percent.

All of this means that a pregnant woman achieves a higher concentration of an inspired gas in her lungs. As concentration increases, so does the amount absorbed. This effect is heightened further by the increased blood flow to the lungs that occurs during pregnancy. The fatty constituents of the blood (plasma lipids) increase significantly during pregnancy so that absorption of gases which dissolve in fat will increase.[7] (Examples of such fat-soluble substances commonly found in industry are benzene, toluene, and other solvents.)

Weight gain is one of the most obvious changes in pregnancy. The fetus, placenta, amniotic fluid, and growth of the uterus account for part of this gain. There is also extensive storage of fat, particularly during the first half of pregnancy.[8] This is thought to be a protective device for energy storage in case of hardship. At any rate, this expands the depot where fat-soluble toxins, like pesticides and organic solvents, can be stored.

Studies have demonstrated that women eliminate benzene more slowly from their blood than men do; this is attributed to their higher body fat. As the fat acquired during pregnancy is lost after delivery, it is possible that the stored toxins are released once again into the women's bloodstream. One study of pesticide levels in the blood of pregnant women lends credence to this theory, as blood pesticide levels dropped slightly at delivery and gradually rose subsequently.[9]

All of the tissues of the body are constantly being broken down and regenerated. During pregnancy the rate of turnover of bone is accelerated due to the increased production of two hormones, cortisol and parathyroid hormone. The overall replacement of bone matches its breakdown, so that there is no net loss during pregnancy. Certain toxic substances like lead, the antibiotic tetracycline, and strontium-90 are stored in bone. They are in an inactive form while stored in bone and can exert damage only when circulating in the bloodstream. It seems reasonable to suppose that bone resorption and turnover allow the release of these toxins, and therefore a second round of exposure to them for the woman. Experimental evidence suggesting that there is mobilization of stored lead in pregnant rats supports this possibility.[10]

Two hazardous metals, lead and cadmium, are absorbed by the same specialized transport system the gut has for calcium. This transport system becomes more efficient during pregnancy, so that calcium absorption increases. A secondary consequence may be increased absorption of these stowaway toxins. For example, a pregnant woman whose diet is deficient in calcium or iron and who is exposed to lead or cadmium will increase gut absorption of the latter two.[11]

The peak physiological efficiency that characterizes pregnancy may be a double-edged sword, magnifying a pregnant woman's effective exposure to environmental hazards. What does this mean for her health? Very little research has addressed this question. Concern about toxic exposures during pregnancy has always focused on the implications for the fetus. But what happens to the woman?

Ignorance of the specific interaction between pregnancy and certain occupational illnesses has cost some women their lives.

The metal beryllium, once extensively used in the manufacture of fluorescent lamps, is associated with a progressive lung disease called berylliosis. A registry of cases was begun in Massachusetts in 1952. Dr. Harriet Hardy reported in 1965 on the ninety-five women who had died of this disease. Sixty-three of them were pregnant when their condition deteriorated (twenty-eight of these women were not working with beryllium themselves, but received their exposure by handling their husbands' contaminated clothes). In some way pregnancy greatly accelerated the course of the illness. Yet attention was not drawn to this. The beryllium standard proposed by the Occupational Safety and Health Administration nowhere mentions that those women unfortunate enough to have berylliosis may not survive pregnancy.[12]

Benzene is a solvent used widely in industry which damages the blood-forming cells of the bone marrow. In the early part of this century researchers describing benzene-induced illnesses reported that aplastic anemia, a condition where the bone marrow ceases to produce blood cells, often first occurred during pregnancy. These anecdotes have vanished from the medical literature, no further such research has been done, and, again, this possibility is not reflected in the government-issued standard for benzene exposure.[13] Many women workers are exposed to benzene, so the question is of real importance.

Limited research has focused on the interaction between pregnancy and work. What little data we have have not been widely disseminated. In 1977 the American College of Obstetricians and Gynecologists published a book designed expressly to assist the practicing physician care appropriately for the pregnant worker. Despite the availability of this information, few physicians are adequately informed.[14]

In one study, family practitioners in a heavily industrialized area in upstate New York were queried about their knowledge and practices concerning work and pregnancy.[15] Only 25 percent of these physicians obtained occupational histories from their pregnant patients; 65 percent offered no information to their patients about the reproductive risks associated with work conditions; 25 percent were not aware themselves that certain substances commonly used in industrial settings can be hazardous to reproduction. Nor were they informed about the practical realities facing their pregnant patients. Only 33 percent were familiar with New York State's Pregnancy Disability Law (which requires their participation). Fewer than 5 percent expressed any interest in learning anything about union contracts and proceedings regarding pregnancy disability.

Nor were labor organizations more of a resource. A survey of over a dozen major unions revealed them to lack awareness or useful information on this issue.[16] Few of the health and safety staff

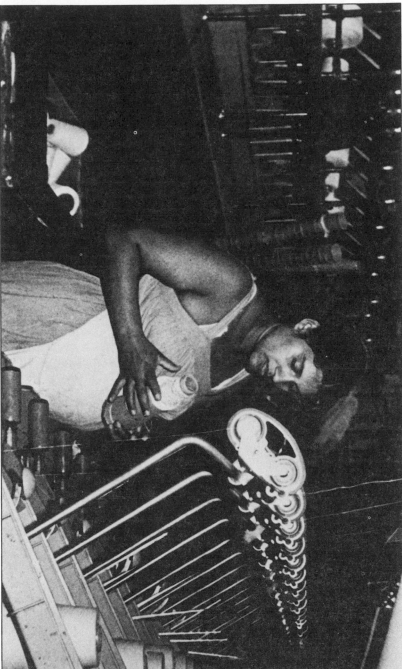

members queried knew anything about the problems their members encountered at work during pregnancy.

The Medical Model

This ignorance is not accidental. It arises from the deeply held conviction that reproduction is a private, not a social, phenomenon, and one for which society is not responsible. This is entwined with the myth that pregnant women are not in the workforce.

In fact, through the first half of this century pregnant women were held to be "unemployable." This meant they were not considered eligible for unemployment compensation, medical coverage, or disability payments. They had no rights vis-à-vis employment. They were not hired, were automatically fired or forced to take lengthy unpaid leaves, lost seniority and promotions, and their jobs were not guaranteed until their return.

Title VII of the Civil Rights Act of 1964 prohibited discrimination on grounds of sex. It required a further amendment—the Pregnancy Discrimination Act (PDA) of 1978—to specifically forbid discrimination against pregnant workers.[17] Its passage was a victory for a coalition of feminist groups, labor unions, and civil rights organizations that jointly lobbied for it. As a result of the long legacy of barring women from power and full participation in public life because of their reproductive capacity, many feminists were afraid that if they drew attention to pregnancy-related needs they would imperil newly gained jobs. Therefore they embraced a model that holds that women are no different from men—that women's needs and characteristics are legitimated only when they can be made analogous to male experiences. In this case pregnancy is legitimated by comparing it to any medical condition that temporarily disables a worker (i.e., a hernia, a broken leg, pneumonia). Pregnancy, however, is not an illness. Rather, it is a unique condition that may be accompanied by special needs, and sometimes by illness. Does such a model succeed in achieving gains for women workers?[18]

The PDA mandated that pregnant women have access to the same fringe benefits as men. In other words, pregnancy could not be singled out as a special condition *not* deserving coverage. This is a significant improvement for those women whose jobs provide such benefits. However, the PDA does not insist upon a minimal benefits package, such as paid (or even unpaid) sick leave, medical coverage, and so on. In short, it guarantees female workers the same rights as men, in a country in which male workers have few guaranteed rights. U.S. workers are not assured of fringe benefits or health care. Only those workers who belong to unions that stipulate these benefits be included in the contract are securely covered. The unorganized frequently have no benefits at all.

Because there are so few social protections, those women whose jobs do provide fringe benefits may continue working throughout pregnancy so as to keep them. A midwife in Connecticut questioned 153 women who had live births in a New Haven hospital during one month in 1981.[19] She found that a woman worked longer during her pregnancy

—if the job provided health coverage;
—if the job provided fringe benefits;
—the less hard the physical labor required;
—the more flexible the work conditions;
—the more years she had at the job; and
—the more skill, training, and status involved in the job.

Many of these women expressed clearly that a principal reason they stayed at work was that they needed the money or the health insurance. (Many also noted satisfaction and enjoyment of their work, however.)

The PDA guarantees pregnant women the same rights as men. The problem is, of course, that men are never pregnant or breast-feeding. A model based on the male as the norm offers an equality of form only; it does not take into account the physical and social realities of women's lives.

One issue that illustrates the inadequacy of the medical model when applied to pregnancy is prenatal care. Because prenatal care does not fit clearly into the disability model (it is preventive, not curative), it appears difficult to deal with. Since neither successful reproduction nor access to health care are seen as job-related or social responsibilities, there has been no conceptual framework with which to approach prenatal care for workers.

Prenatal care is intended to monitor the progress of pregnancy and detect any abnormalities that may signal a problem. Many studies have documented that those who receive prenatal care have significantly improved reproductive outcomes.[20] Interwoven with the medical surveillance is education for labor and delivery, breast-feeding, and care of the newborn. Nevertheless, most physicians and midwives make appointments only during work hours. Only sometimes are there evening or weekend sessions to accommodate those patients who work. Employers often make it very difficult for women to leave regularly for their prenatal appointments:

Surgical intern: I had difficulty getting to appointments with my obstetrician. When I was in my ninth month I traveled uptown to the doctor after being on call all night and then was chewed out for not returning to the hospital [workplace] after the appointment. I was supposed to see the doctor once a week in my last month, but I didn't go, 'cause I couldn't leave. I couldn't go to childbirth classes either.

Factory worker: They're really cracking down on absenteeism. It's hard to get time off for doctors' visits—you have to bring in a note. You have to bring in a note for everything.

One worker was asked to sign a letter stating that she was aware of her attendance problem every time she missed a day for prenatal care appointments.

Another arena in which the medical model proves inadequate is that of leave at time of childbirth. The medical model permits leave only for recuperation from the physical stress of delivery—not for nurturing the new baby or for recuperating from the exhaustion often experienced by the mother.

Moreover, employer hostility toward women, pregnancy, and all regulations protecting workers is expressed through punitive interpretations of the PDA. Claiming that the law prevents them from offering women more than they offer men, many employers have cancelled voluntary unpaid maternity leaves. This is not the only course of action open to them—they could, for instance, extend such an option to new fathers.[21] Instead, many a new mother of a six-week-old infant is forced to search high and low for some form of infant care so that she can return to work (which usually puts an end to breastfeeding as well, since workplaces do not enable her to pump or store breast milk) rather than lose her job.

The only acceptable reason for work absence around pregnancy and childbirth is one based on an illness model, and yet many physicians hesitate to certify a new mother as "disabled," ("she's not sick, she's tired"). In the words of one physician, "Now that we have established that it's just as honorable to be pregnant as to have a heart attack, do society, government, and the taxpayers have an obligation to subsidize every pregnant woman?"[22] Yet without this certification the mother is once again caught between the devil and the deep blue sea: she either returns to work exhausted and forfeits time with the new baby or she loses disability payments or her job:

Worker in a cosmetic factory (6 weeks postpartum): I'm not at all ready to go back to work. The baby isn't sleeping nights, and I'm not getting any rest. I don't feel I can go back yet.

I just got a call from the personnel department. They said I'd be terminated unless I got a [doctor's] note clearing me for work and I return at the end of the disability period. All maternity leaves have been stopped.

I called the union to find out what was happening. They said there will be no more maternity leaves and that we have the ERA to thank for it. They told me to go to the doctor and tell him I'm too nervous, make up excuses to get an extension of disability. You'd think after thirteen years, they would give a person a few months off with her baby.

Worker in a pharmaceutical plant: Before disability, they wanted you out by your fifth month. They didn't have to pay either. Well, the law went into effect and suddenly all changed. No more leaves. If you were going out on pregnancy you had to clear it. They really harassed in the beginning. I don't know if it's tamed down any. It's very hard to get sitters for six-week-olds, especially the hours this plant has. You mostly have to work 7:00 to 3:30. Have to drop the baby 6:00 to 6:30 in order to get to work and get into safety shoes and the whole get-up. Nobody wants to take a baby at that age and that hour of the morning. There was only one leave of absence granted because the baby needed mother's milk or it would have died.

The medical model is completely at a loss when faced with the issue of breastfeeding. The breastfeeding worker is neither ill nor temporarily disabled. She is a fully capable worker who merely requires facilities at work to enable her to pump her breasts and refrigerate the milk until she takes it home for her baby. If she is denied the opportunity to pump her breasts, they may become engorged and her milk supply may drop.

Hostility toward working mothers has been clearly demonstrated by harshly refusing to accommodate their breastfeeding needs. One woman returned to work at an auto assembly plant after her maternity leave with a note from her personal physician stating she was fit and ready to work. The company physician, however, barred her because she was breastfeeding. The company explained: "To allow a nursing mother to work would foist upon the company a burden to bear the resulting inefficiencies of lost production from time spent away from her job." The union grieved and won. The policy was changed, and the company reimbursed the woman for wages lost while banned from the plant.[23]

Another example is that of Linda Eaton, the Iowa City firefighter. She was suspended for nursing her infant in the women's locker room at the fire station during the long hours on duty spent waiting for fire alarms. She took her case to the Iowa Civil Rights Commission and eventually won.[24] In another instance, a federal employee was denied access to the first aid station at work when she wanted to pump her breasts. She took two hours of unpaid leave daily to drive home and breastfeed the baby.[25]

Alternatives: Parental Benefits

These dilemmas confront an ever growing proportion of women in the United States. Of the 3 million women who had live-births in 1972-73, about 42 percent (or 1.3 million) worked during their pregnancies. It is estimated that 85 percent of the female labor force will be pregnant at some point during their working lives.[26] In short, U.S. women are increasingly likely to be working while bearing and raising young children. These women are either contributing significantly to family income or are the family's sole support.

What policies would meet the needs of these women?[27] A vision of a policy that guarantees women opportunities to work and parent assumes the right to health care, as well as societal appreciation of the work involved in bearing and rearing children. Such a program must demand:

—temporary job modification to accommodate the physical changes of pregnancy;
—temporary transfer to a safer job, if the job cannot be adequately modified (both of these with salary and seniority retention);
—paid leave time to attend prenatal classes and medical appointments;
—paid leave for late stages of pregnancy and to recuperate from childbirth;
—paid leave for both/either parent to care for newborn;
—facilities for breastfeeding—i.e., break time and a place for pumping breasts, refrigeration for storage of breast milk; most desirable would be on-site infant care so women can breastfeed during work breaks;
—low-cost, readily accessible, high quality daycare; and
—paid leave for both/either parent to care for sick children.

This is not a utopian fantasy. The United States is *alone* among the industrialized nations of the world in not providing compensation to the working woman at the time of childbirth. Seventy-five countries, including many developing nations, guarantee work leave at the time of delivery—with job, seniority, and pension protection—and payment to replace wages (equal to all or a portion of insured wage, usually provided through the social security system).[28]

In a survey of policies in 14 countries, the minimum paid maternity leave was 12 weeks in Israel; the maximum was 9 months in Sweden; most were 5 to 6 months.[29] Usually part of the leave (generally 6 weeks) is taken before the expected birth. Prenatal and postnatal medical coverage and hospital coverage for delivery are included. Job modification without penalty and the right to nurse at work are also standard. Extended child care leaves—sometimes paid, sometimes unpaid—are common. Sweden is currently the only country that allows fathers to share the benefits and to participate in paid parental leave, although other Scandinavian countries are moving in this direction.

The motivations behind such legislation have usually been:

—to protect the health of mothers and infants;
—to provide incentives to encourage childbearing; and
—to draw women into the labor force in situations of labor shortage.

Neither the public health, labor force, or pronatalist goals are explicitly feminist, i.e., designed for the purpose of ending female subordination and expanding women's options. Yet they do recognize the twentieth-century reality of the importance of jobs and incomes for women. The fact that the benefits are universally popular reflects their positive impact; they have achieved significant improvements in women's lives.

In many European countries, for example, extensive regulations exist to facilitate the combination of employment with motherhood.[30] The costs involved are shifted from the family unit to the larger community or state. Childbearing and rearing are seen, implicitly at least, as social contributions, and therefore as social responsibilities.

These measures enable women to perform the dual roles of worker and mother (actually triple roles—"housewife" is assumed to accompany "mother"). What they leave unchallenged, however, is the assumption that child and home are the primary responsibility of the woman: the inequitable balance between women and men in terms of domestic responsibilities is taken for granted. This is reinforced by the fact that sex segregation in the workforce ensures that men's salaries are higher than women's, so that a family's income will suffer more if the man takes unpaid leave from work. Paternity leave is rarely considered a reasonable option, much less a right. And so the circle goes around again. When sex roles within the family are not questioned, the working woman comes home to plunge immediately into housework and childrearing work. Sweden and Cuba are among the few countries that are explicitly striving to shake up these gender roles.[31] The stated aims of Swedish Parent Insurance and the Cuban Family Code are to enable people to manage both family and job responsibilities, and to promote equitable sharing of these responsibilities between the sexes.

To return—with a crash—to the United States: the lack of "special" maternity benefits here does not serve to disrupt gender roles, but instead, leaves the woman struggling to perform her triple day without any protection from, or recognition of, her burdens. It would be possible to arrive at a social policy that mandates pregnancy-related benefits and parental leaves for workers. As long as women alone are considered responsible for domestic chores and childrearing, then employers will weigh the costs of providing related services versus the benefits of female employment. If men and women were to share these tasks equally, then the costs of providing such support services and benefits will become part of the necessary expense of hiring *workers*. The framework exists: "veterans' preference" acknowledges the importance placed on military defense. Parental benefits would reflect explicit social recognition of the importance of work and parenting in the lives of men and women.

It is, of course, not as easy as all that. Maternity benefits elsewhere occur within the context of universal access to health care and labor organization. In the United States, the right to health care and the right to a safe and healthy workplace compete with the employer's "right" to maximize profits. If employers (as opposed to the state) have to bear the brunt of maternity-related benefits, they may see this as a disincentive for hiring women. This is particularly worrisome in a time, like the present, of high unemployment. On the other hand, growth in employment has been occurring primarily in the service sector which relies heavily on women workers. It thus may not be so easy to avoid hiring women.

There is a tension in the feminist camp as to how to proceed on this point. One group fears that demanding pregnancy and mothering-related benefits will rebound negatively on women and serve as a disincentive for hiring them. This group wants to fight for women's rights within the "equality" model, a model which fits pregnancy into the category of temporary medical disability in order to make it comparable to a male experience. The other contingent insists that we must address concretely the situations experienced by many women and try to alleviate their triple burden. This group also feels that in the United States "equality" has too often meant procedural rights rather than the substantive sharing of resources. Both sides take heart from the recent Supreme Court decision which extended pregnancy-related benefits to male workers' wives. This represents an instance in which rights for women workers were extended to men, rather than being used against women to limit their opportunities.

This could, then, be the basis for a new unity between women's groups and organized labor. The current economic situation mandates that these groups seek out their joint interests. Maternity leave provisions were recently a key demand in a strike by postal workers in Canada.[32] In New York City, at the height of the fiscal crisis, the municipal employees' union, District Council 37, won a clause in their contract guaranteeing three years unpaid leave, with salary and seniority retention, for women or men at the time of childbirth or adoption.[33] Women airline employees, members of the Brotherhood (sic) of Railway and Airline Clerks, became active within their local for the first time in order to defend the right to leave at the time of childbirth or adoption. Through their efforts, a resolution for infant care leave passed at the union's annual meeting.[34]

These seem like meager gains compared to the benefits available to women in other industrialized countries. Yet they indicate that these issues are serving to mobilize at least some U.S. workers. Others could be drawn in to lend support. Those who are concerned with children's welfare and health, those who fight for occupational health, those who are active in parents' groups and community organizations may all find a common meeting ground in defending workers' rights to parenthood. This issue could serve as a springboard from which we can move forward creatively and assert that *all* of women's needs be met. We must be vigilant and organized in order to ensure that any legal or legislative gains not be deformed and used to limit women's rights. A strong women's labor presence is necessary to guarantee women's interests.

Notes

I would like to thank the following people for their critical scrutiny of this chapter: Cindy Dickinson, Nick Freudenberg, Vilma Hunt, Rosalind Petchesky, Susan Pincus, Susan Schechter, Lisa Watson, the NYCOSH Reproductive Rights Committee. My special thanks to Molly McNees and Kathy Murray, who conducted the interviews.

1. This and subsequent quotes from pregnant workers were obtained in an interview study of fifty women in the New York/New Jersey area in 1982. The women interviewed do not represent a scientifically chosen or random sample. Rather, access to them came about through union and personal contacts. While an attempt was made to interview women holding a wide variety of jobs, those interviewed were more highly unionized than is true of the general working female population in this geographic area. Women who speak only Spanish or Chinese were underrepresented. Molly McNees and Kathy Murray conducted the interviews, and the New York Committee for Occupational Safety and Health's Reproductive Hazards Committee participated with the author in the study design.

2. Medical texts dealing with the physiology of pregnancy include: F. Fuchs, ed., *The Endocrinology of Pregnancy* (New York: Harper & Row, 1977); F. E. Hytton and I. Leitch, *The Physiology of Human Pregnancy* (London: Blackwell Scientific Publications, 1971); Jack A. Pritchard and Paul C. McDonald, *Williams Obstetrics*, 15th ed. (New York: Appleton-Century-Crofts, 1976). The American College of Obstetricians and Gynecologists has directly addressed the topic of work and pregnancy in *Guidelines on Pregnancy and Work* (DHEW Order No. SA-5304-75, 1975). See also Vilma Hunt, *Work and the Health of Women* (Boca Raton, FL: CRC Press, 1979).

3. There is an extensive literature on maternal weight gain and birthweight. A selected few such references include: David Rush, Zena Stein, and Mervyn Susser, "A Randomized Controlled Trial of Prenatal Nutritional Supplementation in New York City," *Pediatrics* 66 (1980): 656; Zena Stein et al., *Famine and Human Development: The Dutch Hunger Winter of 1944-45* (New York: Oxford University Press, 1945).

4. C. A. Guzman and R. Caplan, "Cardiorespiratory Response to Exercise During Pregnancy," *American Journal of Obstetrics and Gynecology* 108 (1970): 600.

5. Nina Kleinberg, "Pregnant on the Job: An Exploratory Study of the Experience of Working During Pregnancy," Masters essay, Yale University School of Nursing, 1981.

6. See D. W. Cugell et al., "Pulmonary Function in Pregnancy," *American Review of Tuberculosis* 67 (1953): 568; H. G. Knuttgen and K. Emerson, "Physiological Response to Pregnancy at Rest and During Exercise," *Journal of Applied Physiology* 36 (1974): 549; J. B. L. Gee, B. S. Packer, and J. E. Milten, "Pulmonary Mechanics During Pregnancy," *Journal of Clinical Investigation* 46 (1967): 945; M. L. Pernoll et al., "Ventilation During Rest and Exercise in Pregnancy and Postpartum," *Respiratory Physiology* 25 (1975): 295; M. L. Pernoll et al., "Oxygen Consumption at Rest and During Exercise in Pregnancy," *Respiratory Physiology* 25 (1975): 285.

7. Rebound et al., "Plasma Proteins and Lipids During Pregnancy and Postpartum," *Annales de Biologie Clinique* 25 (1967): 383; A. Svanborg and O. Vikrot, "Plasma Lipid Fractions, Including Individual Phospholipids at Various Stages of Pregnancy," *Acta Medica Scandinavica* 178 (1965): 615.

8. F. E. Hytten et al., "Measurement of Total Body Fat in Man by Absorption of 85Kr," *Clinical Science* 31 (1966): 111.

9. A. Curley, "Insecticides in Plasma and Milk," *Archives of Environmental Health* 18 (1969): 156; A. Kato et al., "Kinetic Studies on Sex Differences in Susceptibility to Chronic Benzene Intoxication with Special Reference to Body Fat Content," *British Journal of Industrial Medicine* 32 (1975): 321; Z. W. Polishuk et al., "Effects of Pregnancy on Storage of Organochlorine Insecticides," *Archives of Environmental Health* 20 (1970): 215.

10. J. P. Bucket et al., "Mobilization of Lead During Pregnancy in Rats," *International Archives of Occupational and Environmental Health* 40

(1977): 33; A. A. Wibowo et al., "Blood Lead and Serum Iron Levels in Non-Occupationally Exposed Males and Females," *International Archives of Occupational and Environmental Health* (1977): 113; L. Ahlgren et al., "In Vivo Determination of Lead in the Skeleton after Occupational Exposure to Lead," *British Journal of Industrial Medicine* 32 (1980): 109.

11. Task Group on Metal Accumulation, "Accumulation of Toxic Metals with Special Reference to Their Absorption, Excretion and Biological Half-Lives," *Environmental Physiology and Biochemistry* 3 (1974): 65; J. Bonnar and A. Goldberg, "The Assessment of Iron Deficiency in Pregnancy," *Scottish Medical Journal* 14 (1969): 209.

12. Harriet Hardy, "Beryllium Poisoning: Lessons on Control and Man-Made Disease," *New England Journal of Medicine* 273 (1965): 1188; R. I. McCallum, I. Rennie, and C. Verity, "Chronic Pulmonary Berylliosis in a Female Chemist," *British Journal of Industrial Medicine* 18 (1961): 133; U.S. Department of Health, Education, and Welfare, National Institute for Occupational Safety and Health, *Beryllium Criteria Document for a Recommended Standard, Occupational Exposure to Beryllium* (HSM 72-10268; Washington, D.C.: U.S. Government Printing Office, 1972).

13. Kato et al., "Kinetic Studies." For corroboratory evidence from animal experimentation, see M. Ikeda, *Toxicology and Applied Pharmacology* 20 (1971): 30 and I. Hirokawa, *Japanese Journal of Medical Science and Biology* 8 (1955): 275. Research from the early part of this century includes: Alice Hamilton, "The Growing Menace of Benzol Poisoning in American Industry," *Journal of the American Medical Association* 78 (1922): 627; L. Selling, "A Preliminary Report of Some Cases of Purpura Hemorrhagia Due to Benzol Poisoning," *Johns Hopkins Hospital Bulletin* 21 (1910): 33; A. R. Smith, "Chronic Benzol Poisoning Among Women Industrial Workers: A Study of the Women Exposed to Benzol Fumes in Six Factories," *Journal of Industrial Hygiene* 10 (1928): 73. See also U.S. Department of Health, Education, and Welfare, Occupational Safety and Health Administration, *Occupational Exposure to Benzene* (Washington, D.C.: U.S. Government Printing Office, 1978); 29 CFR 1910.1028, 43 Fed. Reg. 5918 (10 February 1978), *as amended* 43 Fed. Reg. 27962 (27 June 1978).

14. American College of Obstetricians and Gynecologists, *Guidelines*.

15. Susan Pincus, "Reproductive Hazards in the Workplace: The Possible Role of the Family Physician," *The New York Family Physician*, forthcoming.

16. The author and Carole Oppenheimer designed a survey that was sponsored by CRROW and performed by Antioch law students in 1980. Fifteen unions were questioned about practices and protection regarding workers who were pregnant. While several individual staff members were helpful and provided anecdotal information, there were no systematic means of retrieving the data.

17. Pregnancy Discrimination Act, 42 U.S.C. 2000e (k).

18. Nancy S. Erickson, "Pregnancy Discrimination: An Analytical Ap-

proach," Women's Rights Law Reporter 5 (Winter-Spring 1979): 83-105; Ann C. Hill, "Protection of Women Workers and the Courts: A Legal Case History," Feminist Studies 5 (Summer 1979): 247-73; Wendy W. Williams, "Special Treatment Versus Equal Treatment," Women's Rights Law Reporter 7 (1982): 175. See also Alice Kessler-Harris's chapter in this volume. The author is indebted to Wendy Williams and Joan Burton for endlessly battling this out with her. Debby Bachrach, Carole Oppenheimer, Ros Petchesky, Nancy Stearns, and the Reproductive Hazards Committee of the New York Committee for Occupational Safety and Health all helped in refining and clarifying these ideas.

19. Kleinberg, Pregnant on the Job.
20. Steven L. Gortmaker, "The Effects of Prenatal Care upon the Health of the Newborn," American Journal of Public Health 69 (1979): 653-60; Samuel Schwartz and John H. Vinyard, "Prenatal Care and Prematurity," Public Health Reports 80 (1965): 237-48; Milton Terris and Marvin Glassner, "A Life Table Analysis of the Relation of Prenatal Care to Prematurity," American Journal of Public Health 64 (1974): 869; Milton Terris and Edwin Gold, "An Epidemiologic Study of Prematurity: Relation to Prenatal Care, Birth Interval, Residential History and Outcome of Previous Pregnancies," American Journal of Obstetrics and Gynecology 103 (1969): 371-79.
21. Deanna Stropes, "The Committee for Infant Care Leave: A Local Union's Struggle," paper delivered at Forum on Pregnancy and Work, New York Committee for Occupational Safety and Health, New York, January 1982. See also "Paternity Battle," New York Times, 12 December 1982, which recounts the story of an engineer who wanted to take unpaid paternity leave and was told by his employer that the company would not guarantee his job or his seniority rights.
22. "Symposium: Working in Pregnancy: How Long? How Hard? What's Your Role?" Contemporary Ob/Gyn 16 (1980): 154-66.
23. Ford Motor Company (Rawsonville Plant), personal communication with Judy Scott.
24. "Female Firefighter Wins Breast-Feeding Case," New York Times, 21 March 1980, p. B4.
25. Judy Mann, "Nursing Mother's Story Has Yet Another Chapter," Washington Post, 9 July 1980, p. C1.
26. Gerry E. Hendershott, "Pregnant Workers in the United States," Advance Data 11, U.S. Department of Health, Education, and Welfare, Vital and Health Statistics of the National Center for Health Statistics (Washington, D.C.: U.S. Government Printing Office, 1977).
27. See section on "Women's Dual Roles" in Women's Labor Project, Bargaining for Equality (San Francisco: WLP, 1980) for legal and collective bargaining approaches in the United States.
28. International Labour Office, Employment of Women with Family Responsibilities (Geneva: ILO, 1978), and Equal Treatment for Men and Women Workers: Workers with Family Responsibilities (Geneva: ILO, 1979); U.S. Department of Health, Education, and Welfare, Social

Security Administration, *Social Security Programs Throughout the World* (Washington, D.C.: U.S. Government Printing Office, 1980).

29. Sheila Kamerman, "Maternity and Parental Benefits and Leaves: An International Review," *Impact on Policy Series Monograph No. 1* (New York: Columbia University Center for the Social Sciences, 1980).

30. International Labour Office, *Work and Family Life: The Role of the Social Infrastructure in Eastern European Countries* (Geneva: ILO, 1980); Gail W. Lapidus, "Occupational Segregation and Public Policy: A Comparative Analysis of American and Soviet Patterns," in *Women and the Workplace*, eds. Martha Blaxall and Barbara Reagan (Chicago: University of Chicago Press, 1976).

31. See Kamerman, *Maternity and Parental Benefits*, for information about Swedish Parent Insurance. For discussion of the Cuban Family Code, see Margaret Randall, "Introducing the Family Code" and Carollee Bengelsdorf and Alice Hageman, "Emerging from Under-development: Women and Work in Cuba," in *Capitalist Patriarchy and the Case for Socialist Feminism*, ed. Zillah Eisenstein (New York: Monthly Review Press, 1979). See also Maxine Molyneux, "Socialist Societies Old and New: Progress Toward Women's Emancipation?" *Monthly Review* 34, no. 3 (July-August 1982): 56-100.

32. *New York Times*, 1 July 1981, p. 5.

33. The Citywide Contract, 1 July 1980–30 June 1982, Article 5: Time and Leave: 20.

34. Stropes, "The Committee for Infant-Care Leave."

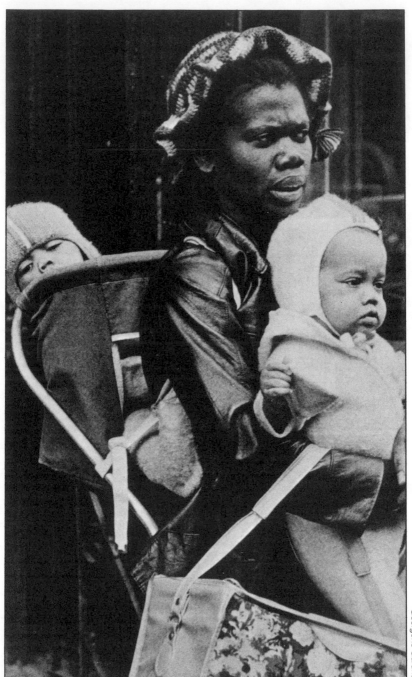

Part 3
On the Homefront: Women at Home and in the Community

Introduction

While it is widely believed that women belong in the home, it is not widely understood that what they do there is work. They work "keeping house," they work as wives, and they work as mothers, yet these activities are not generally recognized or respected as work because they receive no direct remuneration. As Ruth Milkman has put it, "Housework is a labor of love in a society whose universal standard of value is money."[1] A major feminist contribution has been to focus on this unseen labor and to explore its characteristics. Because this is a book about work hazards, the aspect of domestic work under scrutiny in this section will be its attendant occupational hazards.

This is a complex issue and one fundamental to feminist analysis.[2] Examination of these hazards reveals that they result not only from the use of toxic materials in the home (many of them the same materials that threaten the health of industrial workers), but from the structural characteristics of the work itself. Wifework and motherwork place the worker (wife/mother) at risk because of the stress she undergoes. As Harriet Rosenberg tells us in chapter 11, this stress comes about for four reasons:

(1) Because of the enormity of the tasks assumed to fall within the "job description," and the Sysiphus-like nature of tasks that have no clear end product and have to be endlessly repeated (i.e., preparing meals, bathing children, washing laundry).

(2) Because of the impossible nature of the assignment: however sensitive, soothing, and supportive a woman may be, she cannot sufficiently patch up the psychic bruising that the husband or child experiences daily in the outside world and she thus risks feelings of personal failure.

(3) Because of the multiplicity of her burdens—frequently she is a member of the paid labor force as well.

(4) Because of the privatized and isolated nature of the work experience, so that her heavy workload and/or the abuses experienced remain "personal" and invisible.

The idealized image of housewives as nonworkers in domestic havens is linked to the subordination of women in the paid labor force. The longstanding justification for paying women less in every job category is that their true vocation is as wives and mothers. Recently, as we saw in the previous section, women have been excluded from certain "hazardous" jobs and sent back to their (implicitly safe) homes.

But are they safe? We hope to explode this myth by demonstrating that work in the home is both hazardous and arduous, thus giving the lie to the "protective" concern for women that supposedly motivates such exclusionary policies. Clearly, it does not help women to remove them from the hazardous (paid) workplace if doing so puts them in the hazardous (unpaid) home. Moreover, the dichotomy between work and home is untenable because toxic industrial products are often sold for home use. Worker health is threatened in the production process, communities are polluted by industrial waste, and consumer health is threatened through use of the products. The world cannot be neatly compartmentalized between workplace and community.

But this overlap evokes the possibility of united resistance. Within the constraints of the housewife-mother role, women have been militant fighters against threats to health at home and in the community. Housewives and mothers have been tenant organizers, boycott leaders, anti-inflation fighters, and so forth. Miners' wives have demonstrated clearly, through militant and creative strike support activities, that the (paid) workplace and the community are inseparably related.[3] This activism is important, and must be examined to determine in which circumstances a woman's acceptance of her role has led to activism, and how this experience has in turn led to a shake-up of her traditional roles. It is only on the basis of this sort of knowledge that our future strategies can be devised.

Nick Freudenberg and Ellen Zaltzberg have attempted to extract tentative answers to these questions from interviews and survey responses. They found many environmental activists to be women who took their job description as housewife very seriously: it was concern for the well-being of their children and the sanctity of the home that catapulted these mothers into the public arena. The skills acquired as housewife and mother—intimate familiarity with the community, involvement in local organizations (block associations, church and parent groups), and sensitivity to others were all highly pertinent to this kind of organizing activity. Their experiences as organizers had politicizing consequences for these women. They had to make forays into the public domain, making use of (and demands upon) public resources, and they had to break through the privatized bonds to make explicit the similarities of their personal experiences and to connect them with the larger social picture.

Those women whose work lies within the household know that the paid workplace impinges upon the private world. Workers go home. The money they earn, the psychic toll taken by their job conditions, their work-related illnesses and accidents, the contaminants they unwittingly transport on hair, skin, and clothes—all these help determine the events and quality of life at home. Industries are located in, or near, communities. Their physical characteristics, wastes, and by-products, and their choice of those to whom they offer employment, drastically affect the surrounding communities. Both of the chapters in this section suggest ways in which women can be in the forefront in promoting a more unified view of social life, and point to the possibility of alliances and coalitions that can work to bring about changes to improve life at work, life at home.

Notes

1. Ruth Milkman, "Women's Work and the Economic Crisis: Some Lessons of the Great Depression," *Review of Radical Political Economics* 8, no. 1 (Spring 1976).
2. Various analyses of domestic labor include: Margaret Benston, "The Political Economy of Women's Liberation," *Monthly Review* 21, no. 4 (September 1969); Mariarosa Dalla Costa, *The Power of Women and the Subversion of the Community* (Bristol, England: Falling Wall Press, 1972); Eli Zaretsky, "Capitalism, the Family, and Personal Life," *Socialist Revolution* 3, nos. 1-2 (January-April 1973), and no. 3 (May-June 1973). For further references see Zillah R. Eisenstein, ed., *Capitalist Patriarchy and the Case for Socialist Feminism* (New York: Monthly Review Press, 1979), p. 172.
3. My thanks to Hal Benenson for criticizing an approach that solely emphasizes resistance at the point of production. See his book review, "The Reorganization of U.S. Manufacturing Industry and Workers' Experience, 1880-1920: A Review of *Bureaucracy and the Labor Process* by Dan Clawsen," *Insurgent Sociologist* 11, no. 3 (Summer 1982). See also Barry Brodsky, "Tenants First: FHA Tenants Organize in Massachusetts," *Radical America* 9, no. 2 (1975); Frances Fox Piven and Richard Cloward, *Regulating the Poor* (New York: Pantheon, 1971); Batya Weinbaum and Amy Bridges, "The Other Side of the Paycheck," in *Capitalist Patriarchy*.

11
The Home Is the Workplace: Hazards, Stress, and Pollutants in the Household

Harriet G. Rosenberg

Domestic Labor: Invisible Work

One of the central struggles of the women's movement since its rebirth in the 1960s has been focused on the issue of domestic labor, the unpaid work women do in the home. Despite the fact that the media frequently portray feminists as anti-housewife, it has been the women's movement that has drawn attention to the long hours of work that women put into the home, the economic importance of that work to the economy in general, and the social and economic costs that would accrue if that labor were purchased in the marketplace.[1] What have drawn the anger of the media and the male establishment, however, are not the calls for payment for housework, or for pension rights for women outside the paid labor force, but the feminist insistence that housework is not a natural, sex-linked, God-given characteristic of being female. Women have argued that there are no genetic, hormonal, or sacred reasons why only some people should do childcare, shop, cook meals, do laundry, and soothe the frayed tempers of others. Yet it has been hard for women to struggle against sex bias in the paid labor force, and even harder for them to point out that such bias also exists in the home.[2]

It is the aim of this chapter to show that a rigid sexual division of labor in the household contributes to significant health and safety hazards for women who work in the home. One of the key features of the division of labor by sex in the household is that it perpetuates a widely held ideology that what women do in the home is not really work. This basic myth, as we shall see, serves to obscure the often stressful and physically hazardous nature of domestic labor. Women marry and have children to fulfill basic human needs for love, intimacy, and security; but the work that accompanies wifedom and motherhood also requires skill, training, and experience.

Workers are not expected to love their jobs. If they do so even some of the time, they are considered lucky. Housewives, on the other hand, are considered to be married to their jobs and are under enormous pressure not to admit or analyze the negative aspects of the work they do.[3] When they do so, however, they are setting the stage for allying themselves with waged workers who are also struggling for safer, healthier working conditions, in which they will be treated with dignity.

Despite the increasing number of women who work for wages, over one-third of married women in the United States and Canada are still full-time housewives. It is the largest occupational category for women in our society. And women who work for wages outside the home continue to bear the major responsibility for housework and childcare. They work a double day. In addition, many women work at domestic labor as waged workers. These women are servants, nannies, cleaners. They work in homes and office buildings, often under extremely exploitative conditions. Those who "live-in" as maids may face eighty-hour weeks with salaries below the minimum wage, sexual harassment, racial insults, and threats of deportation if they are immigrants.[4] Thus while I will concentrate on women who are full-time homemakers, the issues are of concern to all women who do domestic labor, whether they are paid or not, and whether they work in their own homes or not.

Housework, Wifework, Motherwork

Those who benefit from the services that women perform in the household may glorify the work publicly but once in a while we get a hint of what they really think of it. For example, in 1973 a British magistrate sentenced a man to clean an old-age pensioner's flat as punishment for a minor misdemeanor. Other judges were impressed by this tactic and copied it. A woman reporter in London clarified the deeper social lesson to be drawn from this new practice in sentencing:

> It may come as a surprise to the magistrate that thousands of women in this country are interned for varying periods of time, week in and week out, performing the ultimate deterrent known as "housework." Many are finding it increasingly difficult to remember what offence they committed in the first place.[5]

Women work hard in the home. Yet the popular image persists that housewives are lazy, pampered, and lucky because they do not have to punch timeclocks in the "real world." This view was espoused by a Toronto alderman to explain why so few women held upper level jobs in City Hall. Women in his view were too lazy "to get off their backs" and go to work.[6]

This viewpoint implies that the locus of "real work" is in the "real world." The home is where men relax after working "out there." The household is thus not defined as a place where work is done. And where no work is done, there are no workers, no training programs, no workplace dangers, no sick leave, no compensation for overtime, no paid vacation, no benefits.

We live in a society in which people are not encouraged to notice and understand the working conditions of their neighbors, or how their own jobs fit into the larger production picture. Information about the labor process is sparse. Our children don't take courses in school about the conditions under which red pop, jeans, or ball-point pens are made. Television commercials regularly tell us that elves make certain brands of cookies and crackers and giants make frozen vegetables.

Although we tend to label people by occupational category—what they do for a wage—we use these labels to help describe status and earning capacity, not how people actually spend their time. Thus, when a person is labelled "housewife," we know very little about what she does on a day-to-day basis. We are conditioned not to ask about the nature of the labor process but to judge a person by the status of the job. And the job of housewife has a low status.[7] Since the labor process involved in housework is not acknowledged or experienced as work, it is invisible.

For these reasons working conditions in the home have rarely been studied.[8] Yet women who do domestic labor face difficult, stressful, and often hazardous conditions. These physical hazards are ignored or denied. This is in large part because women are publicly defined as *consumers* not *workers*. They are targets of multimillion dollar advertising campaigns that try to get them to buy certain products but do not inform them of any potential dangers of these products—after all, the home is a haven and nothing produced for use there could be dangerous. Nevertheless, many products that routinely enter the home, as well as the very materials of which it is built, pose serious health and safety threats.

There are three major interlocking aspects of the work women do in the home: *housework*, *motherwork*, and *wifework*. These jobs are of course interrelated, but they can be analytically separated. *Housework* includes the cluster of tasks that are involved with cleaning, maintaining, and repairing the home, with the purchase and preparation of food, with doing laundry, and with mending clothes. The fact that we live in a primarily urban capitalist society, and are dependent on wage labor, shapes much of the nature of housework. A wage must come into the household in order for it to survive. That wage is transformed into food, products, and services that maintain and reproduce the labor power of the wage earner (among others) on a daily basis so that he or she can go back to work the next day. The male wage-earner may see the results of housework as his reward for selling his labor power,[9] but housework also provides these services to those who do not earn wages: to children, the unemployed, the sick, and the elderly. Housework makes it possible for people to be clothed, bathed, fed, and refreshed.

When a women gives birth to or adopts a child, the amount of work she has to do increases significantly. Motherwork is the culturally organized set of tasks that are part of feeding, clothing, nurturing, and socializing a child (or children) until he or she can leave home and become self-supporting. These care-giving aspects of motherwork can also extend to dependent family members who are not children, such as parents, in-laws, and other relatives, whether they live in the household or not. Motherwork can thus imply the maintenance of extensive support and care-giving networks outside the household.

The physical aspects of the job, which include interrupted sleep and heavy lifting, are intertwined with deep emotional and psychological aspects. These can be experienced as internal or external pressures as to how mothering should be conducted. Mothers usually experience their work in very personal terms, but in social terms their job is to produce the next generation of workers (and often to care for former workers as well). Like housework, this job is intimately connected to the "outside" world of consumer products, expert advice-givers, and social agencies, although it is mythologized as being a private project.

Motherwork and housework are jobs that are not necessarily sex-linked and could be held by men as well as women. In fact, breaking down the division of labor by sex, as well as socializing these jobs, would be the first step in their redesign.

Wifework at first glance may appear to be more sex-linked. It is part of housework in the sense that it helps the male wage-earner return to his job the next day psychologically refreshed. What women do in this context may be thought of as emotional housework. Wifework is the job of listening and sculpting conversations to suit a man.[10] It is the job of soothing, comforting, and having sex with one man exclusively. It is the job of attending to a husband's needs before he knows that he has them.[11] And it is the job of always putting those needs before one's own. Good wives avert crises by developing special kinds of organizational forethought which enable them to plan days, weeks, months, and even years ahead.

Women who do not live up to expectations (their own or others') are accused of being "bad wives"—accusations that can even be used to justify physical attack.

Women who do the jobs of motherwork, housework, and wifework thus face a number of hazards. In the following sections we will examine two of the most pressing of these in more detail—physical and psychological stress, and exposure to toxic products used in the home.

Stress

Stress is a health hazard that many workers confront. Teachers, health workers, police, and firefighters are among those who deal with high levels of occupational stress, but any worker who is in a job where the demands are high and the ability to control the situation low is subject to a high level of stress.[12] The following list of common sources of stress was prepared for waged work outside the home. However, as we shall see, it also applies to housework.[13]

(1) *Lack of participation in decision-making.* Women sometimes experience motherwork, especially in combination with housework and wifework, as exhausting and depressing because they have little scope for real decision-making. In fact, every small decision a woman makes during the day becomes a demand in itself. As one mother of young children put it:

> It drove me crazy just deciding what to wear or what to eat. Because it wasn't only me, I had to decide for the kids and for my husband. Laundry after laundry . . . meal after meal. And you get to decide between Cheer and Tide, between Campbell's and Lipton. . . . Great choices, eh?[14]

Such pseudo-choices have no fundamental impact on the overall structure of the working conditions of domestic labor. They are simply part of the ideology of "freedom of choice" under capitalism which diverts attention away from larger issues by focusing attention on the trivialities of minor consumer choices.

In the household, the wage-earner's decision takes precedence. Women move households to follow their partners' jobs. A household's status is often rigidly determined by the husband's career.[15] And for most women, directly or indirectly, it is the experts who set the conditions of birth and childbearing—even the most intimate encounters with mates are circumscribed by expert definitions of appropriate sexual expression for women.[16] Further, women's household schedules are determined by the schedules of infants, school-age children, and the male wage-earner. Women are rarely "their own bosses."

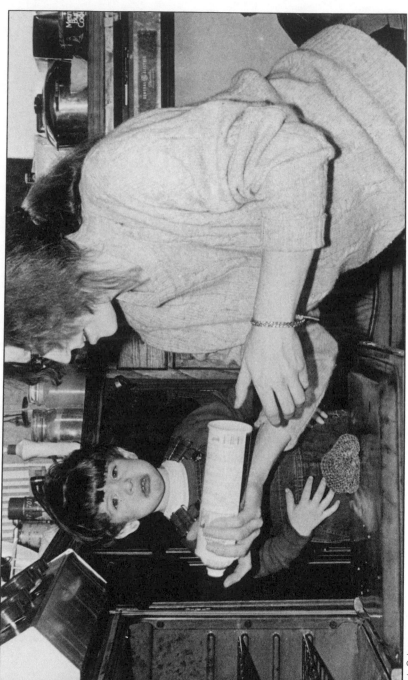

(2) Low job satisfaction. Housewives in London, England, interviewed about the work aspects of their roles indicated dissatisfaction as the dominant emotion. They hated the monotony, fragmentation, and loneliness of their jobs.[17] Since housewives are told that their work is their nature—part of their self-definition of womanhood—job dissatisfaction can be read back to them as personal "craziness." A family therapist had this to say about a client who didn't like housework:

> A young woman who received superior ratings as a schoolteacher refused to cook or shop for food since she considered this beneath her. . . . She seemed to expect her family as well as her therapist to be completely accepting of her *passive dependent attitude* that it was beneath her dignity to fulfill this aspect of a *woman's role.*[18]

Women who react to the stress of domestic labor by becoming depressed are not suffering from neurotic confusions about their role. They are expressing on-the-job stress symptoms. These symptoms are common. A study of depression and marriage in London found that working-class married women with young children living at home had the highest rates of depression recorded in the survey.[19] Depression among women at home is much the same as the job burn-out experienced by workers in the helping professions—doctors, nurses, therapists, social workers, etc.—whose work situations include high demands, long hours, little support, insufficient resources, emergencies, dangers, and risks.[20]

(3) No opportunity to learn new skills. The routine aspects of housework can become numbing and monotonous. The multiplicity of tasks and the constant demands make learning new skills difficult. Furthermore, when skills are acquired they are rarely recognized as such. Women's skills in cleaning and repairing are devalued as "household hints" in chatty little articles or books. Their accumulated knowledge is not explored or built on as a form of scientific inquiry. It is constantly dispersed, traded as discrete bits of disembodied information. Women's crafts—such as sewing, knitting, and quilting—rarely receive public attention and are undervalued in artistic and financial terms.

(4) Too slow or too fast a pace. Domestic labor combines too slow and too fast a pace. Contrast the long nights of infant feeding or caring for a sick family member with the hectic atmosphere of meal preparation and serving while attending the scheduling needs of all household members. If the principal wage-earner in the household is doing shift work, the scheduling demands on the housewife are enormous. As one housewife trying to cope with a screaming

infant, four children just home from school, meal preparation, and a husband trying to sleep and demanding quiet, put it, "The worst thing about this job is the working conditions. I always feel fractured because I have to do several things at once. I feel so frazzled."[21]

There have been many studies attempting to calculate just how many hours a day women work in the home. A recent study estimates that women with no children work 35 hours a week, while mothers with 4 or more children work 61 hours a week.[22]

Women who are employed for wages outside the home can expect to work an additional 19 hours in the home on top of their regular 35- to 40-hour week if they have no children, and an additional 32 to 37 hours a week if they have 4 or more children.[23]

(5) *Confinement to the work area.* Loneliness and isolation are the dominant concerns that women express about their working conditions in the home. The feeling of being trapped is especially common among mothers with young children. Some psychiatrists have dismissed this constriction on women's lives as a manifestation of some unresolved inner problem, particularly in the postpartum period, and have prescribed drugs to ease depression. The medical profession has argued that twenty-four-hour-a-day shifts are part of the role of being a mother and that suicidal fantasies, feelings of intense anger, bouts of crying, lack of feeling, or conflicts with mates or other children are signs of poor individual adjustment to the feminine role.[24]

The struggle for high quality accessible daycare is an important aspect of job redesign that can lessen the stress and isolation of motherwork.

(6) *Discrimination and rigid work roles.* The stress-producing conditions that women experience in the household are fundamentally the same as the stressors they experience in waged work outside the house. This is not surprising, since much of the work women do outside the home is devalued in the same way that housework is. Health workers, bank tellers, food industry workers, and assembly-line workers have to cope with a pervasive sexism and discrimination that undervalues their work and can involve demands for personal service or even sexual attention from male bosses. In fact, women are often seen as housewives wherever they work. Until recently such demands for personal services have not been seen as out of place in the waged workplace precisely because women are supposed to be available for such tasks on a twenty-four-hour basis.

Many women seek to escape the low status and harassment of waged work by becoming wives and mothers—only to find that their escape has been illusory, an escape into captivity.[25]

(7) Lack of job security. Women who are deserted, divorced, or whose partners die become displaced homemakers. One writer has described their situation this way:

They were Total Women. Perfect. Careerists in Home-making. Mid-game the rules change: Marriage is no longer a lifetime engagement. [A wife is] . . . fired from marriage. She is a walking obsolescence, tossed on the scrap heap of laid-off wives.[26]

"Displaced homemaker" is a term that was coined to deal with the special problems of women over forty-five who lose their jobs in the household and are forced onto a labor market that discriminates against them because of their age and lack of skills. Such women are too young to receive old-age benefits and may no longer have children young enough to be eligible for government assistance. They are an unknown and hidden group of women, whose numbers have not yet been accurately counted, although the Alliance for Displaced Homemakers has estimated that there are potentially 15 million women in this category in the United States alone.

These laid-off workers have fewer rights than do other workers. Displaced homemakers are not eligible for unemployment benefits that might help them retrain themselves. They are not protected by unions, whose contractual clauses might also help with retraining. Their skills are rarely recognized by employers because they are not backed up by an earning history. They cannot count on the courts to grant alimony, which would also facilitate retraining. As a Florida lawyer has noted, "Rehabilitative alimony [is granted] for the shortest period deemed necessary to get the wife back on the job market." A woman who worked to put her husband through college is rarely granted the equivalent opportunity.[27]

In the United States, according to a 1975 study, only 14 percent of divorces involved alimony awards. Fewer than 50 percent of divorced women are granted financial support for their children.[28] And the rate of default on payments is high: in Canada a 1975 study revealed that women are granted child support in only 44 percent of divorces, and that less than half of them receive payment regularly.[29]

Women who leave or are pushed out of their jobs as housewives require legal protection, including revised divorce laws, marriage or cohabitation contracts, access to pensions, retraining programs, and centers that can meet their needs. In today's world, being a housewife is not a secure occupation, and that lack of security is a real source of stress to millions of women.

To this list of workplace stressors may be added one more—abuse.

(8) Abuse. Battering can be an occupational hazard of housework, wifework, and motherwork. It is considered part of a woman's

job to represent the household and family to the outside world.[30] Housework defined as inadequate by a male can be used as a pretext for battering in a society in which men have more power than women and have the privilege of acting out frustration and anger through violent behavior. Men who beat women who they define as bad housewives are even considered justified. As one police officer investigating an abuse case put it, "If it had been my house, I would have beaten my wife for the condition it was in."[31]

The job requirements of wifework also contribute to the possibility of abuse. It is a job that is virtually impossible to do perfectly. It necessitates always being available to service the psychological, emotional, and sexual needs of a partner, mediating the tensions of the outside world and making the household safe, warm, and secure. A woman who is not always supportive, who criticizes her partner, may be considered a rightful object for abuse.

Some men consider sexual refusal, extra-marital affairs, or pregnancy as cues for abuse.[32] Pregnancy, for example, is a visible signal that a wife will be less available to tend to the needs of her mate. It is thus a statement of the conflict that some men see between wifework and motherwork—conflict over who will be the most important object of caregiving.

Women's image of being property, not a worker, is reinforced by the larger social system and is used to keep them in the home despite abuse. As one rural woman explains it, "I was just his possession, and the better isolated he could keep me, the easier it was to keep me from looking for ways to get out."[33]

In addition, many women find that their legal rights stop at the front door. What is assault on the street is permissible in the home. The larger social system thus allows violence as a private matter between husband and wife and so effectively places the family outside the rules and laws of society. To support this covert system, the "proper roles" for men and women based on a division of labor and authority by sex are built into the rules and procedures of other institutions. Representatives of these institutions learn to turn a blind eye to the use of violence by a husband against a wife, in the name of the sanctity of the marriage. The result is that the woman who has been battered looks for help outside her family only to discover that her plea elicits platitudes about the privacy of the home and the proper role of the woman.[34]

Women who work in the home with the threat of abuse hanging over them live with a kind of fear about which we know very little. It may be just as damaging as are the episodes of actual abuse. For battered women, the household is a very dangerous workplace.

Health and Safety Hazards

The experts' advice to women centers on the areas of housework, childhaving and rearing, and sexual performance. Books on these subjects are cheap, written in simple language, and readily available in supermarkets, drugstores, and bookstores. While it is a question how much of this advice is valuable, how much is idiosyncratic, and how much is blatant guilt-inducing propaganda, one thing is clear: we are surrounded by it.

On the other hand, it is very difficult to find information about product or appliance safety. Women who do domestic labor are forced to rely on advertisers for information about the chemical content or safety aspects of their products. When the powerful myth-making machine of advertising enters the household, it swirls around like a white tornado, leaving behind the feeling that nothing bad could happen in these happy homes. However, chemicals, toxic substances, pollutants, and safety hazards do not lose their potency when they cross the threshold of the household. Here I will describe a few of the most common hazards to which household workers are exposed.

(1) *Home-cleaning products*. Table 1 outlines the dangers of some commonplace home-cleaning products. These are items that domestic workers use virtually every day, yet there is almost no product safety information available about them. Many of them are dangerous and some, like dishwashing and laundry detergents, can be lethal to small children.

In fact, the average household has as many as 250 chemicals which, if ingested, could send a child to the hospital.[35] Women who do motherwork in the home and are responsible for the health and safety of their children are surrounded by floor and furniture polish, wax, ink, adhesives, paint, shoepolish, room deodorants, and many other products that are not identified as poisons. The image of happy carefree housewives dancing around their clean and wonderful kitchens costs advertisers millions of dollars a year. Procter and Gamble, for example, spends $300 million a year promoting bliss through use of its detergents, while systematically avoiding any real discussion of their substantial hazards.[36] Yet one study shows that a child in the United States swallows a poisonous substance every *60 seconds*.[37] Since women engaged in motherwork are not informed about how hazardous these common products are, they cannot be held responsible for such accidents. Yet they are accused, or accuse themselves, of being negligent.[38] Mothers absorb the guilt of industrial irresponsibility. Manufacturers should be forced to label all potential poisons adequately, and to specify lethal dosages.

Table 1
Dangers of Home-Cleaning Products

Product	Dangers	Alternatives
Drain Cleaner (lye)[1]	The most dangerous product in home use. Can eat through mouth, skin, stomach, or damage eyes. There is no effective antidote.	Rubber plunger or plumber's snake. Prevent clogging with drain strainer. Use hot water + 1/4 cup washing soda.
Toilet bowl cleaner (ammonia)[2]	Can burn skin on contact, or respiratory tract if inhaled. Liquid from in-tank cleaner harmful if swallowed. Fumes fatal if mixed with chlorine bleach.	Scrub with stiff brush.
Scouring powder[3]	Rapidly absorbed through mucous membranes and scraped skin. Can cause red rash in any area that comes in contact with product.	Salt or baking soda clean and disinfect effectively.
Oven cleaner (lye)[4]	Extremely dangerous. Can burn skin and eyes. Inhaling fumes is hazardous. Some brands don't have childproof closures.	Damp cloth and baking soda. Scrape hardened material with a knife. One commercial product contains no lye.
Chlorine bleach[5]	Can cause corrosive burns if swallowed. Fumes fatal if mixed with ammonia.	Safer when diluted.
Window or glass cleaner[6]	Swallowing can cause nausea or vomiting. Can irritate eyes. Lethal dose for a child is over one pint.	Warm tap water alone or 1/2 cup white vinegar mixed with 1 quart cool water. For chrome, use flour and a dry cloth.

Product	Hazards	Safer use / alternatives
Disinfectants[7]	May irritate skin and eyes. Spray can irritate throat. May cause nausea and diarrhea if swallowed. Lethal dose for small child is 1/5 oz.	Soap and water.
All-purpose cleaner[8]	Hazardous to eyes. Can burn throat and stomach lining if swallowed. Products containing petroleum distillates can cause a fatal lung condition.	Diluted bleach or detergent. A slice of potato removes fingerprints on painted wood.
Dishwashing detergent[9]	A lethal dose for a small child is 2 oz. Enzymes can be highly irritating.	Use less. Rinse dishes immediately after use. Scour with a stiff brush and/or salt and baking soda. Soak burned pots overnight, boil, cool, and scour.
Automatic dishwashing detergent[10]	Major cause of poisoning in children. Irritating to skin, eyes, respiratory tract. Residue on dishes may have long-term effects.	Use less. Vinegar in rinse cuts spotting, leaves less residue to be ingested.
Laundry detergent[11]	A lethal dose for a small child is 1/7 oz. Swallowing can cause nausea, vomiting, diarrhea. A few grains can damage eye cornea if left untended.	Soap powders are safer. Liquid laundry detergents do not contain sodium carbonate, a corrosive present in detergent powders.
Furniture polish[12]	A drop or two of solvent fatal if swallowed. Flammable. Aspiration can cause a form of chemical pneumonia. Nitrosamines (present in some brands) can be absorbed through skin and cause cancer in laboratory animals.	Tsp. of vinegar in a cup water; buff with a dry cloth for wood furniture. Use mineral oil for shine.

Sources:

On *drain cleaners*, see *Calpirg Reports* (June 1981), Factsheet; Center for Science in the Public Interest, *The Household Pollutants Guide* (Garden City, N.Y.: Anchor Books, 1978), pp. 180–90; Joanne Robertson, "Housework Is Hazardous to Your Health," *Pollution Probe* (Toronto), 1982, factsheet; Women's Occupational Health Resource Center, "Factsheet for Women Who Work in the Home," January 1979; "Alkali Products Dangerous to Eyes," *Occupational Health Bulletin* 26, nos. 1–2 (1971): 4.

On *toilet bowl cleaners*, see Robertson, *Housework Is Hazardous to Your Health*; Center for Science in the Public Interest, *Household Pollutants Guide*; "Toilet Bowl Cleaners," *Consumer Reports* 4, no. 3 (March 1975): 157.

On *scouring powder*, see Robertson, "Housework Is Hazardous to Your Health."

On *oven cleaners*, see Robertson, "Housework Is Hazardous to Your Health"; "Oven Cleaners," *Consumer Reports* 45, no. 10 (October 1980): 598–99.

On *chlorine bleach*, see *Calpirg Reports*, Factsheet; Robertson, "Housework Is Hazardous to Your Health."

On *window and glass cleaners*, see *Calpirg Reports*, Factsheet; Robertson, "Housework Is Hazardous to Your Health."

On *disinfectants*, see Robertson, "Housework Is Hazardous to Your Health"; "Household Cleaners," *Consumer Reports* 39, no. 9 (September 1974): 677.

On *all-purpose cleaners*, see *Calpirg Reports*, Factsheet; Robertson, "Housework Is Hazardous to Your Health"; "All-purpose Cleaners," *Consumer Reports* 44, no. 2 (February 1979): 81.

On *dishwashing detergent*, see *Calpirg Reports*, Factsheet; Robertson, "Housework Is Hazardous to Your Health."

On *automatic dishwashing detergent*, see Robertson, "Housework Is Hazardous to Your Health."

On *laundry detergent*, see *Calpirg Reports*, Factsheet; Center for Science in the Public Interest, *Household Pollutants Guide*, pp. 149–50; Emmanuel Sommers, "Risk Assessment for Environmental Health," *Canadian Journal of Public Health* 7 (November–December 1979): 389.

On *furniture polish*, see *Calpirg Reports*, Factsheet; Robertson, "Housework Is Hazardous to Your Health"; "Furniture Polishes," *Consumer Reports* 44, no. 7 (July 1979): 496.

Safer alternatives, such as salt, baking soda, and vinegar, get very little advertising exposure because they are much cheaper than supermarket cleaning compounds. Yet they are as effective as the fancy "improved" chemical cleaners and have been tested by women in the household for generations. They come from the underground storehouse of women's science, more commonly known as household hints. Other alternatives are safer but more labor intensive than commercial cleaners. This is not to suggest that women should work harder: cleaning pots is not a sex-linked activity and anyone with an arm can apply the necessary elbow grease. Finally, it should be noted that these commercial cleaners are so dangerous that they should not be stored under the sink—where kitchen and cabinet designers assume they should go—but should be put on a high shelf and locked up whenever possible. Daycare centers are required by law to do this.

(2) Workplace environment, workplace equipment. The walls of a house do not act as a magical detoxifying barrier. Products that are hazardous in industry remain hazardous in the home. Vinyl chloride (VC), for example, is a chemical that is dangerous at point of production, dangerous in the household, and dangerous at the point of disposal.[39] Some workers exposed to VC have developed cancer; other hazards include hepatitis, chronic bronchitis, skin disease, deafness, vision failure, and liver dysfunction. It is a common chemical, and is used in the production of many plastic products. It is found throughout the house in polyvinyl chloride (PVC) products, and can leach out of a PVC product in its early life. PVC is part of such building and construction materials as pipes, siding, windows, lighting, is in household furnishings and appliances, and is in such products as plastic baby pants, toys, footwear, outerwear, records, food packaging, and plastic bottles. In the United States the industrial threshold limit for VC exposure is set at one part per billion. However, it is such a dangerous substance that labor unions and public interest groups are pressing for a zero-tolerance level. Women, as domestic workers, should be made aware of these dangers and join in this campaign.

Insecticides are another group of products that pose a health hazard, not only to factory and farm workers but also to domestic workers. Housewives are assaulted by advertising campaigns which insist that the elimination of all mold and bugs is absolutely necessary. This cult of cleanliness, which far surpasses public health requirements, encourages consumers to use the chemical equivalent of a cannon to kill an ant.

One such "cannon" is Kepone. It is so dangerous that in 1974 it was banned from industrial production in the United States because it was found to cause damage to the brain, liver, and testes of workers, and cancer in laboratory animals. It was considered so unsafe that no state would bury it, and no disposal company was able to secure permission from the U.S. Environmental Protection Agency (EPA) to burn it. Yet the EPA has approved its sale in household insecticides, and the stipulation that the substance is to be sealed in hard-to-open insect traps is not always complied with.[40] Since such ant and roach traps are often placed on the floor, they pose a serious hazard to young children.

Other common chemicals in pesticides used in the home include arsenates, diazinon, dichlorvos, and DDVP, all of which are extremely dangerous. DDVP, for example, enters the home in hang-up antipest strips and cat and dog flea collars. It is a nerve poison that has cancer-causing properties and may induce genetic alteration. Women who work and live in houses with these strips may be exposed to DDVP for over 100 hours a week. Over 12 million strips are sold annually in the United States alone. In addition, 32 million dogs and 22 million cats wear flea collars containing DDVP.[41]

Gardeners may bring a variety of toxic substances into the home, including 2,4,5-T, a component of Agent Orange, the defoliant used by the U.S. air force in Vietnam.[42] 2,4,5-T has been linked to high rates of miscarriage in areas sprayed with it. Nitrosamines, cancer-causing agents in animals, have routinely been found to contaminate weed killers.[43]

Captan, a fungicide, is extremely hazardous to pregnant women and young children.[44] It has been found to cause cancer and birth defects in pregnant animals. It is used by home gardeners as part of rose and fruit-tree sprays. And, unbeknownst to most people, it is also found in cosmetics, wallpaper paste, vinyl textiles, and polyethylene garbage bags. Yet it has had, until recently, an aura of safety about it. It was tested and approved by Industrial Bio-Test Laboratories in the United States. Unfortunately, IBT test data are alleged to have been falsified and company officials are on trial in Illinois.

Other hazards to those who work full-time in the home stem from construction and insulating materials, which contribute to indoor air pollution.[45] This has become a serious health hazard in North America as soaring heating costs have led to more effective insulation, trapping airborne hazards in the home. Unfortunately, ventilation alone may not be sufficient to dilute indoor pollution to an acceptable point. A 1981 U.S. National Research Council report suggests that better ways must be devised to reduce exposure to indoor contaminants. This is especially crucial for domestic workers who face long-term low-level exposure to potential cancer-causing substances, or to contaminants that may cause respiratory infection and cardiovascular disease. Some of these dangers are listed in Table 2.

(3) Home accidents. Many appliances that women routinely use in the home are potentially hazardous. These dangers are listed in Table 3. Industry claims that women are responsible for any accident that occurs in the home. In a somewhat condescending fashion, "today's woman" is told by an industrial spokesperson that she "has responsibility for much more than how her home looks. She is also legally and morally accountable for the safety of herself and others inside that home."[46] Since home accidents are very serious and rank high among the causes of death, and since 57 percent of all fatal falls in the home involve women,[47] women must demand adequate safety education.

The promotion of highly unnecessary cleaning standards contributes to home accidents. Advertising is unrelenting in its assertion that shiny, and therefore slippery, floor surfaces are a meaningful sign of good housekeeping. Since it is estimated that 38 percent of home accidents result from falls on the level and only 14 percent from heights, it is clear that slippery surfaces are a real danger.[48]

Other causes of home accidents can also be traced to industry. When one person is injured walking through a glass door, it may be considered an individual problem. But when over 250,000 Americans a year are killed or injured in architectural glazing accidents, then we must look to the systemic problems of design, manufacture, and installation.[49] Glass doors and other architecturally used glass in the home is considered so dangerous that the U.S. Consumer Products Safety Commission lists it sixteenth in a list of the one hundred most hazardous consumer products.[50] Consumer groups throughout the United States and Canada have fought to change building codes so that glass with shatter-resistant qualities will become required in house construction.

Fire is another significant contributor to home accidents. Flame retardants, however, are not the solution: when plastics treated with such retardants burn they release large quantities of poisonous smoke. Since 80 percent of fire victims die from smoke inhalation and are not touched by flames, the value of flame retardants is dubious.[51] Furthermore, any burning plastic, treated or not, will release toxic substances, and rooms with plastic rather than wood furniture (common in mobile homes) are characterized by very rapid oxygen depletion.[52] Despite these dangers, plastics manufacturers do not make information about their products' burning

Table 2
Environmental Dangers of the Home Workplace

Pollutant	Danger	Source	Precaution/Alternative
Asbestos[1]	Can irritate lungs. Known carcinogen.	Home insulation, dry-wall patching compounds, ceiling tiles. Some baby powders, humidifiers, hair driers, ironing board covers, and oven mits.	Seal cracks, especially in older homes. Substitute corn starch for baby powers. Use asbestos-free building products.
Lead[2]	High levels can cause irreversible brain damage or death in children. Lead in the environment can be absorbed by pregnant women and lead to miscarriages.	Leaded house paints found in older homes. Dust contaminated by leaded gasoline contributes to 90 percent of all environmental land. Leaded solder in evaporated milk cans, especially serious when used for formula of under-three-year-olds.	If you live in older home with peeling paint, have children's blood tested. Support groups fighting to remove lead from gasoline.
PCBs (polychlorinated biphenyls)[3]	Long-term exposure can lead to liver, heart, blood vessel damage; chronic bronchitis; asthma and limb numbness.	Cork wall tiles (over 1 ppm), drinking straws, kitchen film wrap, plastic baby pants, plastic foam weatherstripping (under 1 ppm).	Banned in Sweden and Canada. U.S. has partial restriction on PCB use.

Formaldehyde[4]	Respiratory problems and allergies. Formaldehyde is cancer-causing in animals. Especially high concentrations found in mobile homes.	Foam insulation. Aldehydes and other organic substances are emitted from formaldehydes used in manufacture of particleboard, plywood, fabrics.	Urea formaldehyde foam is now banned in U.S. and Canada.
Aerosols[5]	Heart problems (cardiac arrythmias); lung cancer. Explosive if heated. Rarely child-proofed. Hydrocarbon or fluorocarbon propellants are also dangerous.	Small aerosolized particles are inhaled deep into lungs (e.g., deodorants, room fresheners, disinfectants). Especially dangerous in poorly ventilated bathrooms.	Avoid products packaged this way. Open windows to dispel unpleasant odors or set out a dish of vanilla and water or vinegar and water. Use soap and water to disinfect.

Sources:

On asbestos, see York-Toronto Lung Association, Environmental Health Hazards in the Community Home, Classroom and Household (Toronto, 1980); United States Committee on Indoor Pollutants, Board on Toxicology and Environmental Health Hazards, Assembly of Life Sciences, National Research Council, Executive Summary, "Indoor Pollutants," p. 7; Emmanuel Sommers, "Risk Assessment for Environmental Health," Canadian Journal of Public Health 7 (November-December 1979): 390.

On lead, see Center for Science in the Public Interest, The Household Pollutants Guide (Garden City, N.Y.: Anchor Books, 1978); York-Toronto Lung Association, Environmental Health Hazards in the Community, pp. 155–61; "While FDA Ponders, Babies Drink Lead," Consumer Reports 38, no. 10 (October 1973): 601–2; "Getting Lead Out—A Tough Problem," Consumer Reports 40, no. 7 (July 1975): 404; J. P. Buchet, H. Roels, G. Humbermont, and R. Lauwerys, "Placental Transfers of Lead, Mercury, Cadmium, and Carbon Monoxide in Women," Environmental Research 15, pp. 494–503; Richard L. O'Connell, "Female and Fetal Responses to Toxic Exposure," National Safety News 119, no. 1 (January 1979): 77–80.

On PCBs, see L. M. Reynolds, "PCB and PCT in Commercially Available Products in Samples of Garbage," Environmental Impact Control Directorate, Environmental Protection Service (Canada), EPS-5-ec-77-2 (1978); York-Toronto Lung Association, Environmental Health Hazards in the Community.

On formaldehyde, see "The Modern New Office or Your Home—A Place to Become Ill," Forum for the Advancement of Toxicology Newsletter 14 (1981): 1–3; U.S. Committee on Indoor Pollutants, "Indoor Pollutants," p. 6; Michael Lafavore, "Clean Air Indoors," Rodale's New Shelter (May/June 1982): 22.

On aerosols, see Center for Science in the Public Interest, Household Pollutants Guide, pp. 34–56.

Table 3
Potential Dangers of Appliances

Pollutant	Dangers	Precaution/Alternative
Gas stove[1]	Gas stoves emit carbon monoxide and nitrogen dioxides in varying amounts. Exposure to carbon monoxide on a day-to-day basis may aggravate or cause a wide range of chronic conditions, including anxiety, physical fatigue, rheumatism, arthritis, muscle pain, and headaches.	Forced draft ventilation to the outside may help. Stoves with pilot lights constantly leak small amounts of pollutants into the house. However, some newer stoves don't use pilot lights.
Refrigerator drip pans[2]	Self-defrosting refrigerators have coils which generate temperatures of 100°F. Below them are drip pans. Bacteria grow in this hot moist climate and circulate into the kitchen air from the front grate even when the fridge door is closed. These bacteria can cause respiratory problems.	Drip trays should be cleaned outdoors once a month.
Microwave ovens[3]	Radiation leakage through faulty seals may result in tissue damage, especially to the eyes, resulting in irreversible cataracts. Nerve tissues and white blood cells are also vulnerable to the thermal effects of microwaves. Some research has indicated fetal abnormalities in mice exposed to low levels of radiation.	Examine microwave ovens for evidence of shipping damage. Never insert objects around door seal or tamper with locks. Do not clean seal with abrasives. Stay at least 3 feet away from oven while it is operating. Do not permit children to operate.

Televisions[4]	In the late 60s some TV sets were found to emit radiation above maximum recommended level.	Avoid older model TVs. The U.S. surgeon general recommends viewing TV from at least 7 feet away.
Lighting[5]	Fluorescent lights, common in kitchens, emit ultraviolet radiation. Exposure may damage the eyes. Minute reactions in the eyes may occur for years until cataracts are produced. Since the eye lens contains no pain receptors, damage may go undetected until a serious problem develops. Persistent exposure recently linked to skin cancer.	Don't overuse fluorescent lighting.
Ionization-type fire detectors[6]	All battery-powered detectors contain radioactive materials confined in metal containers. How effective these containers are in keeping exposure to a minimum is not yet known.	Use photoelectric detectors, which contain no radioactive material.

Sources:

On gas stoves, see Collin High, "Indoor Air Pollution," *Natural History* 10 (1981): 110–17; York-Toronto Lung Association, *Environmental Health Hazards in the Community Home, Classroom, and Household* (Toronto, 1980); Michael Lafavore, "Clean Air Indoors," *Rodale's New Shelter* (May/June 1982): 22.
On refrigerator drip pans, see York-Toronto Lung Association, *Environmental Health Hazards in the Community.*
On microwave ovens, see "Is Microwave Leakage Hazardous?" *Consumer Reports* 40, no. 6 (June 1976): 319–21.
On televisions, see "Possible X-Ray Hazard Revealed in Certain TVs," *Consumer Reports* 40, no. 2 (February 1975): 73.
On lighting, see Center for Science in the Public Interest, *Household Pollutants Guide*, pp. 221–22; Valerie Beral, Helen Shaw, Susan Evans, Gerald Milton, "Malignant Melanoma and Exposure to Flourescent Lighting at Work," *Lancet*, 7 August 1982, pp. 290–93.
On ionization-type detectors, see Center for Science in the Public Interest, *Household Pollutants Guide*, pp. 223–24.

properties easily available to housewives buying plastic furniture, drapes, toys, rugs, foams, lacquers, or adhesives.

All consumers are affected by product safety questions and all suffer from lack of adequate information about, and control over, what enters their homes. Yet since women are charged with the care and protection of households, they are in a particularly difficult situation. Several years ago mothers were encouraged to buy children's sleepwear treated with fire retardants. Tris—one of the products used to treat such sleepwear—was later identified as a potential carcinogen, and in 1977 it was banned in the United States.[53] This episode highlights the extent to which the household can be permeated by all the excesses of an inadequately regulated industry. Industry, however, prefers to imagine that home and work are two separate spheres. It can then ignore its responsibility for home health and safety, and insist that this is the woman's responsibility.

Industry has a different view when it comes to industrial accidents, however. Since a good wife is the custodian of the industrial worker "off-the-job," it is her duty to provide a harmonious home environment so that the worker's mind will be "uncluttered with worry and concern about personal problems."[54] If a woman does not keep her man happy, his attention may lapse and a routine job procedure may become a "crippler—or a killer."[55] This message shifts the responsibility for industrial accidents to bad wives. This equation must be turned on its head: industry must bear responsibility for *household* and *workplace* safety.

Conclusion: Strategies

Women, alone in their households, cannot successfully resist the stresses and hazards of domestic labor. The women's movement has provided significant encouragement in bringing women together to identify and solve their problems. Drop-in centers, self-help groups, newspapers, books, and public education programs for new mothers, displaced homemakers, and battered wives have served women in many ways. They provide immediate crisis support, they break down women's tendency to personalize domestic problems, and they offer the model and experience of collective action for personal and political goals.

The struggles women engage in are varied. They range from fighting for good, inexpensive daycare, to working for changes in divorce laws, to organizing around issues of equal pay for work of equal value. When women realize that the quality of their household environment is determined by forces outside the home, they may also join the struggles of consumer groups and ecology activists to fight the excesses of industry. (See Freudenberg and Zaltzberg in this volume.) These and many other efforts directly or indirectly enhance the power of women who work in the home, offering them new maneuverability and new choices. These struggles break down the isolating barriers between household and community.

But another barrier must also be breached, the division between home and workplace. It is in industry's interest to see these as scparate spheres, but it is not in the interests of women or workers. One obvious link that must be forged is between unions and housewives. This link already exists in the "wives' committees" that sometimes appear to offer support to strikers, but broader and longer term connections need to be made. Women need to know more about household chemicals, pollutants, and hazards— information also sought by union health and safety committees. Unions need to learn that these problems do not stop at the factory gates. Joint educational and political programs mobilizing wage workers and domestic workers can be important in achieving mutually desired goals.

Creating links between home and workplace also has important implications for breaking down the barriers between men and women. The present system that identifies domestic life as a woman's major task and the workplace as a predominantly male sphere creates the conditions whereby men and women can feel exploited by the other. It is not enough to get women into wage work. Men must also be brought into domestic labor—child care, housework, emotional support—in deeper, more committed ways. To do so—by demanding a shorter work week and extensive paternity as well as maternity leave, for instance, will inevitably transform both wage work and domestic labor. The home will no longer be seen as a reward for men's "real" work, but as a worksite itself where both tedious and rewarding tasks are carried out.

Notes

Much of the theoretical material presented in this essay is the outcome of a long and enjoyable collaboration with Meg Luxton. I urge readers who are interested in a fuller discussion of housework as a labor process to read Luxton's book, *More than a Labor of Love* (Toronto: The Women's Press, 1980). Many others kindly shared information and insights, and I wish to extend thanks to Ann Woodsworth and Joanne Robertson of Pollution

Probe in Toronto, Marianne Langton, Paula Webster, Susan Schecter, and most especially Lorna Weir for invaluable assistance in gathering data on household pollutants and hazards.

1. See, for example, Monique Proulx, *Five Million Women: A Study of the Canadian Housewife* (Ottawa: Advisory Council on the Status of Women, 1978), pp. 35-50.
2. Ellen Malos, ed., *The Politics of Housework* (London: Allison and Busby, 1980), pp. 7-43.
3. For the political implications of such analyses see Susan Harding, "Family Reform Movements: Recent Feminism and Its Opposition," *Feminist Studies* 7, no. 1 (1981): 57-75.
4. See Louise Brown, "Today's 'Slaves'—Immigrant Women Working as Maids," *Toronto Star*, 11 January 1979; Norma Drummond and Maria Lee, "Working Paper on Immigrant Women in the Workplace," paper presented to a meeting of the Health Advocacy Unit, Toronto, March 1981; "Domestics," *Wages for Housework Campaign Bulletin* 5, no. 1 (Spring 1981).
5. Quoted in Robert Lekachman, *Economists at Bay: Why the Experts Will Never Solve Your Problems* (New York: McGraw-Hill, 1976), p. 117.
6. *Toronto Star*, 5 March 1982.
7. Margrit Eichler, "The Prestige of Occupation Housewife," in *The Working Sexes*, ed. Patricia Marchak (University of British Columbia: The Institute of Industrial Relations, 1977).
8. A list of exceptions includes: Ann Oakley, *The Sociology of Housework* (Bath: Martin Robinson, 1974) and *Woman's Work: The Housewife Past and Present* (New York: Vintage Books, 1976); Lillian Rubin, *Worlds of Pain: Life in the Working-Class Family* (New York: Basic Books, 1976); Luxton, *More than a Labor of Love*.
9. Rayna Rapp, "Family and Class in Contemporary America: Notes Toward an Understanding of Ideology," *Science and Society* (1979): 278-300.
10. Karen L. Adams and Norma C. Ware, "Sexism and the English Language: The Linguistic Implications of Being a Woman," in *Women: A Feminist Perspective*, ed. Jo Freeman (Palo Alto: Mayfield Publishing Co., 1979), pp. 487-504.
11. Susan Harding, "Women and Words in a Spanish Village," in *Toward an Anthropology of Women*, ed. Rayna R. Reiter (New York: Monthly Review Press, 1975), pp. 290-91.
12. Robert A. Karasek, Sr., "Job Demands, Job Decision Latitude, and Mental Strain: Implications for Job Redesign," *Administrative Science Quarterly* 24 (1979): 285-308.
13. Janet Bertinuson, "The Unseen Hazard: Stress on the Job," *LOHP Monitor*, March-April 1979.
14. Interview with the author in 1981.
15. Dorothy E. Smith, "Women, the Family, and Corporate Capitalism," in *Women in Canada*, ed. Marylee Stephenson (Toronto: New Press, 1973), pp. 2-35.

16. Lillian Rubin, "The Marriage Bed," *Psychology Today*, August 1976.
17. Oakley, *The Sociology of Housework*.
18. I. Boszormenyi-Nagy and G. M. Spark, *Invisible Loyalties: Intergenerational Family Therapy* (New York: Harper and Row), p. 203; emphasis added.
19. G. Brown, M. Chrdchain, and T. Harris, "Social Class and Psychiatric Disturbances Among Women in an Urban Population," *Sociology* 9 (1975): 225-54.
20. Herbert J. Freudenberger and G. Richelson, *Burn-Out* (New York: Doubleday, 1980).
21. Luxton, *More Than a Labor of Love*, p. 196.
22. Proulx, *Five Million Women*, p. 33.
23. Some would argue that these calculations are low because they do not account for the many jobs done simultaneously or for the managerial work of coordinating jobs.
24. Alan Seltzer, "Postpartum Mental Syndrome," *Canadian Family Physician* 26 (1980): 2549. See H. Rosenberg, "Motherwork, Depression, and Stress: Post-Partum Depression as a Symptom of on the Job Stress," paper presented at the Canadian Sociology and Anthropology Association Meetings, Halifax, 1981, for a longer discussion of medical responses to post-partum depression.
25. Hannah Gavron, *The Captive Wife: Conflicts of Household Mothers* (London: Routledge and Kegan Paul, 1966).
26. Rae Andre, *Homemakers: The Forgotten Workers* (Chicago: University of Chicago Press, 1981), p. 189.
27. Ibid., p. 217.
28. Ibid., pp. 217-18.
29. Pearl Goldman, "Violence Against Women in the Family," Master of Laws thesis, McGill University, Montreal, p. 49.
30. Dorothy Smith, "Women, the Family, and Corporate Capitalism," in *Women in Canada*, pp. 2-35.
31. *Calgary Herald*, 29 June 1979. A Michigan police officer at a recent conference stated that even though wife-beating is chronic among police officers, "because they are used to using force to control a situation," they are able to "de-personalize the incidents they cover. Even if they are wife-beaters, I think they lay charges" (*Toronto Globe & Mail*, 22 July 1982). A Winnipeg, Manitoba, study found that wife-batterers were predominantly from three occupational groups: truck driver, police officer, and doctor (unpublished ms. by workers of Osborne House Women's Shelter, Winnipeg, Manitoba, 1977; cited in Linda MacLeod, *Wife Battering in Canada: The Vicious Circle* [Canadian Advisory Council on the Status of Women, Ministry of Supply and Services, Canadian Government Center, Hull, Quebec, 1980], p. 14).
32. On sexual refusal and extramarital affairs, see Peter D. Chimbos, "Marital Violence: A Study of Husband-Wife Homicide," in *The Canadian Family*, ed. K. Ishwaran (New York: Holt, Rinehart, and Winston, 1976), pp. 580-99. See also Susan K. Steinmetz, *The Cycle of Violence:*

Assertive, Aggressive, and Abusive Family Interaction (New York: Praeger, 1977), p. 77.

33. *Toronto Star*, 22 July 1982.

34. MacLeod, *Wife Battering*, p. 30. In Canada, when a parliamentary report on wife-battering was presented to the House of Commons on May 1982, male members of the house burst out laughing. Women MPs and women across Canada protested their "appalling" outburst. A director of a shelter for battered women said: "If one in ten husbands beats his wife and there are 282 seats in the House of Commons, in all likelihood at least 20 of those politicians beat their own wives." *Toronto Star*, 14 May 1982.

35. Survey by the Hospital for Sick Children, (Toronto, Canada), 1979, cited in *Toronto Globe & Mail*, 17 February 1982.

36. "Top 50 Supermarket Product Advertisers," *Progressive Grocer*, December 1976.

37. "Poison in the Home," *The Searcher*, 12 June 1971, p. 15.

38. A common example of the habit for blaming women for poisonings in the home is a pamphlet by the Canadian Pharmaceutical Association entitled "Children and Poison Don't Mix." No mention is made of inadequate labelling or manipulative advertising; instead women are told that "accidental poisoning need not happen . . . it's up to you."

39. Center for Science in the Public Interest, *The Household Pollutants Guide* (Garden City, N.Y.: Anchor Books, 1978), pp. 197-203.

40. *Consumer Reports* 44, no. 6 (June 1979): 364.

41. *Household Pollutants Guide*, pp. 130-31.

42. See Molly Peter, "Eight Women Make a Difference: The Halting of 2,4,5-T," *Women's Health Network*, 19: 4. See also *Household Pollutants Guide*, p. 131; and Lawrence Fishbein, "An Overview of Potential Mutagenic Problems Posed by Some Pesticides and Their Trace Impurities," *Environmental Health Perspectives* 27: 126-27.

43. *Household Pollutants Guide*, p. 131; Fishbein, "An Overview," p. 127.

44. Ross H. Hall, "A New Approach to Pest Control in Canada," *Canadian Environmental Advisory Council*, Report No. 10, July 1981, p. 48; Toby Vigod and Anne Woodsworth, "Captan: The Legacy of the IBT Affair," Submission on Pesticide Law and Policy to the Consultative Committee on IBT Pesticides on Behalf of the Canadian Environmental Law Association and Pollution Probe, February 1982; press release, Pollution Probe (Toronto, Canada), 10 March, 1982. For information on the IBT case, see Keith Schneider, "Faking It," *Amicus Journal* 4, no. 4 (1983): 14–26.

45. Committee on Indoor Pollutants, Board on Toxicology and Environmental Health Hazards, Assembly of Life Sciences, National Research Council (United States), "Indoor Pollutants," Executive Summary, 1981, pp. 1-15.

46. Gloria Naurocki, "Safety Clips: Women and Falls, *National Safety News* 116, no. 1 (1977): 77.

47. "Home Accidents Rank High," *Occupational Health Bulletin* 7–8 (1970): 3–4; and Naurocki, "Safety Clips."

48. "Home Accidents."
49. "The Unseen Menace: A Glass Door," *Dimensions/NBS* 60, no. 2 (1976): 3-5.
50. Ibid.
51. *Household Pollutants Guide*, pp. 191-96.
52. Ibid.; and York-Toronto Lung Association, *Environmental Health Hazards in the Community, Home, Classroom and Workplace*, 1980, p. 45.
53. *Consumer Reports* 45, no. 8 (August 1980): 468-69.
54. Jim Johnson, "How the Little Woman Keeps Her Man Safe," *Industrial Supervisor* 38, no. 9 (1974): 12.
55. Ibid., p. 13.

12
From Grassroots Activism to Political Power: Women Organizing Against Environmental Hazards

Nicholas Freudenberg and Ellen Zaltzberg

Hardeman County, Tennessee[1]

In 1964 the Velsicol Chemical Company brought a 242-acre farm in rural Hardeman County, Tennessee. The company soon dumped 300,000 55-gallon barrels of unknown chemicals on the site. The bulldozer that covered the barrels burst some of them open and their contents seeped into the soil.

In 1967 a U.S. Geological Survey report showed that the chemicals from the dump site were reaching the water wells of the families that lived on the road. No action was taken. Five years later, the Tennessee Department of Public Health ordered Velsicol to close the dump.

By 1977 residents began to notice that their drinking water had a foul odor and taste. Among those who lived near the dump was Nell Grantham, a licensed practical nurse, and her family. Her neighbors included her parents, her brothers and sisters, and their families. The residents' requests for an analysis of their water went unheeded for several months. When the local health department finally ran tests, they looked only for bacteria. Finding none, the health officer said the water was safe.

But Grantham and her relatives were dissatisfied, so they brought a sample of their water to the laboratories of the State Water Quality Division. After making its own tests, the Water Quality Division brought the Granthams some grim views: their water contained twelve chemicals, including five known cancer-causing substances—benzene, chlordane, heptachlor, endrin, and dioxin.

As the state ran more tests, which were then confirmed by the U.S. Environmental Protection Agency (EPA), the Granthams were given ever stricter rules. They were first advised not to drink the water or to cook with it. They were next told not to bathe in it, and then told that vegetables should not be grown on their property, nor animals raised on it. A neighbor's hog was found to be highly contaminated with chemicals. Finally, after several months of having water shipped in by National Guard tank trucks, the residents were connected to the public water system of a nearby town. Eventually the quality of that water was also challenged.

Media coverage forced Velsicol to admit that its dump *might* be the cause of the problem. Meanwhile, the residents were experiencing a host of health problems. Skin rashes were common. A child was born with a serious birth defect. Following that birth, no child was conceived in the area for more than four years. An environmental health survey by scientists from the University of Cincinnati Medical Center found evidence of liver damage in some exposed individuals, which they attributed to the contaminated drinking water.[2]

While residents were frightened by the ill effects they suffered, they were even more alarmed about the future. As Nell Grantham put it, "Who knows? In twenty years my kids may have cancer. I may never have grandchildren. I may not even live to see my kids grown. That's something we don't know. That's something no one knows. But when you've been drinking contaminated water with chemicals that you know can cause cancer, that makes it look worse. My kids are my biggest concern. What kind of life are they gonna have?"[3]

As a result of these problems a group of eighty people living close to the dump have filed a $2.5 billion class action suit against Velsicol Chemical Company. Others have received from $12,000 to $15,000 in out-of-court settlements. The residents have also demonstrated, petitioned, and written countless letters to local, state, and federal officials. As Grantham put it, "I may not get but ten cents [from the suit], but they'll know I've been there—the state of Tennessee and Velsicol too."[4]

Grantham has become a leader of a new statewide coalition, Tennesseans Against Chemical Hazards (TEACH). Composed of eleven community groups across the state, TEACH does public education, legislative lobbying, and supports local action against polluters. It is also seeking a new statewide tax that would require that chemical companies contribute to a fund to clean up abandoned dump sites.

Rutherford, New Jersey[5]

Rutherford, New Jersey, is a comfortable suburb only eight miles from New York City. Many of its residents moved there to escape the more industrial landscape of the surrounding areas. One such family was the Cleffis. For Vivian Cleffi, a housewife, and her husband Jim, a trucker, Rutherford seemed the ideal place to raise their three sons.

Then in 1975 their oldest son, eight-year-old Jimmy, developed a rare form of leukemia. In the waiting room of the New York City cancer specialist who was treating Jimmy, Vivian Cleffi met two other Rutherford parents whose children had leukemia. Alarmed by this unlikely coincidence, Cleffi began making phone calls. With the help of the Parent-Teacher Association at her children's school, she ultimately found eleven cases of leukemia and Hodgkin's disease, a related cancer of the lymph system. Six of the victims had attended the same elementary school.

A group of concerned parents then organized a group called We Who Care, which met regularly with the PTA, church groups, and local health department officials to plan strategy, share information, and investigate rumors. At one meeting held at the school, 700 parents were informed by a New Jersey state epidemiologist that Rutherford's leukemia rate for children aged five to nineteen was six times higher than the national average.

Activists from We Who Care began to look for causes of the cancer cluster. Their research did not reassure them. Forty-two industrial concerns using organic chemicals—many of them known carcinogens—were located within three miles of the school. On two sides of the town is the Hackensack Meadowlands, a swamp that was being sprayed for mosquitos with between 50,000 and 100,000 pounds of insecticides every year. Until it was banned in 1967, DDT, a proven carcinogen, was one of them. Two major highways flanked the town. Automobile exhaust, the single most important air pollutant in the United States, is suspected of contributing to some forms of cancer. Finally, Rutherford sits at the convergence of microwave beams from two airports and an industrial research facility. Some experts believe that microwave radiation can cause cancer.

Faced with organized community concern and a barrage of media coverage, the New Jersey departments of health and environmental protection began investigations. But despite seemingly determined efforts—an epidemiological survey and air, water, and soil sampling—the state was never able to find a specific cause for the cancer cluster.[6]

While the state's failure to pinpoint a cause disappointed the town, We Who Care did not disband. The group brought in its own researchers to conduct further studies. It critiqued the official investigation and forced the state to make further tests. It organized a telephone squad that deluged officials with calls whenever chemical odors appeared in the town. The group's efforts also forced a nearby plant to shut down because it used benzene, a known cause of leukemia when used without adequate precautions.

We Who Care also achieved some long-term results. With the support of labor and environmental groups, it forced New Jersey to establish a cancer registry, an important tool for future epidemiological research. One activist was appointed to the town's board of health, and the town's health department has as a result become more actively involved in environmental health issues. Local newspapers now cover environmental stories regularly. The local PTA developed a cancer prevention education program that has served as a model for schools across the country.

Despite these advances, however, the fear has not left Rutherford. Vivian Cleffi, whose son Jimmy died only three months after he was diagnosed, observed: "You look at the kids and here they are, they're playing in the same rotten air. You look at them and you can't help thinking to yourself, which one of them is going to be next?"[7]

Pine Ridge Reservation, South Dakota[8]

On the Pine Ridge Reservation in South Dakota local members of Women of All Red Nations (WARN), an affiliate of the American Indian Movement, became concerned about high rates of miscarriage and birth defects on their reservation. A household survey and interviews with hospital workers revealed that in one month in 1979, 38 percent of the pregnant women on the reservation suffered miscarriages, compared to the normal rate of between 10 and 20 percent. A doctor at a local hospital issued a report showing extremely high rates of cleft palate and other birth defects, as well as hepatitis, jaundice, and serious diarrhea. Health officials confirmed that the reservation had higher than average rates of bone and gynecological cancers.

WARN investigators uncovered a plethora of environmental hazards. Inadequate sewage treatment facilities had led to fecal contamination of drinking and bathing water. Widespread spraying of pesticides to control grasshoppers and prairie dogs, and of herbicides such as 2,4-D (a component of the Vietnam defoliant Agent Orange), further threatened the water supply.

Tests done by government officials also showed high levels of radioactivity in the water. The reservation is downwind from old mines surrounded by uranium tailings. Furthermore, in the last few years, 12,000 exploratory holes were drilled in the area by energy companies looking for uranium; many of these drill sites had been improperly capped. In 1962 a major spill of radioactive wastes contaminated the Cheyenne River, which flows through the reservation. It was never cleaned up. WARN also suspects that an old air force gunnery range on the reservation was used as a dump site for nuclear waste.

Unlike other groups created specifically to combat environmental problems, WARN is a multi-issue group that existed before the Pine Ridge health hazard situation became known. Founded in 1978, WARN is a national grassroots organization of Native American women that seeks to "protect the health, culture, and lives of their families and communities." Among the other issues the group has addressed are land use for energy development, political repression of Native American activists, sterilization abuse of Native American women, and child care and schooling problems.

WARN's experience in political action guided its response to the health problems and environmental hazards it had uncovered. After completing the health survey, WARN activists called a press conference to announce their preliminary findings. They demanded an independent health study by reputable researchers, emergency shipment of clean drinking water until the existing water supply could be made safe, the development of an ongoing system for monitoring water quality, and an end to further energy development in the area.

To support its demands, WARN obtained affidavits from sympathetic health professionals. It hired independent consultants to test water quality. Its lawyer used the Freedom of Information Act to obtain more evidence from government agencies. Relevant officials in the state and federal governments were besieged with telegrams. On the reservation, the group distributed fact sheets describing the problem and their demands. The community councils of various tribes on the reservation were encouraged to pass resolutions of support. WARN members also met regularly with tribal leaders to pressure them to act. They presented their findings to a United Nations conference on tribal peoples.

As a result of public pressure, the Center for Disease Control conducted an investigation of the Pine Ridge Reservation. Its report concluded that no unusual health problems could be detected, a finding that contradicted the residents' experience. A new privately funded community health program was set up in 1982; its focus, however, was on individual health behavior rather than on environmental hazards. As of 1982, no action to eliminate the hazards had been taken, and no water had been shipped in despite a drought that had left certain areas without drinking water for two weeks. Political and legal action aimed at correcting the situation continues.

Alsea, Oregon[9]

Alsea is a small logging community in rural Oregon. In the spring of 1975 Bonnie Hill, an English teacher at the local high school, suffered a miscarriage. Her search into its cause began a struggle that pitted local women and Alsea's health officer against the U.S. Forest Service, commercial timber companies, and the Dow Chemical Company. Aware that some of her former students had also recently had miscarriages, Hill began an investigation. She contacted these women to find out when the miscarriages had occurred, where the women lived, and what factors they might have in common. Hill also began looking for clues in the medical and scientific literature. She came across an article linking dioxin, a contaminant in the herbicides used in the defoliant Agent Orange, with reproductive problems in monkeys. A call to the Bureau of Land Management revealed that 2,4,5-T, a phenoxyherbicide in Agent Orange, had been sprayed in her area a month before her miscarriage. Foresters spray 2,4,5-T to suppress growth of unwanted vegetation.

Although this process took almost three years, by the spring of 1978 Hill had investigated eleven miscarriages experienced by eight women. All had occurred within several weeks of the spraying season. Hill then began to collect more specific information on spraying practices. Despite the unwillingness of government agencies and timber companies to give her information, she was able to demonstrate that most of the women lived within one-half to two miles of known spray sites.

At this point, the women who had been involved in the survey decided that they needed outside help if they were to take the matter any further. They wrote a letter summarizing their findings to the local county health officer and requested a more systematic study. They also notified the press, local elected officials, and federal agencies of their discovery.

Responding to this pressure, the U.S. Environmental Protection Agency decided to investigate. EPA's involvement in the issue proved problematic, however; not only did it ignore suggestions made by the women who had done the preliminary work, but it hired as a consultant a physician with ties to the timber industry. Nevertheless, its study confirmed that there was a higher rate of miscarriage in the study area than in control regions. Despite challenges to the EPA's methodology (from the timber companies as well as from Bonnie Hill's group), the courts ordered a temporary ban on the spraying of certain phenoxyherbicides.

Dow Chemical Company then challenged the ban in court,

arguing that it was based on inadequate research. Dow offered an alternative explanation which attributed the higher rates of miscarriage to alleged marijuana used among women in Oregon, although it presented no convincing evidence to support this claim. In a 1983 Long Island court case filed by Vietnam veterans exposed to Agent Orange, Dow submitted a motion stating that as early as 1969 (two years before Agent Orange use was halted in Vietnam) both the company and the U.S. government were aware of evidence that the dioxin in 2,4,5,-T might cause birth defects in the children of women exposed to the defoliant. Finally, in October 1983, Dow withdrew 2,4,5,-T from the market "because of public concern and public misinformation." Their decision marked a victory for the women of Alsea.

Harlem, New York City[10]

While taking her child to school in Harlem one day in 1978, Helene Brathwaite noticed a white powder flaking off the ceilings in the corridors of the school. Having recently watched a television report on asbestos problems in schools, she became concerned. As the newly elected president of the school's Parents' Association, she felt she ought to investigate.

The response to her initial questioning of the school custodian was unsatisfactory, but after persistent inquiries her fears were confirmed: asbestos was flaking off the ceiling in several places in the school. A work order had been sent in for repairs, but no remedial action had been taken. The school authorities were not especially concerned. Yes, they would correct the situation, but it posed no imminent hazard to the children.

Brathwaite and other officers of the Parents' Association were not reassured. They had read that asbestos was one of the most potent cancer-causing substances known. A few reports in the literature showed that some children had gotten asbestos-related cancer after only brief exposure to asbestos dust brought home from work on their fathers' clothing. Since it takes between ten and thirty years for asbestos to cause cancer, the parents felt that their children faced a lifetime of concern over the possibility.

With its own funds, the Parents' Association hired a private laboratory to conduct tests in the schools. They also contacted public interest groups and environmental health experts. When the report came in that there were high levels of asbestos in the school, the Parents' Association decided to act, and called a community meeting to present the findings. At the meeting the parents decided that the school had to be closed, but they also insisted that their children's education not be disrupted: entire classes, with their teachers, must be bussed to neighboring schools. The parents also demanded a voice in determining the procedures to be used to correct the hazard. Not only did they refuse a band-aid repair job, but they also suggested specific methods for protecting the workers who made the repairs.

Brathwaite helped to organize a telephone hot line to answer parents' questions and to dispel rumors. Regular media coverage and some support from elected officials helped keep the pressure on the school board. A boycott of the school by the parents finally forced official action. Ultimately, the school was closed for seven months. More than $100,000 was spent on repairs, leading most parents to feel that the school was relatively safe.

But there were failures as well. A plan for ongoing health testing and follow-up surveys for the exposed children never materialized. This lack of baseline data will make it difficult to assess whether the asbestos did in fact contribute to any health problems that arise in the future.

A survey by the New York City Board of Education in 1977 showed that more than four hundred schools had asbestos problems. Although the Harlem parents developed a model for remediation, few other schools have been repaired as extensively, though many have worse problems.

The five case histories just described are not isolated events. Toxic chemicals and other hazardous materials pose a serious and growing threat to the health of all people in the United States. The air we breathe, the water we drink, the land on which we build our homes and schools, and the highways we travel are being contaminated by a constantly expanding brew of health-damaging substances. Between 1940 and 1980 the production of synthetic chemicals increased from 10 billion pounds to more than 350 billion pounds a year.[11] Each year, 1,000 new compounds are added to the estimated 70,000 chemicals already in regular use.[12]

In 1980, the United States produced 125 billion pounds of hazardous waste, enough to fill approximately 3,000 Love Canals.[13] By the year 2000, current annual production of hazardous wastes is expected to double.[14] In the mid-1970s, 90 percent of hazardous wastes were being disposed of by environmentally unsound methods.[15] These wastes have contributed to groundwater contamination on a local basis in all parts of the nation and on a regional basis in some heavily populated and industrialized areas. The House Subcommittee on Environment, Energy, and Natural Resources in 1980 listed 250 dump sites that "present a great potential threat to drinking water supplies."[16] Once a water supply source is contaminated it is nearly impossible to detoxify it.

Nor are toxic chemical threats to health limited to waste products. Each year more than 1 billion pounds of pesticides are sprayed on our crops, forests, gardens, and roadways.[17] Agricultural experts believe that even greater amounts will be needed in the future to maintain current levels of agricultural and lumber production.

The transportation of hazardous materials poses another set of risks. Every second over 125 tons of hazardous chemicals move onto the nation's highways, rails, and waterways.[18] In 1978 there were 18,000 accidents involving rail, highway, and water transport of dangerous substances, an eightfold increase since 1971.[19] Injuries from these incidents increased by 400 percent in the same period.[20] An accident involving a truck transporting nuclear wastes could cause a major disaster. According to data from the Oak Ridge National Laboratory, the nuclear industry will have to ship over 75,000 truckloads of used and dangerous fuel over the next twenty-five years.[21] While the likelihood of a serious accident is low, the consequences, according to one expert, could include "thousands of prompt or latent cancer deaths and injuries."[22]

Nuclear power creates still other hazards. In 1980 the 69 licensed and operable atomic reactors in the United States reported 3,804 mishaps.[23] The Nuclear Regulatory Commission's first national survey in 1981 found fifteen of fifty plants "below average in management control, maintenance, radiation and fire protection, and overall compliance with operating regulations."[24] The most persistent problem is the disposal of high-level radioactive wastes, some of which remain dangerous for 250,000 years. Although no permanent burial place has yet been found for these wastes, commercial nuclear power plants have more than 8,000 tons of them in temporary storage tanks.[25] Military activities, especially the production of nuclear weapons, have generated even more such waste.[26]

A variety of other suspected or proven hazards exist across the United States: high voltage powerlines, improperly disposed mining wastes, industrial emissions sent directly into the air or water, testing and storage of military products such as nerve gas or other weapons, contamination of animal or human food.[27]

What are the health consequences of human exposure to the array of chemicals and other toxic substances contaminating our environment? Unfortunately, scientific evidence is limited. Research is difficult for several reasons: few toxic chemicals are found in isolation from others, many carcinogens do not cause cancer until between ten and thirty years after exposure, government and industry have not seen environmental health research as a priority. Nevertheless, combining the evidence that exists with anecdotal reports from disaster areas gives no cause for complacency. Known or suspected carcinogens have been found at dump sites and in public drinking water around the country.[28] Communities situated near toxic disposal sites have reported higher than average rates of spontaneous abortion, congenital anomalies, kidney and liver disorders, and skin problems.[29] While few of these findings have been confirmed by rigorous epidemiological studies, the persistence and recurrence of similar complaints lends weight to a causal relationship.

Pesticide exposure has been linked to cancer, liver disease, skin disorders, and altered semen quality.[30] Widespread spraying of pesticides and herbicides on croplands, forests, gardens, and highway and railroad rights-of-way means that millions of people have some contact with these substances. Pesticides have been found in human breast milk throughout the country.[31]

Exposure to low-level radiation has been associated with higher rates of leukemia, thyroid disorders, birth defects and mental retardation, and other illnesses.[32] While scientists debate what levels of radiation endanger health, there is as yet no proof that any amount of exposure is safe.

Deaths from accidents involving the transport of hazardous materials are few so far, but the potential for disaster is great. In many urban areas hundreds of trucks carrying toxic materials cross residential streets daily. A single explosion or spill could kill or injure thousands of people.

Environmental disasters can create psychological as well as physical damage. Research at Three Mile Island in Pennsylvania, as well as reports from Love Canal, show mental distress, family disruption, and emotional disturbances among children as sequels of those episodes.[33]

The most convincing evidence of the risk of exposure to environmental contaminants, however, comes from the occupational setting. Each year, 100,000 U.S. workers die from occupational illnesses, and almost 400,000 new cases of occupational diseases are recognized.[34] Nine of every ten U.S. industrial workers are inadequately protected against exposure to at least one of the most common industrial chemicals.[35] A government report estimated that between 20 and 40 percent of all cancers are related to workplace exposure.[36] U.S. workers are the canaries sent into the mine for the U.S. people. As the silenced canaries warned the miners of imminent danger, so too do workers who experience disease and death serve as a warning to the general population of what is in store for all of us should we fail to control human contact with toxic materials.

Over the last two decades, the environmental and labor movements have helped to win passage of federal legislation designed to control human exposure to toxic chemicals. The Clean Air and Water Acts, the Toxic Substances Control Act, the Resource Conservation and Recovery Act, the Safe Drinking Water Act, the Occupational Safety and Health Act, among others, have created a foothold for environmentalism within the federal bureaucracy. In the 1970s the Environmental Protection Agency, the Council on Environmental Quality, and the Occupational Safety and Health Administration became arenas in which environmentalists and corporations battled over regulatory policy. But during the Reagan administration the federal government's already limited commitment to environmental protection has plummeted. By the end of fiscal 1982, Reagan had cut EPA's staff by 40 percent.[37] The administration has attempted to weaken regulations on hazardous wastes, lead, and air pollution.[38] Enforcement of existing laws has dropped precipitously.[39] In 1983 Congressional investigators alleged that high EPA officials doctored government reports, delayed the cleanup of toxic dump sites in order to benefit the electoral campaigns of Republicans, and refused to turn over data on enforcement actions to Congress. As a result of this scandal, President Reagan was forced to replace the entire top management of that agency.[40] But the new team of former corporate managers brought into the executive suite took no action to reverse EPA's pro-business orientation.

This drop in federal action on the environment comes despite broad public support for such protection. Recent polls by the *New York Times* and Louis Harris show that a majority of the U.S. people favor continued strong protection of the environment, even if it requires economic sacrifice.[41] According to the Harris poll, 80 percent of the public believes that the Clean Air Act should be strengthened or maintained, rather than weakened.[42]

The increase in environmental threats to health and the decline in government action to protect people account for the groundswell of community opposition to pollution. The case histories illustrate both the range and depth of this opposition. In this section, we discuss in more detail the role that women have played in organizing community opposition to toxic chemicals and other hazardous materials, and assess the impact of environmental activism on the lives of the women involved and on the environmental movement.

The discussion is based on three sources: First, we interviewed a dozen women active in environmental organizing, asking them to describe their struggles and the problems they encountered. Second, we conducted a survey of community groups involved in environmental health action around the country as part of a broader research project investigating citizen involvement in controlling environmental health hazards. Names of grassroots organizations were solicited from national and local environmental, public interest, health, and women's groups. A total of 242 groups received questionnaires; 110 (45 percent) answered. Respondents were asked about the nature of the hazard they were fighting, the health problems observed, the methods of community education and organization used, and the processes and structure of their group. While the sample is not necessarily representative of all local groups involved in the control of environmental hazards, it does include a broad cross-section of such groups from every region of the country. Finally, we reviewed some of the feminist literature on women's role in community organizing, looking for similarities and differences between women's involvement in environmental organizing and their participation in other kinds of community work, e.g., struggles over housing, health care, or education.

The Role of Women

Women played a key role in each of the community groups we interviewed. They made the telephone calls, stuffed the envelopes, organized the demonstrations, and wrote the press releases. While the survey showed that the vast majority (96 percent) of local environmental groups included both males and females, our interviews revealed that women often constitute the backbone of local organizations. In each of the groups we studied in depth, virtually all the most active members were women. Groups were four times more likely to have leadership that was mostly female than mostly male; however, the majority of groups (80 percent) reported leaders of both sexes.

Other investigators have observed that women play a key role in tenant organizing in New York City, neighborhood organizing in England, and in the current disarmament movement.[43] Several aspects of women's social roles in the family and community, and in their broader socialization, may explain this involvement. In our survey we asked respondents to rank various concerns that motivated people in their region to take action against an environmental hazard. The concern that ranked highest was the fear that the hazard might endanger children and future generations.

Because women have traditionally been responsible for most child care, it is not surprising that they should feel the need to counter threats to their children's health. Their intimate contact with children, their feelings of responsibility for them, and their

Bill Dyviniak, *Buffalo Evening News*

daily observations make women aware of changes in children's health. When asked why women participated actively in the fight against a toxic dump site, Lois Gibbs, a leader of the Love Canal struggle, replied simply, "Motherly instinct."[44] Helene Brathwaite, explaining the mothers' involvement in ridding her child's school of asbestos, said, "We're related to children in a more intimate way. We care and want to take care of children. I felt I was responsible for all these children now."[45] Women's concern for children need not be predicated on biological instincts. Rather, Brathwaite's sense of responsibility for "all these children" shows that in a social struggle familial bonds can be extended into the community.

For women who are full-time housewives or mothers, environmental issues can take on a special salience because of their greater contact with the physical environment of the community. Nell Grantham's awareness and activism around the issue of contaminated water developed in part because it was she who cooked, washed, and bathed the children. Cynthia Cockburn, a British feminist sociologist, has observed that in their roles as mothers and wives women are more likely than men to come into contact with local government services, such as the school or health care system.[46] It is these very contacts that create the opportunity for learning about and organizing against threats to health. It was in the doctor's office that Vivian Cleffi discovered other cases of leukemia in Rutherford. Both there and in Harlem, the school parents' associations played a key role in the organizing drive.

Our survey asked environmental activists which community groups they had used to spread the word about a hazard. Among the most common answers were block and neighborhood organizations, church and temple groups, and medical offices. Most frequent of all was neighbor-to-neighbor conversations. These are social networks in which women usually play dominant roles. Ronald Lawson and Stephen Barton, in their study of sex roles in the tenants' movement in New York City, came up with similar findings: they reported that women dominated the membership of tenants' organizations of all kinds and played a leadership role in organizations within a building.[47] Just as women's practice in child care reflects and is reinforced by their socialization, so too does their engagement in community networks mirror their social training. Lawson and Barton argue that "female socialization for 'interpersonal orientation, empathy sensitivity, nurturance and supportiveness' often develops a greater interpersonal sensitivity that is important to organizing, especially where people are fearful and distrustful."[48]

As Nell Grantham put it, "Women have a bigger mouth for

spreading information. We compare more—our children, their health, our water."[49] For Bonnie Hill, it was conversations with her former students which made her suspect an unusually high rate of miscarriages in her Oregon town. On the Pine Ridge Reservation, women's discussions about their health problems first brought that issue to attention.

While we lack sufficient data to draw firm conclusions as to why men get involved in environmental struggles, our impressions are that it is often for quite different reasons. For instance, Edwina Cosgriff, a leader of a successful fight to prevent the siting of huge liquid natural gas (LNG) tanks on Staten Island in New York City, has noted that men became more involved in the issue when they learned that the tanks might increase their electricity rates; women were involved from the start because of their fears of an explosion.[50] On the other hand, where the correction of an environmental hazard is perceived to threaten jobs, men have often been reluctant to take action. Corporations often play on these fears in an attempt to divide communities. Some activists have been able to counter these threats. Lois Gibbs of the Love Canal Homeowners' Association has described how men braved the threat of being fired by the Hooker Chemical Company in order to join the struggle to clean up Love Canal.[51]

A final point to consider in explaining women's prominence in community environmental struggles is that since this is a new problem, established mechanisms for resolving these crises are lacking. In our society, when official institutions are created to resolve a problem they tend to be controlled by men and located far from the neighborhood. But since community environmental hazards such as toxic wastes, nuclear power, and pesticide spraying are relatively recent phenomena, it is possible that there is a power vacuum, a free social space, that women are particularly well suited to fill because of their skills, networks, and socialization.

How Class, Race, Occupation, and Ideology Affect Environmental Activism

While the media image of the new environmental activist may be of a white middle-class suburban housewife, in fact people from all regions, all classes, and all ethnic groups have acted to protect their communities. As one activist from a multiracial community trying to force the clean-up of a toxic dump put it, "Chemicals don't know about skin color."

But like other social problems in the United States, the impact of environmental hazards differs by class and race. Truck routes for hazardous materials, for example, are more likely to pass through working class or poor communities than wealthier ones. Although a comfortable, mostly white suburb like Rutherford, New Jersey, may be downwind from several chemical factories, a mostly black city like Newark has such factories, as well as warehouses and dump sites, *within* its residential neighborhoods.

As the case histories illustrate, women of different socioeconomic classes and races have engaged in action against environmental hazards. Their style of organizing, their problems, and their perspectives have differed, reflecting the varied family structures, financial resources, social networks, cultures, and political realities of the various communities. While blacks and other urban people of color may be less likely to tackle environmental issues because other concerns—such as employment or housing—are perceived to be more urgent, when they do take on toxic contamination it is seen as a survival issue. Black activists during the Harlem school asbestos controversy and members of a group fighting to prevent the dumping of PCBs in a mostly black county in rural North Carolina assumed that the failure of the authorities to act to clean up the hazard was simply one more aspect of a broader attack on the living conditions of minorities.[52] Previous struggles (i.e., the battle for community control of the schools in New York City) had helped teach people political skills.

For Native Americans, environmental issues have been inextricably linked with the basic right to self-determination and survival. Perhaps as a result Native American activist groups have the most sophisticated political understanding of how the issues of energy development, environmental hazards, and reproductive freedom are related. As multinational companies have moved to exploit natural resources on the reservations, policies that would depopulate these areas have been vigorously pursued. Pat Bellanger, a member of Women of All Red Nations, explained, "It's genocide what they are doing. . . . The highest percentage of sterilizations are where the energy deposits are greatest. Northern Cheyenne [in Wyoming], for example, is almost 80 percent sterilized. Eighty percent of all the Indian women of child-bearing age in that area have been sterilized. In this same area, where the energy is so concentrated, there is the highest number of child placements, foster care, outside of our own families. We see the tie very clearly between energy and the family."[53]

In contrast, middle- or working-class whites involved in environmental struggles often assume that they can trust their government. Only after they become bitterly disillusioned do they mobilize politically.

Communities, depending upon whether they were rural, urban, or suburban, seem to use different communications networks. In cities, neighborhood associations, churches, parents' associations, and sometimes labor unions form the coalitions that fight environmental hazards. In the suburbs, property owners' associations as well as parent groups are often a key element. While farmers' groups often participate in some of the rural fights (i.e., the battle against high voltage powerlines in Minnesota),[54] a key organizational tactic in sparsely populated areas is person-to-person contact. The lack of other structured groups necessitates this approach.

How does women's occupational status affect their participation in community environmental struggles? According to our survey, housewives are more commonly group leaders than any other single type of worker. Nevertheless, a significant proportion of female group leaders also hold paying jobs, as teachers, health workers, clerks, or secretaries. Other research also suggests that paid work does not block women from community participation. Based on a survey in a working-class and low-income neighborhood, Sandra Schoenberg concludes that, compared to women who stay at home, "Women who do paid work were significantly more likely to attend a neighborhood meeting, and to have made an effort for a neighborhood organization in the previous six months."[55] Similarly, in their study of women's involvement in tenant organizing, Lawson and Barton conclude that outside employment does not seem to deter participation in building organizations.[56]

While quantitative evidence on the effect of paid work on environmental activism is lacking, our interviews indicate that paid work plus child care responsibilities and housework do make community organizing more difficult. As one Rutherford mother explained, "I'm working full-time now, so I don't have as much time as I did before. Traveling around the state or going to meetings every night just isn't possible."[57] Perhaps flexible organizational forms have enabled some environmental groups to support and accommodate those members with family responsibilities.

Just as race, class, and occupational status affect how women participate in environmental struggles, so too does previous political experience and political ideology. Our interviews indicate that most activists involved in community environmental issues do not have prior experience in political movements. Some feminist groups, however, have begun to work against environmental health hazards. These "ecofeminists" have been active in fights against nuclear power plants and nuclear weaponry. For these women, their environmental activism springs from a worldview that combines feminism, pacifism, and ecological concerns.[58]

The Consequences of Women's Involvement
in Environmental Health Hazards

Community environmental struggles have occasionally won con-crete victories: construction of a gas tank or toxic waste facility has been halted, families have been relocated at government expense, a nuclear power plant has been shut down, a school with asbestos problems has been adequately repaired. Although it is impossible to measure the lives saved or the diseases prevented by these successes, there can be no doubt that some children, some families, some neighborhoods are healthier as a result of community action.

Perhaps as important, however, have been the changes in women's lives as a result of these struggles. An activist from Love Canal explained the impact of her involvement in the struggle there: " I was quite shy before, but now I guess I'm an extrovert."[59] And a woman active in a fight against toxic contamination of drinking water in a small town in New Hampshire told a reporter: "When it comes home to roost, you'd be surprised how quickly private citizens can become adept at pressuring congressmen, doing complex research, making calls and generally raising hell to protect your family and your town."[60]

Women have learned how to organize petition campaigns, call press conferences, and plan strategy. These activities not only take them out of the home, but they also provide them with a new self-confidence. Said one of the leaders of the fight to block the LNG tanks on Staten Island, "Now I feel I can get involved and make a difference."[61] And Helene Brathwaite assessed the lessons of her experience: "I'm as competent now in the problem-solving area as they [the experts] are, so my approach isn't a mealymouthed one. Automatically, I expect flak, lies, placation, pacification . . . that people want me to go home and go to bed. But if a problem comes up again, I know exactly what to do."[62]

Women's engagement in environmental struggles has also changed their family lives. Some of the husbands of the activists who were interviewed help more with cooking and child care. Several women told us that their political activity has brought them a new respect and admiration from their children.

Despite these positive results, there have also been costs—for the women organizers, their families, and their communities. For many women their new-found commitment threatens their rela-tionships. At the least, there were complaints: "Aren't you over-doing it?" asked a husband of a Rutherford activist. "I've got to listen to the radio to know what the hell you're up to," complained one Love Canal husband. For others the long hours away from home, the new independence and new self-confidence led to shake-ups which culminated in divorce or separation. Nevertheless, in our survey only 11 percent of the groups actually reported that one or more of their members had a problem with a male partner objecting to his spouse's involvement in community action.

Inevitably, activism generates opposition. Many of the women we interviewed told us that some of their neighbors thought they were crazy. Nearly a third of the groups reported that neighbors occasionally opposed their efforts to correct a hazard. Often employers threatened that if the environmentalists prevailed jobs would be lost. In hard times, this form of economic blackmail can be very effective in muting opposition.

Some activists were harassed more directly. The members of the Staten Island group had their finances and personal lives examined by a private investigator hired by the utility company.[63] In Alsea, Oregon, Dow Chemical initiated a smear campaign against those activists who opposed it—the charge that the excess miscarriage rates were due to alleged marijuana use was part of it.[64]

When the community disruption caused by protests is added to the frustration caused by government inaction and the physical and emotional impact of the hazard itself, the results can be devastating for both women and their communities. As Dianne Sheley, a social worker who helped families during the Love Canal crisis, explained to a journalist, "These people always believed that government would take care of them. Starting three years ago they found that no one would take care of them. Every reason they had to trust in their country was taken away from them. They've been lied to, treated like they were crazy, and they've had to fight people they were in awe of, people like the governor and other authorities."[65]

A former Love Canal resident and activist, now separated from her husband, discussed the magnitude of the disaster: "I think people are a lot worse off now emotionally. . . . You can't go back to the way life was before. It's like starting new but I don't think any of us are going to feel secure again. We can never start fresh."[66] At Love Canal, a neighborhood was broken up to save its people. The cost of that dislocation will probably never be calculated.

In her classic essay, "Women and the Subversion of the Community," the Italian feminist Mariarosa Dalla Costa wrote:

> In the sociality of struggle women discover and exercise a power that effectively gives them a new identity. This new identity is and can only be a new degree of social power. . . . [Women's] point of departure must be precisely this willingness to destroy the role of the housewife in order to begin to come together with other women, not only as neighbors and

friends, but as workmates and anti-workmates; thus breaking the tradition of the privatized female, with all its rivalry, and reconstructing a real solidarity among women: not solidarity for defense but solidarity for attack, for the organization of the struggle.[67]

Have women involved in community environmental struggles defined a new role for themselves? While our response must be tentative, we suggest some preliminary answers based on the evidence we have gathered.

First, we believe that the women we interviewed perceived their involvement in environmental action as an extension of traditional female roles rather than as a challenge to these roles. As Cockburn observed in her analysis of women's role in community struggles in Great Britain, women became active when "what they considered their very reason for existing, the maintenance of home and children [was] threatened."[68] Yet in the process of carrying out their traditional responsibilities, these activists were in fact transformed. They learned new skills, gained self-confidence, and at least to an extent exercised political power. In confronting the government agencies or corporations responsible for the problem, they developed a new understanding of the political system. At the same time, however, relationships were broken up, neighborhoods polarized, and a certain faith and trust in society was destroyed. Whether these losses were part of a painful but ultimately rewarding process of transformation or whether they were final outcomes in themselves cannot yet be determined.

The Impact of Women's Involvement

In the last decade or so the environmental movement has broadened from a primarily middle-class phenomenon concerned about wildlife protection, pollution, conservation, and overpopulation into a much wider movement addressing the effect of industrial development on human health. The disasters at Love Canal and Three Mile Island, the anti-nuclear power movement, the growing concern about cancer, and now the movement against nuclear war have all contributed to this transformation.

As community organizers against environmental hazards, women both reflect and help create this new consciousness. Women's socially determined concern to protect the health of their families, their communities, and future generations have played a crucial role in the growth of environmental organizing. Women's active involvement in environmental organizing promises not only the possibility of reaching the 51 percent of the population that is female; it also helps to ensure that the focus of organizing will be on the compelling issue of health.

On a more tactical level, women seem to have contributed flexibility and an innovative spirit to environmental organizing. Like the Women's Strike for Peace, which used the traditional female roles of mother and wife to disarm and ridicule the House Committee on Un-American Activities in the early 1960s,[69] environmental groups have used sacrosanct images to confront corporations and the government. At Love Canal, women held a Mother's Day rally in front of the Hooker Chemical Company. On Staten Island, women and infants in baby carriages blocked cement trucks at the construction site of the LNG tanks. At another point in that struggle, an organizer wrote Pat Nixon, then the First Lady, "a woman-to-woman letter, explaining why I was afraid for my family."[70] The response to the letter stated that the storage tanks were "as safe as the gas tank in your car"—and preceded by one day an LNG explosion on Staten Island that killed forty workers.

When images of women protecting the health of their families are picked up by the mass media, they have a powerful impact on public opinion. Dow Chemical's allegation of marijuana use in Oregon or the New York State Department of Health's dismissal of the Love Canal mothers' survey (which showed high rates of birth defects) as "useless housewife data" were desperate attempts to counter these popular images. While the use of conventional images risks reinforcing stereotypes, it can also contribute to a redefinition of roles. Lois Gibbs the housewife is also Lois Gibbs the militant, implacable organizer.

According to our survey, many community environmental groups had organizational structures similar to those of the early women's movement. Decisions were usually made by discussing a problem until a consensus was reached. A few groups rotated leadership; others stressed participatory democracy. "My only function as president," said one leader, "is to activate a phone chain for meetings." Another respondent explained, "We decide we need to get together, we decide what needs to be done, and then we divide up jobs and do them."

While we do not have evidence as to the origin of these organizational forms, it does seem clear that the informal structures and the lack of hierarchy help to keep people involved. It also seems plausible that women's training in social interactions and empathy helps them to participate effectively in a group of this kind.

Another parallel between the women's and environmental movements is the integration of personal concerns, such as family health, with political action. Environmental groups have also used nonviolent but active forms of resistance, i.e., the Love Canal mothers' die-in at Hooker Chemical. A detailed examination of how movements learn from one another is beyond the scope of this chapter, but clearly environmental activists have used the forms and tactics developed by earlier social movements.

Women environmental activists have also suggested new approaches to the definition of issues and the building of coalitions. As noted earlier, Women of All Red Nations has been particularly skillful in connecting environmental hazards, energy development, and abuses of reproductive freedom. Such links create the possibility of movements that transcend a single constituency. Other groups that cross over current political boundaries are those that address both occupational and environmental threats, those that look at the immediate and long-term health dangers posed by weapons and military programs, and those antinuclear groups that combine work on health and safety hazards with research into alternative energy development. The ecofeminists have attempted to join pacifism, civil disobedience, feminism, and environmental concerns into a coherent philosophy.

The New Right's ability to mobilize a political constituency in the last decade has been attributed in part to its efforts to reach women on issues of home, family, and community. While the New Right has its own narrow definition of what these terms mean (and thus organizes women against their own real interests), nevertheless it has been the issues of abortion, teenage pregnancy, school bussing and prayer, and the Equal Rights Amendment that have brought some women into the political arena. Thus environmental issues offer the women's movement and the Left an opportunity to contest the New Right's definition of our problems. Concern about the well-being of their families, their children, future generations, and their communities has motivated many women to organize against environmental hazards. The threats to health have come very clearly from major corporations and the government that protects these companies. Most environmental activists do not have a developed anticapitalist consciousness, but they usually hate the corporations that are making them sick and wrecking their communities, and they hate the government officials who lie to them and ridicule their concerns. They understand, albeit tentatively, the need to build alliances that cross class and race lines. Moreover, unlike the New Right, the perceived enemy is not other women, activists, or people of color: it is the companies and the government. Environmental organizing places the economic system that puts profit above human health firmly on the political agenda.

It would be a mistake, however, to assume that environmental organizing is inherently progressive. Women's attempts to safeguard their families have sometimes sought simply to perpetuate traditional roles and responsibilities. The temperance movement is one such example. Right-wing organizing against water fluoridation illustrates how an environmental issue can be defined from a conservative perspective. In theory, at least, a grassroots environmental movement is vulnerable to the New Right. Nevertheless, we believe that the current environmental movement can become an important part of a progressive mass movement in the years to come. In order to protect our families, our children, and our communities, we must attack the real forces that are destroying them. And that attack will require a transformation of women's role in society. Rather than the strictly private functions of "homemaking" or commuting between home and paid job, women will have to be out in the community—mobilizing their neighbors, speaking in public, researching problems, and confronting corporations and the government. And the changes that women will have to undergo to protect their families and communities will of necessity change men as well.

The growth of movements that can challenge both environmental pollution and women's oppression requires all groups to reexamine how they define issues and choose allies. Feminists will have to look for ways to connect reproductive rights struggles with the fight against toxic chemicals. Environmentalists will have to understand that access to safe abortions and easily available child care are necessary conditions for women's active political participation. Labor activists will need to find ways to include women and community groups in campaigns for safe working conditions and against plant shutdowns.

The history of uneasy relationships among environmental groups, labor unions, feminists, and leftists means that building these new coalitions and alliances will not be easy. But the offensive launched against these groups by the Reagan administration, the New Right, and the big corporations has created new imperatives and new opportunities. Across the country, community groups have begun to organize multiconstituency coalitions to protect people against environmental hazards. Women have played a key role in that organizing. The next step is to link these community organizations into a broader movement that can convert grassroots energy into political power.

Notes

1. The case history is based on the following sources: "Together We Can Do It: Fighting Toxic Hazards in Tennessee: Interview with Nell Grantham," *Southern Exposure* 9, no. 3 (Fall 1981): 42-47; and author interview with Nell Grantham, October 1981.
2. C. S. Clark et al., "An Environmental Health Survey of Drinking Water Contamination by Leachate from a Pesticide Waste Dump in Hardeman County, Tennessee," *Archives of Environmental Health* 37, no. 1 (1982): 9-18.
3. "Together We Can Do It," p. 45.
4. Ibid., p. 46.
5. The case history is based on the following sources: Rick Levine, "Cancer Town," *New Times*, 7 August 1978, pp. 21-32; *New York Times*, 4 April 1978, p. 69; 15 April 1978, p. 51; 2 May 1978, p. 2; 10 May 1978, p. 25; and authors' interview with Carol Froehlich and Louisa Nichols, December 1981.
6. William Halperin et al., "Epidemiological Investigation of Clusters of Leukemia and Hodgkin's Disease in Rutherford, New Jersey," *Journal of the Medical Society of New Jersey* 77, no. 4 (1980): 267-73.
7. Quoted in Levine, "Cancer Town," p. 32.
8. The case history is based on the following sources: Kris Melroe, "On the Edge of Extinction," *Off Our Backs* 9, no. 5 (May 1979): 8-9; Women of All Red Nations (WARN), "Pine Ridge Reservation Health Study," February 1980 (mimeo); Lorelei Means and Madonna Gilbert, "Radiation: 'Dangerous to Pine Ridge Women,' WARN Study Says," *Akwesasne Notes*, Early Spring 1980, pp. 22-23; WARN, "Report to the Russell Tribunal: Continued Genocide of the Lakota People: Corporate Contamination of Their Water," October 1980; and telephone interview with Jacqueline Huber, attorney for WARN, April 1982.
9. The case history is based on the following sources: Norton Kalishman, A. K. Hottle, and Bonnie Hill, "A Grassroots Concern about Herbicide Spraying Leads to Nationwide Ban," paper presented at the Annual Meeting of the American Public Health Association, New York, New York, November 1979; Joseph Bell, "What Happened to My Baby?" *McCalls*, January 1980, pp. 12, 15, 16, 22; and Northwest Coalition for Alternatives to Pesticides Staff, "The Saga of 2,4,5-T," *NCAP News* 3, no. 1 (Fall-Winter 1981-82): 4-7; David Burnham, "Dow Says U.S. Knew Dioxin Peril of Agent Orange," *New York Times*, 5 May 1983, p.A:18; John Holusha, "Dow Halts Fight to Sell Herbicide," *New York Times*, 15 October 1983, p. 6.
10. The case history is based on the following sources: *New York Times*, 15 November 1978, II:2; 21 November 1978, II:2, 6 December 1978, II:2; and author interview with Helene Brathwaite, January 1982.
11. Debra L. Davis and Brian H. Magee, "Cancer and Industrial Chemical Production," *Science* 206 (1979): 1356-57.
12. *Los Angeles Times*, 31 December 1979.
13. Ralph Nader, Ronald Brownstein, and John Richard, eds., *Who's Poisoning America?* (San Francisco: Sierra Club Books, 1981), p. 24.

14. Ibid.
15. U.S. Environmental Protection Agency, Office of Solid Waste, *Everybody's Problem: Hazardous Wastes: SW-826* (Washington, D.C.: U.S. Government Printing Office, 1980).
16. *New York Times*, 20 September 1980, p. 45.
17. *New York Times*, 25 May 1982, p. C:1, 7.
18. U.S. Congress, Senate, Committee on Commerce, Science, and Transportation, *Hazardous Materials Transportation: A Review and Analysis of the Department of Transportation Regulatory Program* (Washington, D.C.: U.S. Government Printing Office, 1979).
19. Ibid.
20. Ibid.
21. Nuclear Information and Resource Center, *Nuclear Waste: Where It Comes From* (Washington, D.C.: NIRC, 1981).
22. Leonard Solon, "Public Health Perspectives in the Highway Routing of Radioactive Materials Through Populated Areas," testimony to the U.S. Department of Transportation, Materials Transportation Bureau, November 1978.
23. *New York Times*, 28 July 1981, p. B4.
24. Cited in the *New York Times*, 13 September 1981, p. 48.
25. *New York Times*, 25 August 1982, p. A12.
26. Ibid.
27. See, for example: on powerlines, Nancy Wertheimer and Ed Leeper, "Electrical Wiring Configurations and Childhood Cancer," *American Journal of Epidemiology* 109 (1979): 273-84; on mining wastes, Kai Erikson, *Everything in Its Path* (New York: Simon & Schuster, 1976); on industrial emissions, National Clean Air Coalition, *Toxic Air Pollutants* (Washington, DC: National Clean Air Coalition, 1982) and Council on Environmental Quality, *Contamination of Ground Water by Toxic Organic Chemicals* (Washington, D.C.: U.S. Government Printing Office, 1981); on military products, Rocky Flats Action Group, *Local Hazard, Global Threat* (Denver: Rocky Flats Action Group, 1977); and on food contamination, Mary Wolff, Henry Anderson, and Irving Selikoff, "Human Tissue Burdens of Halegonated Aromatic Chemicals in Michigan," *Journal of the American Medical Association* 247 (1982): 2112-16.
28. Council on Environmental Quality, *Contamination of Ground Water*.
29. Clark et al., "An Environmental Health Survey of Drinking Water Contamination"; Thomas Maugh, "Just How Hazardous Are Dumps?" *Science* 215 (1982): 490-93; *New York Times*, 8 July 1982, p. B4; 2 January 1982, pp. 1 and 7; 28 December 1981, p. A16.
30. Ephraim Kahn, "Pesticide-Related Illness in California Farm Workers," *Journal of Occupational Medicine* 18 (1976): 693-96; Samuel Epstein, *The Politics of Cancer* (New York: Anchor Press, 1979), pp. 242-81; U.S. Department of Health, Education, and Welfare, *Report of the Secretary's Commission on Pesticides and Their Relationship to Environmental Health* (Washington, D.C.: U.S. Government Printing Office, 1969); T. H. Milby and D. Wharton, "Epidemiological Assess-

ment of Occupationally Related, Chemically Induced Sperm Count Suppression," *Journal of Occupational Medicine* 22 (1980): 77-82.

31. M. Kroger, "Insecticide Residues in Human Milk," *Journal of Pediatrics* 80 (1972): 401.

32. *New York Times*, 26 September 1982, p. E20; Jean L. Marx, "Low-Level Radiation: Just How Bad Is It?" *Science* 204 (1979): 160-64.

33. *New York Times*, 13 June 1982, p. E10; David Weinberg, "Breakdown, Love Canal's Walking Wounded," *Village Voice*, 15-25 September 1981, pp. 1, 10-13.

34. National Institute for Occupational Safety and Health, *President's Report on Occupational Safety and Health* (Washington, D.C.: U.S. Government Printing Office, 1972).

35. National Institute for Occupational Safety and Health, *National Occupational Hazard Survey*, vol. 3 (Washington, D.C.: U.S. Government Printing Office, 1977).

36. National Cancer Institute, National Institute of Environmental Health Sciences, and National Institute of Occupational Safety and Health, *Estimates of the Fraction of Cancer Incidence in the United States Attributable to Occupational Factors* (Washington, D.C.: U.S. Government Printing Office, 1979).

37. William Drayton, "Can Half Do Twice As Much?" *Amicus Journal* 3 (Winter 1982): 21-24.

38. Marjorie Sun, "EPA Relaxes Hazardous Waste Rules," *Science* 216 (1982): 275-76; *New York Times*, 19 February 1982; 16 September 1982.

39. *New York Times*, 22 July 1982, p. A17.

40. Jim Jubak and Richard Asinof, "Scapegoats and Deep Throats," *Environmental Action* 14, no. 8 (1983): 8-15.

41. *New York Times*, 4 October 1981, p. 30; Louis Harris, "Hands off the Clean Air Act," *Amicus Journal* 3 (Winter 1982): 27-30.

42. Harris, "Hands Off the Clean Air Act."

43. Ronald Lawson and Stephen Barton, "Sex Roles in Social Movements: A Case Study of the Tenant Movement in New York City," *Signs* 6 (Winter 1980): 230-47; Cynthia Cockburn, *The Local State* (London: Pluto Press, 1977), p. 177.

44. Lois Gibbs, "What We Learned from Love Canal," speech at Conference on Hazardous Materials in the Metropolitan Region, Columbia University, New York, New York, June 1981.

45. Author interview with Helene Brathwaite, January 1982.

46. Cockburn, *The Local State*, pp. 58-60.

47. Lawson and Barton, "Sex Roles in Social Movements."

48. Ibid.

49. Interview with Nell Grantham, October 1981.

50. Authors' interview with Edwina Cosgriff, November 1981.

51. Gibbs, "What We Learned from Love Canal."

52. Alex Charns, "PCB Protest Unites County," *In These Times*, 29 September-5 October 1982, pp. 5-6.

53. Quoted in Melroe, "On the Edge of Extinction," p. 8.

272 / Nicholas Freudenberg and Ellen Zaltzberg

54. Barry M. Casper and Paul David Wellstone, *Powerline* (Amherst: University of Massachusetts Press, 1981).
55. Sandra Perlman Schoenberg, "Some Trends in the Community Participation of Women in their Neighborhoods," *Signs* 5, no. 3 (suppl.) (1980): 5261-68.
56. Lawson and Barton, "Sex Roles in Social Movements."
57. Interview with Carol Froelich.
58. Susan Koen and Nina Swain, *Ain't Nowhere We Can Run: Handbook for Women on the Nuclear Mentality* (Norwich, VT: Women Against Nuclear Development, 1980).
59. Quoted in Weinberg, "Breakdown," p. 11.
60. Quoted in the *New York Times*, 23 August 1981, p. 61.
61. Interview with Edwina Cosgriff.
62. Interview with Helene Brathwaite.
63. Interview with Edwina Cosgriff.
64. Bell, "What Happened to My Baby?" p. 22.
65. Quoted in Weinberg, "Breakdown," p. 10.
66. Quoted in ibid., pp. 10-11.
67. Mariarosa Dalla Costa, "Women and the Subversion of the Community," in *The Power of Women and the Subversion of the Community*, ed. Mariarosa Dalla Costa and Selma James (Bristol, England: Falling Wall Press, 1972), pp. 36-38.
68. Cockburn, *The Local State*, p. 177.
69. Amy Swerdlow, "Ladies' Day at the Capitol: Women's Strike for Peace Versus HUAC," *Feminist Studies* 8 (1982): 493-520.
70. Interview with Edwina Cosgriff.

Notes on Contributors

Robin Baker has a masters in public health and is director of the Labor Occupational Health Program at the University of California, Berkeley. A former director of the Project on Health and Safety in Electronics (PHASE) and founding member of ECOSH, she continues to serve on the governing board of the Santa Clara Center for Occupational Safety and Health.

Wendy Chavkin is a physician whose background is in obstetrics-gynecology and occupational health. She was a member of the board of Coalition of the Reproductive Rights of Workers (CRROW), chairs the Reproductive Rights Committee of NYCOSH, and has consulted for unions and community groups on the issue of environmental hazards to reproduction. She currently works with the New York City Department of Health on reproductive and occupational health issues.

Linda Coleman is a registered nurse who has worked in New York City hospitals for the last five years. She is active in the women's health movement, and is also a writer and freelance photographer.

Peggy Crull has a doctorate in developmental psychology from Columbia University and taught for six years at Herbert H. Lehman College before becoming research director of Working Women's Institute. At the Institute, a national center for information on sexual harassment on the job, she designed a number of studies on the origin and effects of sexual harassment which became the basis for her expert testimony in several ground-breaking legal cases. She is presently writing a self-help book for women which combines theory and practical information on this issue.

Cindy Dickinson is presently completing her masters in nurse-midwifery and public health (in epidemiology) at Columbia University. She has worked as a staff nurse in New York City hospitals and is a member of Nurses' Network and the NYCOSH Reproductive Rights Committee.

Jane Fleishman is a labor educator in occupational health and workers' compensation for the state of Connecticut. She has a masters degree in labor studies and has been active in the labor movement through her membership in the American Federation of Teachers. She has worked in the past as a clerical worker, helped organize a working women's organization, was active in a clerical workers' union, and is one of the founders of ConnectiCOSH.

Nicholas Freudenberg is a doctorate in public health and an associate professor and director of the program in community health education at the Hunter College School of Health Sciences. He is the author of *Not in Our Backyards! Community Struggles for Health and the Environment* (Monthly Review Press, 1984), and has been active in environmental health organizing in New York metropolitan area.

Maureen Hatch has a doctorate in epidemiology from Columbia University. She is interested in reproductive health, especially male reproductive function; in occupation and environment as risk factors; and in computerized surveillance systems for epidemiological purposes. She writes frequently on the subject of occupation, environment, and reproductive health.

Mary Sue Henifin is a consultant at the Women's Occupational Health Resource Center at Columbia University School of Public Health, where she also received her Master's of Public Health in environmental science. She recently edited *Biological Woman— The Convenient Myth* and co-authored (with Jeanne Stellman) *Office Work Can Be Dangerous to Your Health.*

Sonia Jasso has a masters in city planning and wrote her thesis on farmworker pesticide exposure. She has worked for the National Association of Farmworker Organizations, and is currently research director of the Labor Council for Latin American Advancement, AFL-CIO, in Washington, D.C.

Alice Kessler-Harris is professor of history at Hofstra University. She has been involved for many years with a worker education program in collaboration with District 65, UAW. She is the author of *Women Have Always Worked* (1980) and, most recently, of *Out* to Work: A History of Wage-Earning Women in the United States (1982).

Maria Mazorra has a masters in public health and has worked as an industrial hygienist for the National Association of Farmworker Organizations in their OSHA program. She was a member of the board of directors of Coalition for the Reproductive Rights of Workers (CRROW), and is currently a medical student in New Jersey.

Leith Mullings studied nursing as an undergraduate, and went on to receive her Ph.D. in anthropology from the University of Chicago in 1975. She teaches at City College and the City University of New York Graduate Center, and is the author of several articles and a book, Ideology and Change: Mental Healing in Urban Ghana (Berkeley and Los Angeles: University of California Press, 1984). She is the mother of two small children and a founding member of the Harlem chapter of Women for Racial and Economic Equality (WREE).

Harriet Rosenberg teaches anthropology and women's studies at York University, Downsview, Ontario, Canada. Her research interests include studies of stress and burn-out in the postpartum period. Her academic investigations for this article have been augmented by many years of systematic participant observation in the household. She has recently written (with M. Fitzgerald) Surviving in the City: Urbanization in the Third World (Oxfam-Canada, 1983).

Judith A. Scott is associate general counsel of the United Mine Workers of America (UMWA). She has served as legislative representative with the Industrial Union Department (AFL-CIO), assistant general counsel at the United Auto Workers, and counsel to the American Federation of State, County, and Municipal Employees. While at the UAW, she specialized in employment discrimination matters, including exclusionary policies. She is co-author of the 1983 edition of Organizing and the Law.

Sharon Woodrow has a masters in public health and is the safety training coordinator at the Santa Clara County Office of Education. As a former director of the Project on Health and Safety in Electronics, she maintains an active role in the Santa Clara Center for Occupational Safety and Health and is a member of its governing board.

Ellen Zaltzberg is a registered nurse and a community health educator with a special interest in occupational and environmental health. She is currently working as a health counselor at New York City Tecnical College, where she is also an instructor teaching human sexuality. Women's health/reproductive rights/sexuality are an ongoing political-education interest, and she has been an active member of the Committee for Abortion Rights and Against Sterilization Abuse (CARASA).

Eula Bingham is professor of environmental health and vice-president for graduate studies and research at the University of Cincinnati. From 1977 to 1981 she was assistant secretary of labor for occupational safety and health. Before that she was a teacher and researcher at the University of Cincinnati's College of Medicine. She continues to publish in the field of occupational and environmental health, and to work with local groups throughout the United States and Europe on environmental health issues. In addition, she has been active in speaking for and promoting the passage of right-to-know legislation in various states and communities.